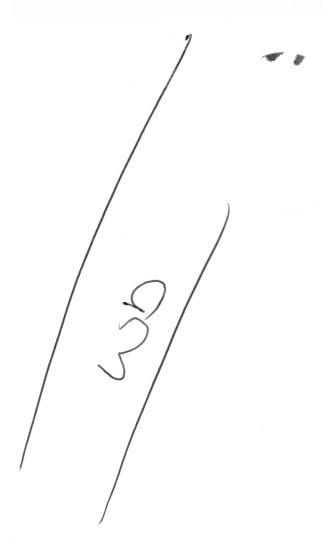

OLDHAM COLLEGE

THE MUSICAL AS DRAMA

THE MUSICAL AS DRAMA

A STUDY OF THE PRINCIPLES AND
CONVENTIONS BEHIND MUSICAL
SHOWS FROM KERN TO SONDHEIM

SCOTT MCMILLIN

PRINCETON UNIVERSITY PRESS

PRINCETON AND OXFORD

Copyright © 2006 by Princeton University Press
Published by Princeton University Press, 41 William Street, Princeton,
New Jersey 08540
In the United Kingdom: Princeton University Press, 3 Market Place,
Woodstock, Oxfordshire OX20 1SY

Library of Congress Cataloging-in-Publication Data

McMillin, Scott.
   The musical as drama / Scott McMillin.
      p. cm.
   Includes bibliographical references and index.
   ISBN-13: 978-0-691-12730-9 (hardcover : alk. paper)
   ISBN-10: 0-691-12730-1 (hardcover : alk. paper)
   1. Musicals—United States—History and criticism.   I. Title.
   ML2054.M353 2006
   792.60973—dc22   2006005429

British Library Cataloging-in-Publication Data is available

This book has been composed in Janson Typeface
Printed on acid-free paper. ∞
pup.princeton.edu
Printed in the United States of America

10 9 8 7 6 5 4

CONTENTS

ILLUSTRATIONS

PREFACE

A NUMBER of writers on the theatre and its history have come to think of the Broadway musical as one of the most important forms of American drama we have, and my aim in this book is to put that belief into concrete terms by discussing the principles and conventions that lie behind the best-known shows. There are good books on the major Broadway composers and lyricists; of these, two books on Sondheim, Stephen Banfield's *Sondheim's Broadway Musicals* (1993) and Steve Swagne's *How Sondheim Found His Sound* (2005), strike me as the clearest sign that serious work is now being done on a form of theatre that was once passed off as trivial entertainment. Raymond Knapp's *The American Musical and the Formation of National Identity* (2004) effectively places the musical in a context of American social and cultural history. Methods of musical analysis have been brought to bear on the genre, with Joseph Swain's shrewd book of this kind now in its second edition (*The Broadway Musical*, 2002). Geoffrey Block, whose study of major musicals (*Enchanted Evenings*, 1997) shows how such archives as the Performing Arts Library at Lincoln Center and the Music Division of the Library of Congress can be put to critical uses, has launched a series of volumes on individual composers. Ethan Mordden's decade-by-decade account of Broadway shows is essential reading for anyone interested in the American theatre, and the amount of sheer chronicle detail that has been searched out and published in works such as Richard C. Norton's three-volume *Chronology of American Musical Theater* (2002) and Gerald Bordman's *The American Musical Theatre* (3rd ed., 2001) is scholarly testimony to the value now being placed on this form of theatre.

I mention only some of the recent good books that are available if one wants to get a grasp on the musical. But I am not aware of a book that brings the musical before us as an aesthetic entity, a genre of drama with definable conventions around which one can think about the musical as a form of art. My chapters are not primarily about Kern or Rodgers and Hammerstein or the Gershwins. They are primarily about the orchestra, or the book and the numbers, or the chorus line— elements one takes for granted as the conventions of the show. Conventions are things we rarely think about, and our taking them for granted renders invisible the aesthetic work that is always going on. To study the aesthetics of an art form is to stop taking things for granted and to start thinking about the assumptions that shape our interests. I want to know what those interests are, not in order to say "I like this" but in order to say what it is I like in terms that belong to the staging of the drama itself, its books and numbers, its songs and dances, its routines. There is even a bit about the curtain and how it was used in what theatre people used to know as "in one" staging. That is an aesthetic matter, too.

If there seems to be a stretch between the specific elements of theatre practice and the aesthetics of musical drama, that is intended. Thinking about the practices and experiences of real theatre has convinced me that the theory usually applied to the musical overlooks the most important feature of the dramatic genre. The important feature is the incongruity between book and number, between what I describe as two orders of time, the progressive time of plot and the repetitive time of music, yet the theory that usually attends the musical would iron out this incongruity in the name of integration. Integration holds a tremendous theoretical position in regard to opera, but the musical is not a stepchild of opera, opera manqué, opera that does not make the grade but gets sidetracked into popular entertainment. The musical is a dramatic genre of its own, and in order to put solid ground under this point, I have turned to theorists and philosophers who spent much time themselves in real theatres. Richard Wagner, Bertolt Brecht, and Søren Kierkegaard are guideposts to the theoretical argument— Wagner on the side of integration in full-blown opera, Brecht and Kierkegaard on the side of disjunction between book and number in the musical.

In my courses on musical theatre at Cornell University,

where I introduced the subject into the curriculum about six years ago, I ask the students not to wonder if the musical is up to the standards of the university but if the standards of the university are up to dealing with the musical. Can we bring our ways of academic thinking to bear on this form of American drama? Can we talk aesthetically about musicals? The challenge is not to the musicals, which are staged across the country—in commercial theatres, in high school theatres, in dinner theatres, and on street corners (I have seen parts of *My Fair Lady* on a street corner)—without any help from university teachers and students. The musical does not need the university, but it may well be that the university needs the musical, as a valid subject of academic study. There is a challenge involved, and it is offered to the universities: are we in universities able to use our methods of analysis—historical, musical, literary, philosophical—and still get this form of popular entertainment right?

In answering this question, I am first concerned to describe the continuity of the musical's aesthetic form across its history, from the shows of the 1920s and 1930s, which themselves were based on conventions reaching back to the later nineteenth century, to the shows that seem most vivid in the musical theatre today. I am not writing a history of the genre, and I have omitted many examples that would have to be included in a historical survey. Still, there is a historical trajectory underpinning the argument, according to which *Oklahoma!* was not a revolution in the musical so much as an extension of the musical's range and later shows such as *West Side Story* and *Cabaret* and *A Chorus Line* represent further extensions of the capabilities of the form. This is how the historical silhouette appears when one thinks about the aesthetics of the genre. However, I am not writing a history, nor am I erecting a taxonomy of the form. There are types and subtypes of the musical's broader conventions, but I am trying to describe those broader conventions themselves, briefly, perhaps readably, and without encyclopedic hopes.

I have tried to keep the focus on a small number of musicals, to which I keep returning as different aspects of the genre come under discussion. I have picked broadly known musicals in order to avoid spending time on plot summaries and other general introductory information. I keep coming back to *Show Boat, Lady in the Dark, Oklahoma!, Carousel, Guys and Dolls, My Fair Lady, West Side Story, Cabaret, A Chorus Line, Phantom of the Opera, Follies, Pacific Overtures,* and *Sweeney Todd.* Other shows are discussed here and there—*Sally* has a few paragraphs, as do *On Your Toes, Boys from Syracuse,* and *Gypsy*—but the argument is consistently grounded in the group of major musicals just listed. *A Chorus Line* threads its way into one chapter after another as the book progresses; I find it one of the defining examples of the musical. Stephen Sondheim, Richard Rodgers, and Oscar Hammerstein II are the writers mentioned most frequently—Rodgers and Hammerstein in the earlier chapters, Sondheim in the later ones. The final chapter dwells especially on Sondheim because his musicals tend to reflect on their own means of production, a habit of thought he learned from Hammerstein. Sondheim writes musicals that are about musicals even when they are also about something else. There is such an instinct for musical theatre in his work that his shows reflect on their own conventions and become commentaries on the aesthetics of the form. I cannot stay away from a Sondheim show if it is at all within reach, and the reason is that Sondheim makes me think about what I am doing when I am there, at his show. He is not the only writer who does that, but he does it consistently, and he learned to do it from immersion in the history of the genre, where Rodgers and Hammerstein are the most important figures.

It is only shorthand that lets us talk of "a Sondheim show" or "a Rodgers and Hammerstein show." Many other individuals leave their visible imprint on a show as we know it. As just one example, *Follies* should be identified as by Stephen Sondheim and James Goldman, directed by Hal Prince and Michael Bennett, with choreography by Michael Bennett, scene design by Boris Aronson, orchestration by Jonathan Tunick, and so on. I call it a Sondheim show anyway, to save space, but here, at the beginning, I would like to list some members of the creative team behind each of the frequently mentioned titles, along with the year of the original production and publication details for the libretto when one is in print. The description of the creative team could be expanded in each case to include the costumers, the conductors, the sound technicians, the producers, and others. The musical is intensely collaborative, and my list is meant only to suggest that, not exhaust it.

Boys from Syracuse. 1938. Music, Richard Rodgers. Book, George Abbott. Lyrics, Lorenz Hart. Direction, George Abbott. Settings, Jo Mielziner. Choreography, George Balanchine. Orchestration, Hans Spialek.

Cabaret. 1966. Music, John Kander. Book, Joe Masteroff. Lyrics, Fred Ebb. Direction, Harold Prince. Choreography, Ron Field. Orchestration, Don Walker. Dance arrangements, David Baker. Libretto published by Random House, 1967.

Carousel. 1945. Music, Richard Rodgers. Book and lyrics, Oscar Hammerstein II. Direction, Rouben Mamoulian. Choreography, Agnes de Mille. Settings, Jo Mielziner. Orchestration, Don Walker. Ballet piano arrangements, Trude Rittman. Libretto published in a Modern Library edition, *Six Plays by Rodgers and Hammerstein.*

A Chorus Line. 1975. Music, Marvin Hamlisch. Lyrics, Edward Kleban. Book, James Kirkwood and Nicholas Dante. Director, Michael Bennett. Choreography, Michael Bennett and Bob Avian. Orchestration, Billy Byers, Hershey Kay, and Jonathan Tunick. Libretto published by Applause Books, 1995.

Follies. 1971. Music and lyrics, Stephen Sondheim. Book, James Goldman. Direction, Hal Prince and Michael Bennett. Choreography, Michael Bennett. Settings, Boris Aronson. Orchestration, Jonathan Tunick. Dance music arrangements, John Berkman. Libretto published by Random House, 1971. Revised edition published by Theatre Communications Group, 2001.

Guys and Dolls. 1950. Music and lyrics, Frank Loesser. Book, Jo Swerling and Abe Burrows. Direction, George Kaufman. Choreography, Michael Kidd. Settings, Jo Mielziner. Orchestration, George Bassman and Ted Royal. Libretto published in *From the American Drama,* ed. Eric Bentley (New York: Doubleday, 1956).

Lady in the Dark. 1941. Music, Kurt Weill. Book, Moss Hart.

Lyrics, Ira Gershwin. Direction, Moss Hart. Musical sequences staged by Hassard Short. Orchestration, Kurt Weill. Settings, Harry Horner.

My Fair Lady. 1956. Music, Frederick Loewe. Book and lyrics, Alan Jay Lerner. Direction, Moss Hart. Choreography, Hanya Holm. Settings, Oliver Smith. Orchestration, Robert Russell Bennett and Philip J. Lang. Dance music arrangements, Trude Rittman. Libretto published together with Shaw's *Pygmalion* (with scenes from the film version) by Signet, 1980

Oklahoma! 1943. Music, Richard Rodgers. Book and lyrics, Oscar Hammerstein II. Direction, Rouben Mamoulian. Choreography, Agnes de Mille. Settings, Lemuel Ayers. Orchestration, Robert Russell Bennett. Libretto published by Random House, 1943. Also available in a Modern Library edition, *Six Plays by Rodgers and Hammerstein*.

On Your Toes. 1936. Music, Richard Rodgers. Book, George Abbott, Lorenz Hart, and Richard Rodgers. Lyrics, Lorenz Hart. Direction, Worthington Miner and George Abbott. Choreography, Georges Balanchine. Settings, Jo Mielziner. Orchestration, Hans Spialek.

Pacific Overtures. 1976. Music and lyrics, Stephen Sondheim. Book, John Weideman. Additional material, Hugh Wheeler. Direction, Hal Prince. Choreography, Patricia Birch. Settings, Boris Aronson. Orchestration, Jonathan Tunick. Libretto published by Theatre Communications Group, 1991.

Phantom of the Opera. 1986. Music, Andrew Lloyd Webber. Book, Richard Stilgoe and Andrew Lloyd Webber. Lyrics, Charles Hart. Direction, Hal Prince. Choreography, Gillian Lynne. Settings, Maria Bjornson. Orchestration, David Cullen and Andrew Lloyd Webber. Libretto published in George Perry, *The Complete Phantom of the Opera* (New York: Henry Holt, 1988).

Show Boat. 1927. Music, Jerome Kern. Book and lyrics, Oscar Hammerstein II. Direction, Zeke Colvan and Oscar Hammerstein II. Choreography, Sammy Lee. Settings, Joseph Urban. Orchestration, Robert Russell Bennett.

Sunday in the Park with George. 1984. Music and lyrics, Stephen Sondheim. Book, James Lapine. Direction, James Lapine. Set-

tings, Tony Straiges. Movement, Randolyn Zinn. Orchestration,
Michael Starobin. Libretto published by Dodd, Mead, 1986.
Sweeney Todd. 1979. Music and lyrics, Stephen Sondheim. Book,
Hugh Wheeler. Direction, Harold Prince. Choreography, Larry
Fuller. Settings, Eugene Lee. Orchestration, Jonathan Tunick.
Libretto published by Applause Books, 1991.
West Side Story. 1957. Music, Leonard Bernstein. Book, Arthur Lau-
rents. Lyrics, Stephen Sondheim. Direction and choreography,
Jerome Robbins. Settings, Oliver Smith. Orchestration, Leonard
Bernstein and Sid Ramin. Libretto published in *Ten Great Musi-
cals of the American Theatre*, ed. Stanley Richards (Radnor, PA:
Chiltern Books, 1973).

ACKNOWLEDGMENTS

Scores of people have helped me in this work and influenced
the outcome. I would like to single out those who contributed
something specific that I could name even if they could not. I
have included some people who worked with me on musicals
or who accompanied me on countless trips to the theatre and
told me what was wrong, or sometimes right, with my reactions. On the latter score, as on many others, the champion is
my wife, Sally, who keeps me going in every way.

The others I list in alphabetical order, with great apprecia-
tion: Allison Bailey, Ron Barclay, David Carey, Marvin Carl-
son, Cynthia Chase, Lenore Coral, Jonathan Culler, Sandor
Goodhart, Tom Herson, Louise and Neil Hertz, Judith Holli-
day, Kit and Rob Hume, Dan Jerrold, Justin Leader, William
Losa, Genevieve Love, Marianne Marsh, Andrew McMillin,
Judith Milhaus, Adam Perl, Amanda Perl, Harry Shaw, Tiffany
Stern, and Tamsen Wolff.

My editor at Princeton University Press, Fred Appel, has
supported this book from the beginning, and the anonymous
readers he found to review the manuscript have been helpful
on matters large and small. Many members of the Press staff
have helped to move this book along, and I am grateful for their

uncommon professionalism. The copyediting by Marjorie Pan-
nell was especially notable. I am also indebted to the staffs of the
Sidney Cox Music Library at Cornell University and the Music
and Rare Books Room of the British Library.

Portions of chapter 1 were published earlier in slightly different form in "Brecht and Sondheim: An Unholy Alliance" in
the *Brecht Yearbook*, 30 (2005), and I am indebted to the editor,
Stephen Brockmann, for permission to use this material.

Quotations from "The Surrey with the Fringe on Top,"
copyright © 1943 by Williamson Music, copyright renewed,
international copyright secured, all rights reserved. Used by
permission.

THE MUSICAL AS DRAMA

Chapter One

INTEGRATION AND DIFFERENCE

INTEGRATION: FROM WAGNER TO BROADWAY

THE American musical has been accompanied by a theory easily believed so long as it remains unexamined. The theory is that of the "integrated musical," according to which all elements of a show—plot, character, song, dance, orchestration, and setting—should blend together into a unity, a seamless whole. Richard Rodgers and Oscar Hammerstein II were articulate proponents of this idea, and the historical moment when integration arrived on Broadway is often said, not least of all by Rodgers and Hammerstein, to have been the opening of *Oklahoma!* in March 1943. As Rodgers later put it, "when a show works perfectly, it's because all the individual parts complement each other and fit together. No single element overshadows any other. . . . That's what made *Oklahoma!* work. . . . It was a work created by many that gave the impression of having been created by one."[1] Hammerstein's version of the theory concerned the unity between music and libretto: the composer/lyricist "expresses the story in his medium just as the librettist expresses the story in his. Or, more accurately, they weld their two crafts and two kinds of talent into a single expression. This is the great secret of the well-integrated musical play. It is not so much a method as a state of mind, or rather a state for two minds, an attitude of unity."[2]

There was nothing new about those statements insofar as they pertained to the action and character of what had long been called musical comedy. In 1917 Jerome Kern said that

---

[1] Rodgers, *Musical Stages*, p. 227.
[2] Hammerstein, *Lyrics*, p. 15.

"musical numbers should carry on the action of the play, and should be representative of the personalities of the characters who sing them," and in 1924 Hammerstein refused to list the numbers in *Rose Marie* because he did not want to detract from the close fit between book and number he thought the show possessed.[3] The best composers and librettists have always wanted that close articulation. The statements of Rodgers and Hammerstein in 1943 pushed the idea further. Read closely, they are about the unity of the collaborators who made the musical rather than about the unity of the musical itself. They have a "two minds as one" air about them.

Although the collaboration of Rodgers and Hammerstein is one of the high points of American drama, the musical has always depended on teamwork among composer, lyricist, librettist, choreographer, stage director, music director, designer, costumer, orchestrator, and others. When a show put together by so many creative minds takes to the stage via the creative minds and bodies of the performers and actually works, even comes across the footlights as something special, an experience for an audience to remember for the rest of their lives (as happened with *Oklahoma!*), one knows that the efforts of many have produced an extraordinary event. Great elation accompanies the run of a hit musical, and everyone involved knows the feeling. But that does not mean that the product of all this cooperation has been smoothed out into a unified work of art. When a musical is working well, I feel the crackle of difference, not the smoothness of unity, even when the numbers dovetail with the book. It takes things different from one another to be thought of as integrated in the first place, and I find that the musical depends more on the differences that make the close fit interesting than on the suppression of difference in a seamless whole. *Difference* can be felt between the book and the numbers, between the songs and dances, between dance and spoken dialogue—and these are the elements that integration is supposed to have unified. Sometimes the elements *are* integrated,

[3] The Kern quotation is in Bordman, *Jerome Kern: His Life and Music*, p. 149. For *Rose Marie*, see Bordman, *The American Musical Theatre*, p. 392.

but I still feel the difference. When the orchestra introduces a tune that causes characters who have been speaking dialogue to break into song or dance, the music has changed the book into something different—a number—and the characters acquire a different dimension, the ability to perform that number.[4]

The disparity between speech and song was a problem long studied in opera, where integration became the governing aesthetic in the nineteenth century. "The passage from one to the other [speech to song] is always shocking and ridiculous," Rousseau wrote in the eighteenth century. "It is the height of absurdity that at the instant of passion we should change voices to speak a song."[5] Recitative in the place of spoken dialogue was an attempt to avoid this problem. Let the dialogue be sung in melodic recitative, let the recitative lead into the aria, and music of one sort or another will be the single register of expression throughout. Nineteenth-century opera intensified the musical register by abolishing recitative and turning the entire drama into formal song. The through-sung operas of the nineteenth century thus had a basis of musical unity to build on, which Wagner further developed into the theory of the *Gesamtkunstwerk* and its titanic realizations in *Tristan und Isolde* and the *Ring*.

Wagner's influence in American culture ran deep in the twentieth century. The leading aesthetic theory at the time Rodgers and Hammerstein were becoming popular was the new criticism, which sought an organic wholeness in works of art, including poetry, drama, music, dance, and novels. Organic wholeness meant that the work of art should grow like fruit on the vine. Radically discordant elements could be yoked

---

[4] I am not the first to voice doubt about integration theory. For skeptical readings of integration in Rodgers and Hammerstein, see Mast, *Can't Help Singin': The American Musical on Stage and Screen*, pp. 201–18; Savran, *A Queer Sort of Materialism: Recontextualizing American Theater*, pp. 29–34; and Most, *Making Americans: Jews and the Broadway Musical*, pp. 12–31. D. A. Miller, *Place for Us*, pp. 1–6, looks beneath integration and finds a "deeper formal discontinuity" between music and drama which he brings to bear on the experience of growing up gay in the era of Rodgers and Hammerstein. Wolf, *A Problem Like Maria: Gender and Sexuality in the American Musical*, pp. 32–43, connects the "fragmented form" of the musical to lesbian subject positions.

[5] Quoted in Poizat, *The Angel's Cry*, p. 54.

together in an integrated whole by the creativity of the artist, an operation that T. S. Eliot famously called "the amalgamation of disparate experience."[6] Eliot came in contact with musical theatre by way of Joseph Kerman, whose influential *Opera as Drama* was solidly based on the new criticism, said nothing at all about musical comedy, and took Wagner and the theory of unity as crucial concerns.[7] Other influential books about drama at mid-century were Eric Bentley's *The Playwright as Thinker* and Francis Fergusson's *The Idea of a Theater*. Bentley took special delight in castigating the musical as "vacuous" (*Oklahoma!*) and half-educated (*One Touch of Venus*). Song and dance are only "embellishments" to drama, said Bentley, whose bias in favor of organic wholeness has a Wagnerian edge: "Every good play has a rhythmic structure and a symphonic unity." Indeed, Wagner was one of Bentley's four heroes of modern drama, along with Ibsen, Shaw, and Strindberg (although Bentley had a sharp eye for false Wagnerianism, too). In *The Idea of a Theater*, Fergusson wrote at length about the Aristotelian "unity of action," ignored the musical, and devoted a chapter to *Tristan und Isolde*.[8]

Thus the best books on drama at midcentury took Wagner seriously and regarded him as a key figure whose influence extended beyond opera to nonmusical drama. They also disregarded the musical, a type of popular entertainment hardly worth study when unity of action was the important dramatic

[6] In his essay "The Metaphysical Poets" in *Selected Essays*, p. 247.

[7] Kerman thought music a further intensification of poetry in the Eliot aesthetic: poetry was an enlargement of ordinary speech, creating nuances of feeling and a heightened sensibility. Kerman accepted that theory of poetry and argued for carrying it a step further into operatic music as an extension and heightening of poetry, but for both Eliot and Kerman, the range of expression was a unified continuum that gained its power by stretching into poetry (Eliot) and into operatic music (Kerman). See Kerman, *Opera as Drama*.

[8] For Bentley on unity, see *Playwright as Thinker*, p. 112. The remarks about musicals are on pp. 6–8. Fergusson treats *Tristan* in chapter 3, on "univocal form" in Wagner and Racine. The Wagnerian connection with the idea of integration in the musical is sharply presented in Most, *Making Americans*, p. 9 and p. 225n7.

consideration.[9] Rodgers and Hammerstein were aware they had a cultural bias to overcome. They did not mention Wagner (although they were well versed in opera) and did not pay much attention to new criticism. But they were among other serious practitioners of the musical who wanted to elevate the cultural status of the form (Gershwin had made the most notable gesture in this direction by writing the Broadway opera *Porgy and Bess* a decade earlier), and they were celebrating the achievement of *Oklahoma!* in ways that reflected the prevailing aesthetic of the mid-twentieth century. They were not alone. "A form which seeks to integrate drama, music, and dance," the conductor Lehman Engel calls the musical, sounding the quasi-Wagnerian note that can be heard in every version of the theory.[10] But the real cultural work being carried out by these writers and practitioners of the musical, I propose, was that of turning Broadway's skill at song-and-dance routines into a new format in which the numbers had important work to do because they were being inserted into the book as a different element, a change of mode, a suspension of the book in favor of music.

My concern is to set the aesthetics of the genre into a perspective that includes earlier shows as well as later and that searches out the already existing principles that Rodgers and Hammerstein used so well. A new theoretical perspective on the musical is necessary now that the form is more than a century old and is proving to be a major form of American drama. The musical has a different aesthetic form from that of nineteenth-century opera. There are musicals today that try to become operatic, as though the musical were a lower form that should strive for an elevated state, and this strikes me as a confusion of genres. The line of achievement that runs from *Oklahoma!* to the musicals of

---

[9] Wagner was not an unqualified success in new critical circles, and the uses to which Nazism had put him were well known. For the cultural milieu of midcentury criticism, a good retrospective essay is Savran's on middlebrow culture in *A Queer Sort of Materialism*.

[10] Engel, *The American Musical Theatre*, p. 76. Like Rodgers and Hammerstein, Engel was well versed in opera but did not mention Wagner in theoretical musings.

Sondheim in the second half of the twentieth century or from *Show Boat* to *Oklahoma!* in the first half is as important as the line of achievement that runs from O'Neill to Williams and Miller and then on to Shepherd in what is still sometimes called the legitimate drama. The musical is the illegitimate drama, and now that the illegitimate has taken its place as a major American artistic accomplishment, it deserves some theoretical thinking that holds true to its own history and form.[11]

Two Orders of Time

The musical's complexity comes in part from the tension between two orders of time, one for the book and one for the numbers. The book represents the plot or the action. It moves (in terms borrowed from Aristotle's *Poetics*) from a beginning through a middle to an end. This is progressive time, in the sense that the ending is different from the beginning—things are not going to be the same after this. Bobby decides to get married, or doesn't, Gaylord returns to Magnolia and sees his daughter on the showboat, two rival gangs act together to carry away Tony's body, Japan takes up a Western way of life. The change occurs somewhere in the middle—the middle makes change possible, keeps the beginning apart from the ending, and lays out the terms by which the two will differ. Middles are crucial to the order of time in the Aristotelian idea of action. Aristotle himself favored moments of "recognition" or "reversal" as turning points leading toward an ending. The books of musicals have turning points, too, and we will read them this way.[12]

[11] African-American drama, now reaching a new point of definition in the plays of August Wilson and reaching back to its own tradition in the theatrical side of the Harlem Renaissance, is the other form to set beside the musical as the high achievement in American drama so far. It too was illegitimate for a time. The aesthetic crossovers between the two are extensive and should be studied.

[12] Examples of recognitions and turning points in musicals are discussed in chapter 2. Aristotole was thinking of tragedy in his definition of dramatic action. Comedy is of lesser magnitude in Aristotle's terms, but for a structural analysis of all plots, with comedy equal to other types, see Frye, *Anatomy of Criticism.*

What makes the musical complex is something the Greek drama had too—the second order of time, which interrupts book time in the form of songs and dances. The choral odes in the Greek drama were danced and sung, and if we knew how they were performed in any detail, we would find Greek tragedy more interesting. Aristotle recognized the need to incorporate the choral odes into the "unity of action" that he found in the best tragedies, but the extant text of the *Poetics* does not give considered thoughts on this problem. Song and Spectacle rank at the bottom of Aristotle's priority list of tragedy's components, as though they were separable from the top categories of Plot and Character. A theory of the musical cannot do this. It has to regard songs and dances as basic elements, equal to plot and character and influential on both.

The songs are stanzaic forms of verse against which the music asserts a broad repetitive pattern, and intricate smaller kinds of repetition occur within the stanzas. Characters who break into song are being enlarged by entering into the second order of time and displaying their mastery of repetitive, lyric form. Shaw's Henry Higgins in the nonmusical *Pygmalion* cannot be imagined breaking into a song. He exists consistently in one order of time. The Henry Higgins of *My Fair Lady* acts in this order of time, too, but he breaks into song in his first scene, and he sings several numbers thereafter. He even dances once. He is not a freewheeling song-and-dance man, but he joins the fandango that develops out of "The Rain in Spain" number, and Eliza is struck by this ("I Could Have Danced All Night"). I am not interested in the question of which is the better form of drama, Shaw's play or the musical based on it. I am interested in the difference between the two, for the change between the two orders of time involved in book and number makes Henry Higgins a different kind of character than he is in Shaw's play, or a character caught up in a different kind of action, and the theory of integration overlooks that difference.

Integration theory would say that songs and dances advance the plot. I can think of songs and dances that do advance the plot, and every reader will think of others. "Marry the Man

Today," near the end of *Guys and Dolls*, makes the two heroines aware of the solution to their romantic problems. Remove the song and the plot will need some new dialogue. The act 1 *finaletto* in the Gershwins' *Of Thee I Sing* conveys elements of plot, as does "A Weekend in the Country," at the end of act 1 of *A Little Night Music*. These are special occasions. But most songs and dances do not advance plots. Usually the book sets forth the turn of plot and the number elaborates it, in the spirit of repetition and the pleasure of difference. Most songs and dances do not further characterization, they change the mode of characterization—difference again. These are the aesthetic principles that all songs and dances follow, including the special occasions that do advance plot and character.

When Sweeney Todd holds his razor over Judge Turpin's throat for the first time and is about to take his revenge (in Sondheim's *Sweeney Todd*, 1979), he pauses to sing a number, "Pretty Women." It is an astonishing moment, the would-be murderer pretending to a bit of male bonding with the rapist he is about to slaughter. Sweeney is lingering over his big moment, changing the mode of expression, caught up in the sardonic delight of idealizing womanhood with the man who has destroyed one woman, Sweeney's wife, and is about to force another, Sweeney's daughter, into marriage. The Judge responds to Sweeney's tune. He sings along—it is a duet between the rapist and his would-be murderer! Then the young lover Anthony breaks in and ruins Sweeney's revenge.

This number gives its own dimension to the scene. It suspends the progress of events, formalizes the relationship between Sweeney and the Judge, turns it into melody and rhyme. Integration theory would say that "Pretty Women" arises out of the situation and is part of Sweeney's delay. It is what ruins the moment of revenge, allowing time for Anthony to arrive just as the razor is about to descend. That is technically true, but it does not account for the effect of the song, which is to add harmony, melody, and rhythm to the ghastly relationship between the revenger and his intended victim. The dimension of song suspends book time in favor of an incongruous moment of lyric time. These two have no business singing with one another, especially not singing so well. In Christopher Bond's *Sweeney Todd*, the source play for the musical, there is no such interplay between the men at this point. Todd draws out his revenge a little, talking as though he were about to reveal his identity. This is dialogue moving toward its goal, then Anthony bursts onto the scene to interrupt the revenge. There is no change of mode, no shift of perspective. It is a good scene, that is all.

The song inserts a lyrical moment into the cause-and-effect progress of the plot, a moment that suspends book time in favor of lyric time, time organized not by cause and effect (which is how book time works) but by principles of repetition (which is how numbers work). There is the repetition of the four-note musical phrase on "pretty women" itself, heard ten times. There is the metrical repetition of four syllables by which "pretty women" matches up to "fascinating," "sipping coffee," "are a wonder," and so on, always in four sixteenth notes compressed into the first beat of a measure. There is the strophic repetition of stanzas by which the song is cast in one of the traditional formats for popular tunes (ABAB'). There is the underlying repetition of a harmonic ninth in the orchestra, established against the tonic and then beating through the chord changes as a hint of something that cannot be resisted until the music itself comes to an end.[13]

This kind of insert is the heart of the musical, any musical. It is lyrical, it gives the pleasure that follows from rhyme, melody, and meter, and it takes effect not because it blends into the plot in the spirit of integration but because it stands apart and declares that there is another order of time in the theatre, not just the cause-and-effect sequencing of plot but the lyrical repetitions of song and dance. I am not saying anything that would have surprised Jerome Kern in 1917, when he made the comment I quoted earlier about songs being suited to the action and the mood of the play, or Rodgers and Ham-

[13] To be exact, I am describing Part II of "Pretty Women." Part I establishes the musical interaction of the two men over the pleasure of "catching fire from one man to the next." It leads into Part II along its own patterns of lyric repetition.

merstein in 1943, when they spoke of the unity of minds that had brought about *Oklahoma!* Kern sought a closer articulation of book and number than many musical comedies of his day provided. Rodgers and Hammerstein wanted the closer articulation, too. Book-and-number formats can be used as license to put anything into a show, and Kern and Rodgers and Hammerstein were not interested in licentiousness any more than Sondheim is. They knew they were making advances in a serious kind of drama, but they knew that the kind already existed—in need of reform to be sure, but already established and ready to be improved upon.

FORMATS: REVUE AND OPERETTA

The musical comes from popular forms of entertainment that sharply maintain the difference between book and number. Indeed, many of the forerunners of the musical do not have a book in the first place. These are the burlesques, the vaudevilles, the extravaganzas, the travesties, the music hall shows, the variety shows, the minstrels, the burlettas—a large and varied group that I will group together as revues, in order to separate them from the other forerunners, the ones with books, which can be called operettas (so long as the name is not taken to mean that they are a form of opera).[14]

The revue might have a story line or a theme, but it does not have a plot. It draws its energy from the one-thing-after-another, now-for-something-entirely-different spirit of the numbers, which are arranged in a running order. The running order calls for a big number at the end of act 1 and a surefire crowd-pleaser as the second number in act 2 (to convince everyone, including the stragglers from the bar, that the second act will be better than the first). If there is a theme or story

---

[14] For a recent and thorough account of these antecedents, see Knapp, *The American Musical and the Formation of National Identity*, chapters 2 and 3, which also have good bibliographic endnotes. Operetta has recently been covered by Lamb, *150 Years of Popular Musical Theatre*. A good older survey is Traubner, *Operetta: A Theatrical History.*

line, it is likely to be absurd. An early revue in London, *Under the Clock* (performed at the Royal Court in 1893), had Sherlock Holmes and Dr. Watson showing Emile Zola around the theatres of the day, all of which were subjected to satire.[15] Or the organizing device might be a satirical revue of the headline events of the year. That was how the original revues, in France, were set up, and the tradition carried over into the "passing shows" of London and New York later in the nineteenth century. Spectacular revues featuring lavish scenery and chorus girls in scanty costumes to go with the songs and dances and comedy sketches also took hold in the later nineteenth century, most famously at the Folies Bergère in Paris from 1886 and in the Ziegfeld *Follies* in New York from 1907. Kern in 1917 and Rodgers and Hammerstein in 1943 (and others at other times) were drawing their kind of theatre away from this tradition, but it would be a mistake to suppose that the rambunctiousness, sexiness, impiety, and occasional beauty of the revue tradition were drained out of the musical as the revue gradually waned and the book show became dominant. All of these qualities remain alive in Kern, in Rodgers and Hammerstein, in the musical generally speaking. (And there still are revues. *Cats* is a thematic revue, and so are the *Forbidden Broadway* satires that appear every so often as parodies of current Broadway shows.)

The revue was the kind of show that depends on a succession of performance numbers rather than on a succession of narrative events. Operettas, by contrast, depended on a succession of narrative events, a plot. Operettas exhibited many different kinds of plot, but they were all book shows. They came to Broadway from London, Paris, and Vienna in the nineteenth century and well into the twentieth century. The reason why they should not be regarded as offspring of opera is that they depended on two elements not central to nineteenth-century opera: satire (especially in the French tradition) and popular social dances such as the polka, the march, and, especially in the Viennese tradition, the waltz. The impudence of

[15] See Mander and Mitcheson, *Revue: A Story in Pictures*, pp. 14–16. Noel Coward's foreword to this book has an account of the running order.

the satire and the scintillations of the waltz, thought to be risqué at first, gave the operetta a broad popular appeal, and its relation to grand opera was largely one of antithesis. Indeed, grand opera is one of the things satirized in operettas.

In New York, by the time the Ziegfeld Follies was launched as a spectacular form of revue, everyone who followed the entertainment scene knew about the operettas of Gilbert and Sullivan, Offenbach, and Johann Strauss. They would soon know about the operettas of Kalman, Lehar, Stolz, Friml, Herbert, and (where the future took shape) Kern. The English Gaiety-type "musical comedies" of the turn of the century were decisively influential on Kern, so I am being brisk in linking him with operetta. But Kern's early shows and the English musical comedies connect with the operetta tradition by being book shows and thus in having a different emphasis from the various kinds of revues we have named, and that distinction is the one that matters here.[16]

Operettas had elaborate plots, usually involving disguise and mistaken identity. The Viennese model emphasized exotic romance in its plots, whereas the French and English models emphasized topical satire, but all used the device of putting one or two leading characters into disguise or settling a mistaken identity upon them. Song is not hard to attain in a plot hinging on disguise or mistaken identity. Disguised characters play a role within a role, and singing is a way of creating the inner role. For disguises as for mistaken identities, the true persons become apparent in their songs, although not necessarily to themselves. Often the characters burst into song *because* they are disguised, literally or psychologically. Or they are in love,

[16] For distinctions between operetta, revue, and musical comedy in the early years, see Mordden, *Make Believe: The Broadway Musical in the 1920s*, chapters 1–4. Norton, *A Chronology of American Musical Theater*, and Bordman, *American Musical Theatre*, detail the different kinds of American musical entertainment. For Kern's connection to English musical comedy, see Bordman, *Jerome Kern*, and Lamb's pamphlet, *Jerome Kern in Edwardian London*. The Viennese operetta has recently been studied in Crittenden, *Johann Strauss and Vienna: Operetta and the Politics of Popular Culture*. The term *review* was first used in New York for *The Passing Show* of 1894, then quickly changed to the French *revue*. See Mander and Mitcheson, *Revue*.

and song is the concentrated way to get to the point. Or they are in a carnival spirit and want to sing and dance in groups— or captured by gypsies who want to sing and dance in groups. If you are in love and at a masked ball, no one knows who you are or everyone thinks you are someone else, and gypsies are waiting to steal you away to their camp where everyone sings and dances, you are in a Viennese operetta, and who could fail to sing at times like these?

But these operetta plots always made room for comic routines and other kinds of show business, and they did not take integration of music and book as a main issue. A theory of integration was not needed for the operetta, although the matter did come up. Johann Strauss, with the example of Wagner near at hand, worked his way into writing through-composed operas. When these proved relatively unsuccessful and he returned to writing operettas, he was heard to complain that the form was rubbish. Sullivan sought higher forms of composition and had bouts of embarrassment over writing music for what he sometimes regarded as Gilbert's silly plots. Operettas appeal to just about everyone and thus can seem lowbrow to a composer yearning for something grand.

The desire to elevate the genre runs through the history of the musical, as though there were something shameful about the operettas and the various kinds of revue that lie behind the form. Integration theory is one product of the desire to elevate the form. My argument is that the principles of disjunction between book and number, and between one number and another, that organized the revue and operetta formats still inform the musical, and there is no point to being ashamed of it. The desire to elevate the form drives the musical of today toward a through-composed form, toward opera manqué, and because the grandiosity of the result fits with the expanding technology of the later twentieth-century theatre, a sumptuous and to my mind overblown kind of musical is created which we can call the integrated musical. I am thinking of the stunning technology required by *Phantom of the Opera*, *Les Misérables*, and *The Lion King*. The genre to which shows of this sort belong is certainly not opera, but they reside uneasily if not unprofitably in the category of the stage musical, too. The aesthetic basis of the Disney and Lloyd Webber kind of musical is technological fantasy. Later I suggest that the genre bearing kinship to these shows is the film musical. But the urgent need, in my opinion, is for a poetics of the stage musical—first, because the stage musical tends to be absorbed into the technological and film musical in the general shuffle of integration theory, and second, because once the stage musical is separated out from integration theory and recognized as a different kind of drama, the genre can be seen to hold fast to its origins in American popular culture. It has the potential to become the kind of socially relevant theatre that Eric Bentley despised it for not being in the age of Rodgers and Hammerstein.

Bentley despised the musical for refusing to acknowledge the drama's political responsibilities. He may have been right about the genre as it existed in the mid-1950s. There had been socially responsible musicals and revues in the 1930s, and Bentley knew these, but he was looking to the mainstream of a form that had been politically innocuous during most of the century. Rodgers and Hammerstein did not write left-wing musicals. Hammerstein was politically progressive, and he did work spots of political awareness into his shows, but when it comes to Indian Territory and what really happened there, *Oklahoma!* is a crying shame.[17] Rodgers and Hammerstein were not writing political drama, but they were setting in motion a further history of the genre in which social and political issues would come to be prominent even in the mainstream. *West Side Story* is about the violence of a younger generation with nothing productive to do. *Cabaret* is about fascism in an urban society caught up in heedless entertainments. *A Chorus Line* is about sexuality in the theatre, which means to an important extent gay sexuality. *Sweeney Todd* is about injustice and the pressure for revenge among the powerless in industrialized cities. People who find these issues unimportant do not pay attention to politics, and the shows I have named are among the most revivable American dramas of the past half-century. They are

---

[17] See Knapp, *The American Musical*, pp. 122–27.

also among the musicals that connect with the broadly popular forms of song-and-dance entertainment that gave rise to the genre in the first place. Rodgers and Hammerstein are the pivotal figures who turned those popular forms into a genre with a future, and that future has political and social relevance.

THE BETTER BOOK

What happened by the time of *Oklahoma!* was not the integration of musical numbers into a unified whole with the book, it was a better book. Many of the successful earlier shows had scanty plots—mere scaffoldings, really, for hanging songs and dances on. They enjoyed the air of the ridiculous in the first place—flappers flapping about at a rich man's birthday party while one of them sallies forth and falls in love with the local cross-Atlantic aviator. This is the first act of the Gershwins' *Funny Face* (1927, book by Fred Thompson and Paul Gerard Smith). The rich man having the birthday party was played by Fred Astaire and the flapper meeting up with the aviator was played by Adele Astaire, Fred's sister. The characters played by the Astaires in the early shows could have crossed over from one book to another with not much more than a change of name. The Astaire characters were multiple characters, I hasten to add, characters doubled because of their extraordinary penchant for song and dance. Their book selves were forgettable, ditzy and inconsequential excuses to give the number selves a chance to shine when they were enlarged into song and dance. The enlargements into song and dance were stunning pieces of theatre. They demanded hours of rehearsal, and when the songs caught on, they emerged out of the show in the form of recordings, by the Astaires and others. Some are still being recorded today.

The books of the standard shows were always comedies, romantic comedies in their conclusions and would-be farces in their pacing. Often they contained a kind of inner revue—a nightclub scene, a ballroom scene, a garden party scene, a theatre scene—episodes that allowed singers, dancers, and comics

FIGURE 1. Fred and Adele Astaire in a pose from *Lady, Be Good*. Billy Rose Theatre Collection, The New York Public Library for the Performing Arts, Astor, Lenox and Tilden Foundations.

to take the stage as part of the narrative. This device has never ceased to be useful, and it developed into the backstage musical—*On Your Toes, Kiss Me, Kate, Follies*, to name just a few examples. The best early example is the Jerome Kern/Guy Bolton/P. G. Wodehouse show *Sally* of 1920, a vehicle for the Ziegfeld star Marilyn Miller and a very good show. But it is the kind of show that would give way to shows with a better book.

Sally begins in a Greenwich Village nightclub where an orphan girl hired as a dishwasher gets a chance to show her talent as a dancer. It then moves through a grand party on a Long Island estate, where the orphan girl disguises herself as a Russian ballerina and performs for influential persons, and ends at the New Amsterdam Theatre on 42nd Street, where influential persons hire the orphan girl to star in a Ziegfeld show and the best-looking influential person offers to marry her. *Sally* was first performed in the New Amsterdam theatre itself, home of the *Follies*, so the final set stood for part of the theatre itself. This is about as metatheatrical as drama can be, but the basic formula at work was used in hundreds of Broadway musicals, and that formula combines revue elements with operetta elements so that just about any kind of number can be called upon in the nightclub, garden party, or Broadway settings of the plot.

A plot like *Sally*'s also depends on unlikely coincidence, the driving convention of farce. Operettas always had a farce lurking in their romantic sentimental stories. Gilbert and Sullivan drew out this potential and made it work. By the time Bolton and Wodehouse were teaming up with Kern for their shows at the Princess Theatre (1915–1918), the British penchant for farce was becoming the standard for the book show. Some wonderful musicals arose from this tendency, but a good farce is tightly made, its unlikely coincidences following one another quickly and relentlessly. The farce interrupted by numbers is rarely good farce, for the principle of interruption basic to the musical becomes an impediment. Numbers must appear at regular intervals. Guy Bolton kept his own kind of running order in mind as he plotted and planned spots for numbers every-so-many pages.[18] One reason most early book shows seem unstageable today is that they are second-rate farces. Another is their excessive topicality, a carryover from the revue tradition, which thrived on up-to-date commentary. In the first fifteen minutes of *Funny Face* there were references to Babe Ruth, the Four Horsemen, Gene Tunney, Cal Coolidge, Jimmy Walker, Henry Ford, H. J. Heinz, Regal Shoes, Armour Meats, Kuppenheimer Buttons, the Hearst newspaper chain, and Paul Swan. Like the revue, the early books were meant to be for-the-moment exercises in nonchalance—Edwardian throwaways, bits of the Jazz Age as casually tossed off as the side kicks and shimmies of the Charleston. (The degree of hard work needed to give this impression of casualness is another matter.) They were busy with topicality, totally up-to-date, and certainly not meant to last down the ages.

Now that it is from down the ages that we view them, the early shows seem dated, and we stage them mainly for their numbers, which are sometimes repackaged into new books. In some cases the abundance of famous songs allows us to preserve the original books, as in *Sally* (where one can watch a rich scion of the Long Island aristocracy sing "Look for the Silver Lining" with the orphan girl tired from washing dishes in the nightclub, and then watch the orphan girl, weary no longer, tap-dance her way through the same song with the disguised Duke of Czechogovinia).[19] Most musicals of the 1910s and 1920s did not have songs as good as "Whip-Poor-Will" or "Wild Rose" or "Look for the Silver Lining" (all from *Sally*). They were urban, breezy, gag-filled comedies about sophisticated zanies who could break into song and dance, and the problem with their books—"one more bit of fluff dealing with flirtations among the 'Tennis, anyone?' Long Island social set," Rodgers complained, after collaborating on a number of them himself—was that they were second-rate, stop-and-go farces

---

[18] Davis, *Bolton and Wodehouse and Kern: The Men Who Made Musical Comedy*, is a mine of information.

[19] Revivals of the original version of *Sally* are rare, but they do occur. I am grateful to the Drama Department of the Catholic University in Washington, D.C., where I saw *Sally* in January 2000.

carried out by characters who were silly, charming, and relentlessly alike.

Oklahoma!, by contrast, concerns women having to run a farm on their own, it concerns a farmhand capable of violence if he cannot have one of those women, it concerns Indian Territory and whether the land will be used for farming or for cattle ranches. (It does not concern the Indians, who are left out of the picture entirely.[20]) Most of the plot owes to Lynn Riggs, who wrote the play on which *Oklahoma!* is based, *Green Grow the Lilacs*. What Rodgers and Hammerstein took over from Riggs was a heroine who has a hard time admitting she has fallen for the hero, not because she is coy and flirtatious and busy with boys at the country club or because she is worn out by washing dishes at a nightclub where she knows she could become a headliner but because she is immature and self-centered—and because she is farming, the hero is a cowboy, and cowboys don't use the land the way farmers do. One reason she *does* commit herself is that she is terrified of the hired hand who has designs on her and is capable of violence if he doesn't get what he wants. The cowboy-hero handles a gun so well that even the hired hand has to worry about him—that is one of the hero's desirable attributes.

I am leaving the numbers out of this description, which sounds more serious than the show itself. The numbers change the tone and make these people sound happy and funny. But the book of *Oklahoma!* does have a serious line, and the challenge taken up by Rodgers and Hammerstein was how to interrupt a potentially serious plot with songs and dances that would not collapse into ridiculousness. The same challenge had been faced by Kern and Hammerstein in *Show Boat*, by Kurt Weill and Paul Green in *Johnny Johnson*, by Weill, Moss Hart, and Ira Gershwin in *Lady in the Dark*, and by some little-remembered composers and librettists of the 1920s and 1930s in whose hands the enterprise *did* collapse into ridiculousness. Challenging book shows were written before *Oklahoma!* But

[20] See Most, " 'We Know We Belong to the Land': The Theatricality of Assimilation in Rodgers and Hammerstein's *Oklahoma!*"

Oklahoma! ran through the war years, and by the time Rodgers and Hammerstein followed with another challenging book show, *Carousel* the Depression was a thing of the past and postwar prosperity was soon to become apparent. The Rodgers and Hammerstein era owes much to the enterprise of two veteran writers, but it also owes much to American economic conditions after the war, conditions that allowed serious composers like Kurt Weill, Frank Loesser, and Leonard Bernstein to look for collaborators who would continue the musical's advance into challenging plots with a hope of mainstream profitable runs.[21]

The wider range of plot resulted in a wider range of character, but the important effect of breaking into song remained the same as it had been when the range of character was narrow. The effect of breaking into song (or dance) is to double the characters into the second order of time, the lyric time of music, so that they gain a formality of expression unavailable to them in the book. Characters like Billy Bigelow and Julie Jordan in *Carousel* have numbers that seem specific to their

[21] See Roost, "Before *Oklahoma!*: A Reappraisal of Musical Theatre During the 1930s." Mordden, *Beautiful Mornin'*, pp. 88–93, argues that the "musical play" replaced the "musical comedy" in the 1940s and makes a strong case for the revised *Show Boat* of 1946 as a sign of the change. For good accounts of Rodgers' decision to collaborate with Hammerstein and of their work together, see Mordden, *Rodgers and Hammerstein*, pp. 17–40; Fordin, *Getting to Know Him: A Biography of Oscar Hammerstein II*, pp. 184–190; and Secrest, *Somewhere for Us: A Biography of Richard Rodgers*, pp. 235–242. John Lahr's way of describing the change brought about by *Oklahoma!* is useful. In a review published in the *New Yorker*, he wrote, "the musical's job description changed, virtually overnight. Anarchic, freewheeling frivolity that traded in joy—in other words, in the comedian's resourcefulness—was renounced for an artful marriage of music and lyrics that traded in narrative. . . . Big names were no longer needed to carry the show; the show itself was the star." Lahr, "O.K. Chorale: An English Take on Rodgers and Hammerstein." Swain, *The Broadway Musical: A Critical and Musical Survey*, p. 95, shows that the innovation in *Oklahoma!* was to reprise parts of its earlier songs almost immediately, as though the number could double back on the intervening dialogue: "the dialogue interrupts the song as much as the song interrupts the dialogue." This seems accurate and is related to the technique of underscoring, which sustains a number even while dialogue takes place. The Bench Scene in *Carousel*, the finest example of reprised number and underscoring, is discussed in chapter 6.

characters, but the effect of the numbers is not so much to advance characterization as to double characterization, by turning Billy Bigelow and Julie Jordan into new versions of themselves, musical versions. Their book versions are one thing, but their musical versions enlarge them into lyrical power. They are said to be the same characters, but clearly they are different, and the incongruity is theatrically arresting. This is the same principle by which Fred and Adele Astaire changed from trivial book selves into interesting song-and-dance selves, only now the book selves aren't trivial. This is a complex and sophisticated kind of dramatic characterization. Behind *Carousel* lies Molnar's *Liliom*, a good play from "legitimate" theatre's modern tradition. The Molnar characters are better drawn than their counterparts in the book of *Carousel*, but they do not have the doubling effect of the songs in *Carousel*. They are more convincing as realistic characters, but the musical gives its characters a dimension that lies beyond realism and increases the range of their presentation. The numbers in the Rodgers and Hammerstein version do not advance the characters or further the book so much as they change the characters and the book into new versions of themselves that play against our normal sense of identity and story. The numbers interrupt our normal sense of character and plot with song and dance, and what we are left with is not the "one" but the "multiple."

I will take up the Rodgers and Hammerstein shows in more detail later. For the moment, the point is that their status in the history of the genre depends on the enlargement they gave to the kinds of book the musical could take up, and not on a transformation of the musical into a quasi-operatic form. There are crossovers between opera and the musical, of course. Opera has always been able to borrow elements of popular music and dance without losing its character as opera. The musical has always been able to borrow elements of opera without losing its character as musical—usually in the spirit of parody in the earlier musicals, but sometimes in the spirit of imitation in the later ones. Opera was always fair game for the musical, and after Rodgers and Hammerstein expanded the range of the book show to include episodes of violence and grief, operatic singing became one of the ways characters could break into song. Opera singers took lead roles in musicals of the 1940s and 1950s, although they played off against musical comedy performers—they were one element of the principle of difference that has always driven the form. Ezio Pinza and Mary Martin together formed an astonishing combination in *South Pacific*. Their musical styles did not belong together, but that was the point. Impudent and eclectic, the musical made the clash of styles into a selling point, with a book that also involved a clash of styles between these two unlikely lovers. This is not the musical becoming the opera. This is the musical expanding its capabilities.[22]

The Concept Musical

After Rodgers and Hammerstein, it seemed that any kind of plot could be turned into a commercial musical. In the mid-1950s, three Maurice Pagnol plays were turned into one show, the Harold Rome/S. N. Behrman *Fanny* (1954), and Homer's *Odyssey* became the Jerome Moross/John LaTouche *Golden Apple* (1954). The key figure in the wake of Rodgers and Hammerstein was Leonard Bernstein, who took on Voltaire's *Candide* and Shakespeare's *Romeo and Juliet*, creating two recordable scores for two revivable books. The Bernstein shows line up with another radical experiment in book writing that is sometimes referred to as the concept musical. The book of a concept musical is often controlled by a theme or a metaphor. Kander and Ebb's *Cabaret* (1966) is one of the earliest concept

[22] Gershwin's *Porgy and Bess* is operatic throughout, demanding a company of classically trained voices. Kurt Weill's *Street Scene* deliberately turns the Rodgers and Hammerstein example in the direction of opera, with several roles calling for operatic singers and giving one of them, the lead soprano, a genuine aria, but it retains the book–number alternation of the musical and inserts popular song formats at will. Frank Loesser's *Most Happy Fellow* brings an operatic singer into contact with musical comedy performers in the *South Pacific* style and goes further toward being through-sung, but no one confuses it with opera.

musicals. Rodgers and Hammerstein had earlier tried highly unusual book shows that smacked of the concept musical, *Allegro* and *Me and Juliet*, and so had Alan Jay Lerner and Kurt Weill in *Love Life*, but these experiments depended on complex and sprawling plots, whereas *Cabaret* knew how to condense an idea into metaphor—the rise of Nazism seems to take place in a seedy Berlin nightclub. (The metaphor was largely created by director Hal Prince.) The heroine, Sally Bowles, leads two lives, one as the girlfriend of the male lead, which is about where she stands in the Christopher Isherwood story and the John Van Druten play on which the musical is based, the other as a singer in a nightclub, where she belts out tunes like the title song. "Life is a cabaret, old chum," she sings in her musical version, celebrating the destructive hedonism she and the others live by in their book selves. Sharpen this doubleness by making her aware of her divided selves, let her become a commentator on the self-destructiveness of her life, and this would be a Brechtian drama. That does not happen, but the song-and-dance formats inserted into the Isherwood story about the rise of Nazism jostle the show into political connections between fascism and popular entertainment, and since audiences at *Cabaret* are themselves watching popular entertainment, the metaphor opens out into the show's performance itself. The concept musical often has such a metadramatic or mirroring effect, a matter discussed in the concluding chapter of this book.

Kander and Ebb went on to another metaphorical concept show, *Chicago*, where vaudeville routines laid out by director and choreographer Bob Fosse comment on the system of justice and imprisonment in Chicago in the 1920s. (Fosse was developing an idea from the play *Chicago* by Maureen Watkins, on which the musical is based.) Roxie Hart, who has ambitions to become a nightclub singer, murders her lover in "real" life and is imprisoned, where she finds that the legal system is already a vaudeville show. By the end, she has teamed up with another murderess/songstress and returned to civilian life, where they also become vaudeville stars. Kander and Ebb and Fosse and Prince were advancing upon the convention by

which characters have two modes of existence in musicals. They
were taking the convention literally, putting show business settings next to "real" settings in Berlin and Chicago and letting
the two overlap.

Cabaret was the turning point for the concept musical. A
long run on Broadway was followed by a successful film version directed by Fosse. *Chicago* then caught up. It seems to
have been ahead of its time in the original production of 1975,
but two decades later it became a Broadway long-running musical, too, and, like *Cabaret*, it was turned into a successful film.

The film of *Cabaret* was made early in the history of the concept musical—1972. In the years just preceding, Sondheim was
teaming with Hal Prince on *Company* (1970) and *Follies* (1971),
two concept shows that, in different ways, look back to the revue tradition without losing contact with the sophistication of
the modern book show. Then, in the same year that *Chicago*
tried to make its way on Broadway, 1975, Michael Bennett
took up the brilliant concept of making a musical, *A Chorus
Line*, about the audition and rehearsal process that lies behind
the musical itself, and Sondheim and Hal Prince mounted *Pacific Overtures*, which used Kabuki stage techniques to deal with
the westernization of Japan. Thus, by 1975, the concept musical had arrived. It had received a jolt of British energy in 1971
with the Lloyd Webber/Tim Rice rock treatment of Scripture
in *Jesus Christ Superstar*, and it would receive another jolt when
Lloyd Webber was inspired to put T. S. Eliot's book of poems,
Old Possum's Book of Practical Cats, into a revue of numbers for
the cats themselves—a concept musical that threatened to run
forever.)

*Cabaret, Company, Follies, Pacific Overtures, Chicago, A Chorus
Line*—these concept musicals are avant-garde Broadway book
shows. Even when they recall the revue tradition, the leading
characters remain throughout the show and their lives change.
The plots of the concept shows are unpredictable and original.
They are driven by confidence that the book has become a
narrative art in itself, requiring new ways of relating book to
number. Some would say the musical became an important

form of drama in the age of Rodgers and Hammerstein, when the book became integrated with the music. I wish to say that the musical was already an important form of drama by the time of Rodgers and Hammerstein, that it never depended on the integration of book and number so much as on the alternation between them, that Rodgers and Hammerstein greatly enlarged the kinds of books that could be used for musicals, and that the age of the concept musical carried this advance in book-and-number formatting to the point that there is virtually nothing that cannot be imagined an effective topic for a musical. The ferment of ideas behind the concept show combines innovation with a strict sense of the musical's history (the revue as called to life in *Follies*), the musical's procedures (the audition and rehearsals of *A Chorus Line*), and the musical's relationships to other forms of theatre (the Kabuki methods in *Pacific Overtures*). The past and the future of the theatre are at issue in the best of them, which one could also say of Elizabethan drama and of other periods of greatness in the theatre, and this could not have happened without the advances made in book writing on Broadway from the time of *Show Boat* through the time of *Oklahoma!* and beyond, to our own time. The musical is arguably the major form of drama produced so far in America.

BRECHT AND THE DRAMA OF DISJUNCTION

It is the difference between book and number that gives the musical its potential as major drama. The European theorist who understood this aesthetic of disjunction most fully and who should stand in the place of Wagner as a challenging and instructive figure for the musical was Bertolt Brecht. That he cannot stand there is a sign of the amalgamation that has always existed between the Broadway theatre and the commercial interests of American show business. Brecht seized on the interruptive quality of the musical number as one means of "alienation" or "estrangement" in drama—the idea that audiences should be held at an emotional distance from the action, able to evaluate what is before them.[23] Indeed, one of Brecht's aims was to repudiate the Wagnerian aesthetic and recognize forms of drama that broke open the assumption of unity as the aim of the action. "When the epic theatre's methods begin to penetrate the opera, the first result is a radical *separation of the elements*," Brecht wrote. "The great struggle for supremacy between words, music, and production . . . can simply be bypassed by radically separating the elements." This "radical separation of the elements" had long been built into the revue formats described in this chapter, which had great attraction for Brecht. When he saw *Oklahoma!* on Broadway in 1946, he praised its plot as providing "scaffolding" for the "inserts" of the numbers, which is a better metaphor than a seamless whole, and when his version of *The Duchess of Malfi* failed in New York, he complained that the cast lacked the technique of the American musical. Zero Mostel and Elsa Lancaster, both trained in vaudeville theatre, were approached by Brecht for leads in his plays. To be sure, he also called the musical an empty form of drama for its political vacuity, but he knew that the song-and-dance format of the musical and the revue was one American source of technique for what he termed Epic Theatre.[24]

The musical is imbued with the capitalistic economic system that Brecht despised. In one of his earliest theoretical statements, appended to his and Kurt Weill's opera *The Rise and Fall of the City of Mahagonny*, Brecht noted that the capitalist apparatus of opera made fodder of the intellectuals who wrote the libretti and the music. The writers think they are producing the artwork, Brecht said, but in fact they are caught up in a system that is controlled by financial interests and is devoted to reproducing the successful formats of the past. The financial

---

[23] The idea is frequent in Brecht but is succinct in "On Music in Drama," in Willett, ed., *Brecht on Theatre*.

[24] Brecht saw *Oklahoma!* on September 30, 1946, accompanied by Ferdinand Reyher, whose diary is the source of information. See Lyon, *Bertolt Brecht in America*, 148–49. A dancer featured in *Oklahoma!*, Joan McCracken, later played Galileo's daughter in the New York production of Charles Laughton's *Galileo*, although Brecht may have had no hand in this bit of casting.

system on Broadway fits Brecht's complaint closely enough, yet innovation has proved to be entirely possible in the musical. The distance the genre has traveled from the early shows of Berlin and Kern through the Rodgers and Hammerstein era of mid-century and then down to the musicals of today shows that the musical is open to change, even though it belongs to the centers of modern capitalism, New York and London.

Certainly there is an enormous amount of formulaic writing in the history of the genre, but one part of Brecht would have understood why a spirit of innovation and experiment was able to push the musical into new territory in every decade of the twentieth century. The musical comes from subversive sources. The spirit of satire and travesty ran strong through both the revue and operetta traditions I have reviewed. More directly, the performers, composers, and lyricists of the early New York musicals came from the Lower East Side, the neighborhood of the Gershwin brothers, Irving Berlin, and Yip Harburg, while much of the music that gave the distinctively American feel and danceability to the early shows, ragtime and then jazz, came to New York from the South and the Midwest by way of Harlem. Broadway, which actually goes some distance toward connecting the Lower East Side and Harlem, found itself in the middle, a thriving ground for the spirit of license and parody so strong at either of its extremes.

That spirit was not enough in itself. It required a formal structure that could be learned and varied by performers as different in training and backgrounds as, say, Irving Berlin singing in Bowery restaurants and Eubie Blake playing piano in Harlem nightclubs. Kern and Gershwin were song pluggers on Tin Pan Alley. The popular song was learned on the job, and it was learned as a crowd-pleaser, but it was also learned as a formal structure. In part the formal structure came from the nineteenth-century parlor song with its verse-chorus format and its sharply defined stanzaic patterns within the chorus. March and polka rhythms crowded in on this format, then especially ragtime crowded in. Berlin, Blake, Gershwin, Kern and, hundreds of other composers, lyricists, and performers of the early twentieth century caught the new rhythms and learned how to produce tunes and verse in the standard formats. The most important thing they learned was how to connect the formats to the idioms of normal speech. When the elevated diction of the nineteenth-century song gave way to the "some of these days" vernacular of common experience, and when the syncopation of ragtime charged the tunes with fresh danceability, the way was open for putting groups of these tunes into stage vehicles of sufficient length to last the evening. The European revue and operetta formats outlined earlier provided the stage vehicles, both uptown and downtown. The result was a new theatrical genre trendy enough to change and tough enough to survive, an aesthetic with staying power.[25]

The musical connects with Brecht more clearly on the aesthetic side than on the political side. It is a matter of aesthetics that the practitioners of the musical wrote the language of ordinary people into popular songs and wrote the songs into stage entertainments that would draw crowds. When the crowds proved large enough to fill theatres, theatres were already waiting, and more could be built. Capitalism thrived on the opportunities for investment that were becoming apparent in the early twentieth century, and those entertainers and composers and lyricists from downtown and uptown were not interested in challenging the system expanding before them. There is no squaring the musical with Brecht's political economics. But the aesthetic basis of the musical is energized by the spirit of disunification that Brecht called for. This spirit can be captured and contained by capitalism, as the history of

[25] Sousa's marches, which have their own kind of syncopation, played a part in the advent of the modern American song. Sousa's turn-of-the century operettas, overlooked in accounts of the musical but fully apparent in the listings of Norton, *Chronology of American Musical Theater*, and Bordman, *American Musical Theatre*, were important in bringing his march-syncopation style into touch with musical theatre. For a historical treatment of song in America, see Hamm, *Yesterdays: Popular Song in America*. For an aesthetic view, see Hamm; see also Forte, *The American Popular Ballad of the Golden Era, 1924–1950*. The development of vernacular song lyrics is covered in Furia, *Poets of Tin Pan Alley*. Brecht's own songs were cut to European strophic patterns different from the Tin Pan Alley models, but the similarities outweigh the differences. See Kowalke, "Brecht and music: Theory and practice."

the musical has no trouble showing. But the aesthetic of disunification also has the potential for resisting structures of
wealth and power. It is a tough aesthetic, originally rooted in
black and immigrant culture and capable of turning the established pieties into song-and-dance routines fraught with social
criticism.

The chapters that follow are not about Brecht and political
drama until the end of the book. I am concerned with the aesthetics of the form, and I want to base my argument on specific
examples from the leading musicals themselves. First I turn attention to a well-known scene from *Oklahoma!*, a scene that
possesses the attributes of integration, to show that the difference between book and number is clear-cut and decisive. Then
I consider another well-known scene from *Oklahoma!* that has
none of the attributes of integration in order to show that the
book-and-number aesthetic is working there, too. I look at
several turning point or recognition scenes from good musicals
in which the book-and-number disjunction is again what
counts. Subsequent chapters take up the most obvious phe-
nomena of musical theatre—the characters break into song,
they often sing in ensembles, there is an orchestra, the crowd
applauds, there is a set—for it is in the conventions we take for
granted that the aesthetics of theatre are most firmly rooted. I
compare a famous show by Andrew Lloyd Webber and one by
Stephen Sondheim, because the aesthetic perspective I offer
suggests that Sondheim is doing the kind of theatre work that
promises an innovative future for the musical genre, while
Lloyd Webber is doing another kind of work. There is little if
anything of Wagner and Brecht in these chapters, but the contrast between their theories that I have sketched here is in the
background. Then, when the aesthetic work is done, a final
chapter asks, What kind of drama is this? and taps into political
theatre for a final remark. Sondheim will be prominent there,
for I believe Sondheim opens the way to political drama, although he makes no claims to that kind of writing himself. And
with Sondheim, Brecht returns to the picture. Sondheim has
little time for the Brechtian, but theory makes for interesting
alliances, and Sondheim and Brecht are an attractive pair, no

matter what either would have thought of the idea. I do not argue that Sondheim is a Brechtian dramatist; that would be pointless and wrong. But I do wish to say that Brecht's theory was right about the artistic form of the musical no matter how rigorously the Broadway musical refuses to answer up to his economic and political beliefs, and I do wish to say that Sondheim, who also refuses to answer up to Brecht, works with aesthetic characteristics that Brecht formulated in his own way, and imagines new variations for them.

Chapter Two

THE BOOK AND THE NUMBERS

LYRIC TIME

O F the two orders of time that the musical sets against one another, lyric time—the time of the numbers, as opposed to the time of the book—is the more challenging to think about. Lyric time counts on repetition, which often passes unnoticed, and that is why it is challenging. We do not think about repetition, although it is going on all around us, or in us. We assume we are making progress in our affairs, and we would rather think about that.

Repetition in song and dance fools everyone with its complexity. Popular songs seem simple and direct in performance, but once one looks at the contraption to see how it works—I borrow the phrasing from Auden, who said that is what should be done to poems—one is surprised at the layers of craft that combine to give the illusion of simplicity.[1]

All popular songs share this intricacy to some extent—it comes from the combination of melodic, rhythmic, and lyric patterns of repetition. Music gains meaning through the accretion of repeated combinations of phrases and rhythms, and dancers give body to these patterns through the repetitive gestures and

---

[1] Auden, *"The Dyer's Hand" and Other Essays*, pp. 50–51. Repeated elements can only be understood in relation to material that does not recur. Nonrecurring elements create a different context for each repetition, with the result that each repetition refers to its previous manifestation over a ground of difference. Theodor Adorno's theory of music, with Beethoven as the leading point of reference, provides a full definition of repetition in this sense. Clear guidance is available in Jarvis, *Adorno: A Critical Introduction*, pp. 124–37. Adorno's writings on Beethoven have been collected in *Beethoven: The Philosophy of Music*, ed. Tiedemann.

movements of their own discipline, which reflect the music and reinvent it at the same time. Song brings words into contact with these pulsations by adding its own possibilities of repetition.

"I Got Rhythm," from the Gershwins' *Girl Crazy* (1930), has an AABA musical structure. It is like thousands of popular songs in this regard—AABA is the most common format. The music of A is repeated once, then different music is heard as B, then A is repeated again. Three times the music of A is heard, with B serving to keep the second A apart from the third. The words to each A strain of music call out "I got" this, "I got" that, "I got my man, who can ask for anything more," and since there are three A strains of music, the "I got" phrases add up to eight (one is missed, on "In green pastures"), three of them being the refrain "I got my man, who can ask for anything more." Then the refrain is repeated once more as a coda. This kind of repetition would be intolerable in conversation, but it is normal and even enjoyable in a lyric and musical structure, that celebrates doing things again and again.

A dull song will keep its repetitions in line with one another.[2] A smart song counts on differences among its types of repetition, so they swing against one another. Each "I got" phrase ("music," "rhythm," "my man") has the same verse meter (trochaic), and this matches up to a repeated melodic meter: a tied-eighth note followed by a dotted quarter in measure 1 is followed by a dotted quarter followed by a tied eighth in measure 2.[3] That means the tied eighth and dotted quarter in measure 3 is both mirror of measure 2 and repeat of measure 1, and the same could be said twice over of measure 4. Yet the verse repetitions of the "I got" phrases plug along on their one routine until they reach their switcharound on "Who could ask for anything more." The systems of repetition cross over one another. The dotted-quarter motif of the melody runs aslant the duple beat of the musical rhythm, two meters keeping time

<del>---</del>
[2] For a fuller account of dull tunes, see Suisman, "Cue the Pop Ballad, Warn the Critics."

[3] See the analysis in Forte, *The American Popular Ballad of the Golden Era*, p. 20. Knapp, *The American Musical and the Formation of National Identity*, pp. 82–85, also gives a fuller account of this song.

within their own repetitions but not quite with each other, so
that the syncopation is pronounced.

The composition is a study in repeats and mirrors. The patterns do not exactly match each other. They actually jive with
each other, coming close to matching but keeping a little apart,
too, a distance where swing is possible, but they do coincide in
their endings. No one thinks of this song as subtle (especially
after Ethel Merman belted it out in the original production of
Girl Crazy), but it is extremely intricate.

My point is that such a completely worked out structure is
set off from the play in which it occurs by virtue of its syncopation of repetitions. The fashioning of repetition in the number
creates a formality of expression that the book does not have,
and that formality of expression results in a kind of characterization and a kind of dramatic action that the nonmusical play
either does without or must attain through other means. Yet
the formality of expression in musical numbers comes to an
end and the play returns to the book, a return from repetitive
time to progressive time, from lyric to dialectic. Lyric time can
be well paced, book time can be well paced, but what matters
most is the alternation between the two. That is what gives the
musical its lift, its energy, its elation.

An Integrated Number from *Oklahoma!*

An illustration of these two orders of time can be found in a
scene of such close articulation between book and number that
integration might seem the appropriate word. Early in *Oklahoma!* the number "The Surrey with the Fringe on Top" arises
because a cowboy named Curly feels so strongly about taking a
farm woman named Laurey to the box social that he breaks
into song as an imaginative way to get around her resistance.
Laurey has teased him by saying that the only way he can take
a girl to the box social is by having her "ride on behind ole
Dun," his horse. Curly can imagine offering a girl a better way,
which he describes in the intricate repetitions of "Surrey."
First, though, here is the same moment from the source play,

Green Grow the Lilacs, written in 1931 by Lynn Riggs, where Curly describes his fantastic surrey this way:

> A bran' new surrey with fringe on the top four inches long—and *yeller*! And two white horses a-rarin' and faunchin' to go! You'd shore ride like a queen settin' up in *that* carriage! Feel like you had a gold crown set on yer head, 'th diamonds in it big as goose eggs. . . . And this yere rig has got four fine side-curtains, case of a rain. And isinglass winders to look out of! And a red and green lamp set on the dashboard, winkin' like a lightnin' bug![4]

If this is a thrust, it is waiting for a parry. Each statement in dramatic dialogue expects to receive a counter-statement, which occasions more counter-statements, as though the thrust and parry were adding up to something new. The form is dialectical. In Riggs's play, Laurey is not slow to answer Curly's speech about the surrey, and he must then respond in a different way. When a song intervenes in the musical format, however, this dialectical pattern is suspended in favor of lyrical repetitions. Curly singing can repeat himself extensively and variously without being countered. To be exact, he manages the repetitions that are built into the music. The melody repeats in one way, the rhythm in another, the verse in another. His management of the repetitions becomes the dramatic focus, and Laurey becomes a listener. She may indicate her reactions to the song, but she cannot speak for herself without entering the song and making it a duet, or halting it for a moment.

Now look at Hammerstein's lyric revision of Curly's fantasy about the surrey. It has the verse-chorus format of the standard Tin Pan Alley song, which gives the singer a chance to make a little drama out of the song itself, introducing the topic in the verse and elaborating the main point in the chorus.[5] Curly seizes this opportunity with his introductory "When I take you

[4] I use the text of *Green Grow the Lilacs* included in Clark and Davenport, *Nine Modern American Plays*. The quotation is on p. 93.

[5] The verse–chorus structure was used in nineteenth-century minstrel shows, where the chorus really was sung by a chorus. It was usually a refrain, such as "O Susannah, don't you cry for me / I come from Alabama with my banjo on my knee," and the narrative told by the song was conveyed by the

out tonight with me / Honey, here's the way its going to be,"
but let us concentrate on the chorus to the song, which is the
part everyone knows. The stanzas of the chorus fall into the
standard AABA pattern. The music of A is repeated immediately in the second A, then new musical material forms B (the
release or the bridge), then the A tune is heard for a third time.
The rhyme pattern also shifts in B from the couplet plus refrain of A to a quatrain, as follows:

A

Chicks and ducks and geese better scurry
When I take you out in the surrey,
When I take you out in the surrey with the fringe on top!

A

Watch thet fringe and see how it flutters
When I drive them high-steppin' strutters!
Nosey-pokes'll peek through their shutters and their eyes will pop!

B

The wheels are yeller, the upholstery's brown,
The dashboard's genuine leather,
With isinglass curtains y'c'n roll right down
In case there's a change in the weather;

A

Two bright side lights, winkin' and blinkin,'
Ain't no finer rig, I'm a-thinkin'!
You c'n keep yer rig if you're thinkin' 'at I'd keer to swap
Fer that shiny little surrey with the fringe on the top!

Hammerstein's lyric reads the play's dialogue closely and clev-
erly, with the isinglass windows turning into isinglass curtains,

---

succession of verses. Twentieth-century songs do away with the narrative purpose of the verse, which is typically heard only once and is introductory, and
concentrate on the chorus (now usually sung by the solo vocalist), which carries the main burden of the tune. Jerome Kern actually called the chorus "the
burthen." The standard authority on the history of popular songs is Hamm,
Yesterdays: Popular Song in America.

and the "winkin'" dashboard lamp turning into side-lights whose winkin' and blinkin' set one a-thinkin.' One can see why Rodgers and Hammerstein would have been pleased over the integration achieved here. The play's dialogue has been turned to music without losing its cowboy specificity. Curly in the song sounds like Curly in the play. He has not turned into a song-and-dance man. He is Curly in the book and he is Curly in the song. A cowboy. This is not a role for Fred Astaire.

True, but the important point is being overlooked. By turning Curly's dialogue into the closed lyric form of song, Rodgers and Hammerstein have added to his character in much the same way as a Fred Astaire performance added to his character— by creating someone able to turn body and voice into musical repetition. Spoken dialogue is not without rhythm, pace, a beat, tone—all the terms one uses of music—but music puts the terms into patterns of repetition that prose has to do without, producing a character who is enlarged by virtue of being able to keep these patterns going simultaneously.

> Don't you wisht y'd go on ferever,
> Don't you wisht y'd go on ferever?
> Don't you wisht y'd go on ferever and 'ud never stop?

I am quoting from the second chorus of the song now (one of the repetitions is that the AABA structure is itself heard three times). Let the melody of the quoted passage be heard, and repetition will be fixed in its own order of time. The melody is exactly the same for each "Don't you wisht y'd go on ferev—" with a change of melody occurring on each "-er" at the end of the phrase, in a rising pattern that continues beyond the final "ev-er" to go one step higher over a last bit of rhyme on "nev-er stop." The pattern of repetition in the melody and harmony coincides with the pattern of repetition in the lyric so fully, and refuses to coincide at such deft points, that the deepening of character happening before us is a deepening in repetition, a demonstration that this so-called cowboy has a control in voice and body over rhythm, pace, beat, and tone that is like the control in voice and body that Fred Astaire had when he was a song-and-dance man enlarging characters in the silly plots of the 1920s.

Curly does not dance at this point, one might say. But the singer repeats bits of the musical rhythm in his gesture, his movement, his way of putting across the song—singers do have a choreography. He does not dance like Fred Astaire, and Fred Astaire did not sing like this Curly before us, but they both turn body and voice to music instead of speaking prose in their numbers, and the effect on a listener is different from the effect in the prose dialogue of *Green Grow the Lilacs*.

How do listeners react to songs like this one, songs in the popular vein? Toe-tapping is common among listeners, who sometimes snap their fingers too, and might hum the tune or even sing the words. We are looking outside the theatre now, but that is where the most successful songs are meant to go. Dancing gets the body moving, which is what the syncopated repetitions of a popular tune call for. We will later have reason to focus on dance as a major practice in the aesthetic of the musical. For the moment, though, just picture yourself tapping your toe if you are a listener, or dancing with a partner on a ballroom floor if you are a lover, or singing and dancing on a stage if you are a performer, and you will have the basics of lyric time in view. You are taking pleasure in repetition, and you aren't progressing toward any destination beyond the performance of repetition itself. You may be thinking of some other destination, especially if you are a lover, but you won't go there until the song is ended or you break it off. At the end of the song other destinations become possible, and your performance during the song might improve the prospects for the other destinations, but your engagement in the song itself is not dialectical, it is not progressive, it is repetitive.

The listener who matters in the scene at hand is Laurey, the one Curly is trying to impress with his "Surrey" number. Laurey is listening with Aunt Eller, and they are drawn into the rhythm of Curly's song to the point of silently mouthing the

words he sings, the words I quoted above about going on fer-
ever. "(AUNT ELLER's and LAUREY's lips move involuntarily,
shaping the same words)." Laurey is capable of song, too. She
will break out into her own music later, but here she and Aunt
Eller feel the performative charm of Curly's deepening character and silently share the lyric with him.

Riggs's Laurey does not do this. The actress in Riggs's play
cannot mouth Curly's words because he does not repeat his
phrases. People repeat one another's phrases in song because
song is based on patterns of repetition, but book dialogue usually lacks the patterns and people speak for themselves. The
Laurey of *Green Grow the Lilacs* is a simpler and less sentimental character than she is in the musical. She does not fall into
the rhythm of Curly's description. She waits for him to finish
his description, holding herself at a distance, getting a coun-
terthrust ready:

> LAUREY. Whur'd you git sich a rig at? (*With explosive laughter*) Anh,
> I bet he's went and h'ard it over to Claremore, thinkin I'd go
> with him!

She accuses Curly of spending all his money on this rig—now
he has to find somebody to ride in it. He defends himself by
pretending that he has made the whole thing up, and she gets
after him for lying to her. Hammerstein uses all of this—
later. But his Laurey has gotten caught up in Curly's lyric,
and she has to draw back after the second chorus in time to
regain her hoydenish defenses. When she does draw back,
Hammerstein virtually copies the Riggs dialogue for a moment. But there is a telling difference. The musical insists
on orchestral underscoring while Hammerstein uses Riggs's
dialogue. The musical register cannot be allowed to lapse,
not yet. The stretch of prose will be followed by the third
chorus of the song, and the orchestral continuity must be
maintained, so that the order of musical time will carry
through to the real conclusion.

Here is the Riggs dialogue that Hammerstein turns into the
final stanza.

CURLY . . . Don't you wish they *was* sich a rig, though? Nen you
could go to the party and do a hoe-down til mornin' 'f you was a
mind to. Nen drive home 'th the sun a-peakin' at you over the
ridge, purty and fine.

Laurey will have none of this in Riggs. "I ain't wantin' to do no
hoe-down till mornin'," she complains, and in a few seconds
she has slammed the door on Curly. She stalks out in Hammerstein's book too, but something else has happened to her
during the final stanza of the song. The stage direction introducing the third stanza reads: "The music, which had become
more turbulent to match the scene, now softens," and Curly
"sings very softly":

A

I can see the stars gittin' blurry
When we ride back home in the surrey,
Ridin' slowly home in the surrey with the fringe on top.

A

I can feel the day gittin' older,
Feel a sleepy head near my shoulder,
Noddin', droopin' close to my shoulder till it falls, kerplop!

B

The sun is swimmin' on the rim of a hill,
The moon is takin' a header,
And jist as I'm thinkin all the earth is still,
A lark'll wake up in the medder. . . .

A

Hush! You bird, my baby's a-sleepin'—
Maybe got a dream worth a-keepin'
(*Soothing and slower*)
Whoa! You team, and jist keep a-creepin' at a slow clip-clop.
Don't you hurry with the surrey with the fringe on the top.

This is exactly where the divide between the two orders
of time can be seen most clearly. The pace of the song has

slowed, as though Curly is dreaming the thing. Laurey falls for this too—she might even have her head on his shoulder at this point. The song's ending is marked by a gentle cadence to the tonic in the orchestra just as Curly repeats the title of the tune. Everyone knows that a song is ending. The gap between the end of the song and the resumption of the book is filled with applause. That cannot happen in Riggs's scene and it cannot fail to happen in Rodgers and Hammerstein's scene. And while the applause marks the divide, "Laurey starts slowly to emerge from the enchantment of his description." She has been captivated again, and now she has to get back to her feistiness: "On'y . . . on'y there aint no sich rig. You said you made the whole thing up." The seam is showing here. Hammerstein is reverting to the exchange they had between the second and third choruses, and back to the rest of Riggs's dialogue, which is followed through to her door-slamming exit. The musical underscoring is over now. We are back in the order of book time.

A DIS-INTEGRATED NUMBER FROM *OKLAHOMA!*

Now let us glance at a number from *Oklahoma!* that is not well integrated into the book. When Curly and Laurey finally get on the same wavelength later in act 1, they sing "People Will Say We're in Love," which moved out of the show and became a standard popular song. It does not fit the plot very well. Laurey sings "Don't please my folks too much," but she has no folks in the book. Her parents are dead, and she and her aunt are trying to run the farm together. That is a main point of the plot, but the song contradicts it. "Sweetheart," the Laurey of the song calls Curly. Sweetheart? The Laurey in the book would never call a cowboy "Sweetheart." This song makes a poor fit with plot and character, yet no one has ever complained about the poor fit before. I am only pretending to complain. Like everyone else, I am glad to hear this love duet sung by two good singers in *Oklahoma!* It is high time they sang together, these two. We have seen their musical selves before, in their solos. Now they are pretending not to be in love yet, but everyone knows they have fallen for each other—because they sing the same tune and repeat it the same way.[6]

The song works this way. The lyric structure is AABA, and the A sections depend on melodic leaps of a fifth on each "Don't" phrase:

> Don't throw bouquets at me,
> Don't please my folks too much.
> Don't laugh at my jokes too much.

Then the A sections answer these leaps with some tight chromatic writing on the refrain, "People will say we're in love." The chromatic motif stands out on the bridge or B section, the part that keeps the second A away from the third A. But the tight chromatic writing in the bridge occurs only after a dramatic drop of a fifth on the one "Don't" phrase which occurs in B—"Don't start"—as though what rises a fifth after every other "Don't" ought to drop a fifth after this one. We could go on about the patterns of repetition that give this duet its lift, but the point is that this beautifully crafted song is not well integrated into *Oklahoma!*, it does not fit its plot and character, it violates the theory of the unified musical, and no one cares. Integration is not the point. The book has been interrupted for a good song about love, giving Laurey and Curly a chance to switch into performance mode, and the musical is finding its groove.

RECOGNITIONS AND TURNING POINTS

Rodgers and Hammerstein show tunes are thought to "forward the action," as though the book were actually making progress through the lyrics of the numbers. It is more accurate to say that the plot is suspended for the time of the number,

---

[6] Hammerstein originally wrote a different duet in this position, "Someone Will Teach You," with lyrics more in keeping with Laurey's character. This can be seen in an early script entitled "*Green Grow the Lilacs*: Musical Version," now in the Performing Arts Library at Lincoln Center, No. NCOF 1942. I have not found music for this lyric.

which carries the characters into new versions of themselves.[7]
On rare occasions this new dimension of characterization does
contain an element of plot, but the book usually repeats the bit
of plot incorporated into song on these occasions anyhow, and
the most frequent phenomenon is for the plot to come to a
standstill during the time required for the song and then to resume when the song is ended. Yet there is often an impression
that the plot has advanced. Lyric time has reached its conclusion, creating the illusion that it was the plot that was moving
along. It wasn't, it was the performance of the number, but il-
lusions count for a great deal in the theatre and deserve to be
taken seriously.

One technique is to make a number refer to a crucial recognition on the part of the singing character. The singing character cannot do anything about the recognition while the song
continues (apart from sing about it, which is the other dimension), but the recognition belongs to this character alone, and
it is important. In *Carousel* (1945), Billy Bigelow discovers (in
the book) that he is going to be a father and realizes that he
will have to find a way to get money, perhaps even by stealing
it. Molnar's *Liliom*, the play on which *Carousel* is based, does
not give the circus barker even one line about this, the recognition is so obvious. In one of their finest decisions Rodgers
and Hammerstein gave him a number titled "Soliloquy," which
consists of two songs strung together, one about the possibility
of a son ("My Boy Bill"), the other about the possibility of a
daughter ("My Little Girl"), and blended the tunes with other
song segments ("I wonder what he'll think of me," "I don't
give a damn what he does") to give the impression of a musical
structure that is open to the character's expressiveness—the
impression of an aria, in other words. But the segments come
out of popular tune formats too (as they do in some arias), and

[7] See Knapp, *The American Musical*, p. 12: "music notoriously does not un-
fold in 'real time,' but rather imposes a kind of suspended animation so as to
intensify selected emotional moments, and through this dramatic hiatus di-
rects us all the more urgently to see behind the mask/makeup/costume of the
performer—even as he or she embodies the role being played even more fully
through the enactment of song."

THE BOOK AND THE NUMBERS 43

"Soliloquy" never loses touch with its sources in American song. That is its genius. It builds several songs and segments into a continuous number neatly connected to the book and gives the baritone playing Billy Bigelow a shining moment of recognition (and a high G at the end), both for his voice and for his character's realization of impending fatherhood. This was real innovation in the mid-1940s. It was not the first pseudo-aria in American musicals, but it was the first to let a character sing his way into his most important recognition in the plot. Then the number comes to a close and the book resumes. The Billy Bigelow of the shining moment of recognition goes back to being Molnar's foolish circus barker and lets himself be suckered into a futile robbery, in which he is killed. There is a difference between the character of the singing Billy Bigelow who makes recognitions and the foolish Billy Bigelow who is killed in the robbery attempt, and this difference is not the deepening of a psychological entity but change of mode in the characterization itself. There are two Billys, only one of them capable of hitting the high G (the original Billy, John Raitt, sometimes managed a high B-flat), and the startling, enlivening fact is that they are projected by the same performer, adept in both orders of time, the book and the number.

I would like to examine some turning point or recognition songs from the era of Rodgers and Hammerstein and its aftermath, in the spirit of admiration for the strong connections composers and librettists and lyricists learned to make between book and number. These are numbers that verge on including plot elements within their structures, thus seeming to unite book and number. We will see that even when book and number are closely coordinated, the two remain distinct from one another.

GUYS AND DOLLS

A turning point changes the direction of the plot in some decisive way. *Reversal* is another name for it. In most musicals the reversal is a scene in which the lovers, having encountered obstacles in their romance, find their way to reconciliation and eventual marriage. This is the standard turn in most romantic comedy, musical or not, and the thrust and parry of dialogue is normally the medium in which it occurs. Musicals often insert a number at this point, in order to celebrate the turn toward romance, and in the Rodgers and Hammerstein era the impression of integrated book and number was gained by articulating the book and number so closely that the turning point seems to occur in the number. This is usually an illusion, but an interesting one.

Guys and Dolls (1950), the only romantic comedy to stage its reversal in a sewer, has a big song-and-dance number for the gamblers just before the turn occurs. Sky Masterson has hit upon a way to restore his relationship with Miss Sarah Brown. He will stake $1,000 against each of the other gamblers, and he will roll them for their souls. If he wins, they must attend the Salvation Army prayer meeting that night—a gesture that will balance the offense the same gamblers committed the night before, when they stole into the mission to hold their crap game. Miss Sarah Brown has broken off her relationship with Sky over that contretemps. "What kind of doll are you?" she is asked at that point: "A Mission doll," she replies, and leaves Sky (so she thinks) once and for all. Now in the sewer because all other locations are unavailable, Sky will become a "Mission guy" by outgambling the gamblers and bringing them into the mission for prayer. He will also help to save the mission, which is threatened by falling attendance.

"Luck Be a Lady Tonight" is the number that leads up to the decisive throw of the dice. Remove the number and Sky will still win his bet. The plot will be intact, but the scene will lose its power, because the dramatic interest is in the elaboration that the song-and-dance number gives to the gamblers' concern for "Lady Luck." They are entering the lyric order of time, where they extend their characters by showing themselves as terrific dancers, and the plot is not advancing at all. Musical repetition is giving the pulse to the scene (it is an unusually repetitive melody and harmony) and the plot is suspended. To be exact, the reversal occurs during the blackout at the end of

FIGURE 2. The turning point in *Guys and Dolls*. Robert Alda as Sky Masterson, rolling the dice to win the gamblers' souls in the original production. Museum of the City of New York.

the number, when Sky finally rolls the dice after everyone has been singing and dancing at some length. The final beat occurs on the "Ha!" of the gamblers as Sky throws the dice. We don't see the outcome of the roll, but we don't need to. The reversal takes effect when the book resumes in the next scene. Sky has won. The gamblers are on their way to the Mission, and the book is now able to proceed to a reconciliation between the lovers.

It transpires that a second pair of lovers, Nathan Detroit and Miss Adelaide, also find themselves headed for marriage as a result of Sky's climactic throw of the dice. But they do not

understand this at first. The degree of impudence in this wonderful plot cannot be overestimated. Not only does the turning point occur during a blackout moment in a sewer, but it is
also misunderstood by the female partner in the second romantic relationship, Miss Adelaide, who encounters Nathan
on his way to the Mission. Nathan reports that he is going to a
prayer meeting. Thirteen years she has been engaged to this
man, and this is the last straw. "That's the biggest lie you ever
told me," Miss Adelaide retorts, but it is actually the truth. He
is going to a prayer meeting. Sky won the roll. When Miss
Adelaide discovers that Nathan was actually telling the truth
for once, she is willing to try for a marriage again, and this
time it works.

That the turning point for both romances has taken place in
a sewer is a stroke of genius, not only because it answers to the
lower origins of the musical itself (which goes back to the "illegitimate," nonpatented theatres of later eighteenth-century
and earlier nineteenth-century England, where melodrama and
burletta were allowed, comedy and tragedy being reserved for
the patent houses at Covent Garden, Drury Lane, and the
Haymarket) but also because it opens a new dimension to the
space of the stage. Musicals tend to fill the surface stage with
dance and song, but this musical discovers the space "under"
the stage when Nicely-Nicely Johnson is asked the persistent
question of this plot, "Where's the crap game?" and replies
that it is about ten minutes' walk "this way" and climbs down a
manhole in the stage. The sewer scene may be the low point of
modern drama, and it deserves full credit for this.

We should glance at two remaining songs from this show, so
neatly are they inserted into the book. In both cases, something other than integration is having the main dramatic effect. "Sit Down, You're Rocking the Boat" is Nicely-Nicely
Johnson's testimony at the prayer meeting. It is a terrific "11
o'clock" number, a showstopper to rouse everyone near the
end of the evening, and *Guys and Dolls* would be reduced without it. But it does not advance the plot. The mission has been
saved once the gamblers have trooped into the prayer meeting,
and what this number adds is a comic elaboration of that

point.[8] It blossoms into an ensemble number, with the gamblers and the mission workers all dancing and singing together—and this is what matters, the ensemble elaboration of a point already established by the book, an episode of elation in formal song-and-dance terms.

"Marry the Man Today" is the other number, and in this case there truly is a recognition scene within the time of the number. The two heroines have introduced themselves to each other and they realize they share a problem. Adelaide has discovered that Nathan really was going to a prayer meeting, so she can forgive him and get him to marry her. Both heroines are a little worried that they are in love with unreliable men, gamblers. Then they break into a lyric about shopping for clothes and groceries when they are really thinking about shopping for husbands, and as the number develops they come to agree that the gamblers can be married first and reformed later. The drama of the number is not that point, which is ordinary, but the performance of the duet, which brings the Mission Doll and the Nightclub Doll into exact coordination with each other and lets them show their combined control over the situation. The singing of the duet is the meaning of the episode. This is the same principle as the earlier one, where the singing of the ensemble is the meaning. Musical performance has a dramatic meaning *as performance*. A duet has significance as a duet. A chorus has significance as a chorus.

MY FAIR LADY, WEST SIDE STORY

Two outstanding musicals of the mid-1950s, *My Fair Lady* (1956) and *West Side Story* (1957), add reversal or turning point scenes to the plays on which they are otherwise based, Shaw's *Pygmalion* and Shakespeare's *Romeo and Juliet*. *My Fair Lady*

[8] A second turning point occurs when Sarah tells her lie about whether the gamblers held their game in the Mission the previous night. This is also book dialogue. Lt. Brannigan breaks into the scene just as the number is beginning. Perhaps the number keeps him from making arrests, but there are no arrests to be made anyway. This is a prayer meeting!

dramatizes the scene in which the cockney flower girl, Eliza Doolittle, masters upper-class pronunciation under the instruction of Professor Henry Higgins. Shaw's play omits the instruction scene altogether. Shaw was determined to avoid romantic implications between the flower girl and the older professor, so the play steers around the intimacy of the accomplishment that occurs between them and hastens on to the social results of the accomplishment, Eliza's visit to Mrs. Higgins's "at-home" tea. The breakthrough instruction scene first appears in the screen play that Shaw and Gabriel Pascal devised for the 1938 film.[9] Lerner and Loewe followed the film in many respects, and it was perhaps their happiest musical decision to cap the instruction scene with a number celebrating Eliza's success, "The Rain in Spain." The turning point itself, when Eliza actually speaks "the rain in Spain stays mainly in the plain" with correct pronunciation, occurs as a book scene. It is a dialectical exchange—Higgins shows some feeling for Eliza's exhaustion, and she responds by learning his way of speech. The number is reserved for the elation that follows. It elaborates the turning point, but the turning point itself belongs to the book. "I think she's got it!" cries Higgins as the orchestra picks up on "Spain" with habanera underscoring, and the change into lyric time follows with wonderful effect. The elevated feeling of song is perfectly in keeping with the change from exhaustion to delight in the characters. The difference in the characters matches the difference in mode, as the number takes over from the book. But the number does take over. A change of mode is noticeable. The humor by which Higgins's hard-handed instruction about rain and Spain becomes a tango beat, and a song-and-dance number in which even the professor participates is wholehearted and appropriate. Its effect could not be attained in book mode.

In *West Side Story*, the love potion device from *Romeo and Juliet* is replaced by one of Arthur Laurents's best book scenes. Shakespeare's plot depends on a prevented message. The mes-

---

[9] The relationship between film and musical is described in Block, *Enchanted Evenings: The Broadway Musical from* Show Boat *to Sondheim*, pp. 232 ff.

senger is trapped by plague restrictions and cannot deliver the news to Romeo that Juliet is alive. This is reported, not dramatized, and the Laurents scene is better. Anita is taunted by the white gang of Jets for her color and her gender, and the gang prevents her from reaching Tony with the news she is trying to bring him from Maria. A mambo is playing on a jukebox. This is picked up by the orchestra, which sets a dance rhythm, and the Jets turn the dance rhythm into a savage attack on Anita, virtually a gang rape. "Stop it!" cries Doc, the druggist, and the book resumes with Anita's angry lie: Chino has killed Maria, tell that to your white friend Tony. This good book writing could have been handled without the number, for the Jets are brutal to Anita without dancing about it. The dancing adds a performance element that shifts the Jets into a different mode of characterization, however, and in this case the performance mode is startling. These white boys had seemed sympathetic, even charming, a few minutes earlier, in "Officer Krupke." Now they are ready to be rapists. The numbers turn them now one way, now another, and the most disturbing thing is that they are good performers both ways. The dance number carries them beyond the racism and misogyny of the book scene and makes the violence inherent in both racisim and misogyny break into what from one viewpoint is a near rape and from another is brilliant dancing.

GYPSY

Sondheim has tried at times to tighten the connection between book and number so that the gap of difference would seem to disappear. His musicals are solidly based on the distinction between book and number I have been discussing, but the artist and puzzlemaker at work in these shows loves to create paradoxes, such as the number that appears to be the book all of a sudden. The clearest example is "Rose's Turn" in *Gypsy*, where Sondheim's aim was to write a number that did not end at all in the conventional sense, with the audience's applause. Rose would reach her recognition—that she had done everything

"for me" and not for her daughters—and would go on scream-
ing "for me" while the orchestra faded out with scratchy vio-
lins. "A woman having a nervous breakdown should not get applause from the audience," Sondheim thought.[10] There would
be a "chilling moment" in the theatre, then "the daughter
would come out of the wings applauding her, and they would
go on." Shifting the applause function to Louise would have
removed the conventional sign of the gap, the moment of audience applause at the end of a number.

In the *Gypsy* planning, this matter of applause became decisive. When Oscar Hammerstein saw the number during the
tryout run, he advised Sondheim to let the audience do its own
applauding. "The audience is so anxious to applaud her that
they are not listening to the scene that follows," Hammerstein
is reported to have said. So Sondheim let Ethel Merman bring
the number to a close and draw her applause from the audience. Hammerstein was making a practical point in advising
Sondheim to let the number come to a clear ending. I am putting the same point in theoretical terms. The ending of a number normally requires definition in a musical, on the one hand
to let an audience show its appreciation for a strong performance, and on the other, to distinguish the closure of one order of time, the repetitive order of the number, from the resumption of the other, the progressive order of the book. (The
dance-rape in *West Side Story* allows for no applause, though. It
is exceptional.)

LAUREY MAKES UP HER MIND

Finally, in what is often set forth as the classic case of integration, Laurey's dream at the end of act 1 in *Oklahoma!* is a
"recognition" of the mistake she is making by taunting Curly
and pretending to favor Jud. The ballet was originally entitled
"Laurey Makes Up Her Mind," as though the crucial turn of
the plot occurred in the dream, but in fact Laurey goes on to be

---

[10] Secrest, *Stephen Sondheim*, p. 139.

frightened by Jud all over again, at the box social itself in act 2, and she makes up her mind there, too. In an act 2 scene that is strictly book time (and is taken over from the source play, *Green Grow the Lilacs*), she summons the courage to fire Jud from his job on her farm. Then, in an outburst of fear over what Jud will do, she realizes how much she needs Curly. Within the same scene, Curly proposes and she accepts. Should the ballet be removed from the show, Laurey will still make up her mind for Curly, will still summon the courage to fire Jud, and will still fear for her life at Jud's hands. The plot would be intact without the ballet, although *Oklahoma!* would be a good deal less interesting.

For there is no denying the boldness of the ballet interlude. De Mille was following the lead of George Balanchine, who had brought ballet into the musical in several Rodgers and Hart shows of the later 1930s, but Balanchine was intent on broadening the musical to include ballet, while De Mille, intent on that too, was also intent on representing the mind of the heroine under pressure. Heroines had not often had minds in musicals before *Oklahoma!* This heroine even dreams about sex, especially the connection between sexuality and her fear of violence in Jud. To suppose that *Oklahoma!* is about nothing more important than who will take Laurey to the box social, a frequent complaint of critics who look back from the perspective of later and more sophisticated musicals, is to miss the point. Jud is capable of rape if Laurey does go out with him, capable of arson if she doesn't.[11] Critics who think this trivial have perhaps not faced these situations.

The dream-ballet dances out the sexual threat, a nervy episode for a musical of 1943. But it depends for its effectiveness on the difference between number and book, and the exact definition of that difference at the end of the ballet can draw a gasp from the audience. The ballet number ends with Laurey about to be raped by Jud, then book time intrudes with Jud really standing there and saying to the awakening girl: "Wake up,

[11] See Miller, *Rebels with Applause: Broadway's Groundbreaking Musicals*, p. 46, for an accurate view of this scene.

Laurey. It's time to start for the party." The rapist/murderer of the dream is to be her date for the box social! So act 1 ends with Laurey dazed over the collision between the dreamed number and the reality of the book.

Thus, dramatic recognitions or turning points are normally achieved through the dialectic of book scenes, in musical and nonmusical dramas alike. Something else is going on in the musical numbers, no matter how closely articulated with the book they are, and this is what gives the musical its extra layer of dramatic quality. The songs and dances intensify the dramatic moment and give it a special glow of performance. Performance has dramatic significance in itself. This is true of all drama to some extent, but the musical elevates the performance meaning and makes it into the defining quality of the moment. Two characters can express the same thing at the same time in a duet and can do so with a style that controls the situation. That is not the dialectic of the book scene. It is repetitive coordination in body and voice, lyric time being found in the body, twice over. Solos have a glow of performance too, once over. If the character glowing in performance seems different from the same character in the book scenes, this discrepancy is desirable because it fits the discrepancy between the two modes of time that the numbers and the book represent, doubling the kinds of performance involved in presenting what is supposed to be one person. Could Shaw's Henry Higgins ever be imagined larking about in an impromptu Spanish fandango in his parlor with a flower girl? No, but Lerner and Loewe use the additional dimension of musical number to double Higgins's character and treat George Bernard Shaw to a bit of cheek. There is always a bit of cheek in the musical's revision of its sources, a matter we return to later.

One more point about the two orders of time. Everyone understands book time because we think our own lives follow the progressive mode. We have beginnings and endings too, and proceed on the assumption that something important happens in the middle to give shape to things. We do not understand repetition nearly so well, even though it is going on around us and within us, as night turns to day once again, as the heart continues beating. Numbers are based on the time of repetition, and we hardly ever think about this, perhaps because we have a vested interest in progress. Good for the sunrise, we say, good for the heartbeat, but we have to get on with shaping a future. So we go ahead making progress—until a song crosses our minds, or we get caught up in a dance, or do anything musical. There are other ways of repetition that can stop us in our tracks, but music is the way that matters in the songs and dances of number time. These interruptions to book time deepen and complicate the musical, and they are the events that need to be understood in the aesthetics of the form.

Chapter Three

CHARACTER AND THE VOICE
OF THE MUSICAL

ARE THERE REAL PEOPLE IN MUSICALS?

A BETTER book is what made the musical seem to become integrated, a better book that demanded more
care in thinking about the kinds of numbers that would
be able to interrupt these good plots. That is part of the argument so far. But we have not faced the character issue fully
enough. Integration theory holds that the new musicals deep-
ened the psychology of the characters, as though the way now
stood open to the presentation of real people in real situations.
"*West Side Story* is about real people: real life, real love," says
one of the best books on the mid-century musical, Ethan
Mordden's *Everything's Coming Up Roses*.[1] Is this true?

The doubling effect we have described when characters
change from book to number would mean the answer is no, if
by real we mean life as it is normally lived in the world of fact
and event outside the theatre. Book and number routines are
for the stage. Yet Ethan Mordden knows that and still uses
"real" for *West Side Story*. I think he is right, but I want to
know why reality comes to mind when we are obviously dealing with theatrical performance.

The conclusion of *West Side Story* gives us something new in
musicals—a plot that ends in grief. Tony has been killed, and
the grief is left to Maria. In some sense she is real at this point—
as real as stage characters can be. All stage characters have been
transformed beyond real people by being written in the first

[1] Mordden, *Everything's Coming Up Roses*, p. 245.

place, or, to put it another way, by consistently speaking dialogue that normally answers the speech of others and is about to be answered itself. Real people sometimes have such dialectical encounters, but their speech is also packed with purposeless chatter, "noise." The dramatist eliminates the noise and intensifies the dialectic. All dramatists try to do that. Musical drama has a second way of creating intensified character that is not dialectic but lyrical. The idea that characters in either kind of play are "real" means that the dialectical or the lyrical conventions are so well managed that we forget we are watching a play—suspend our disbelief some would say—and fall into the attitude that these are actual people in actual situations. Shakespeare's and Chekhov's characters can be real in this sense too. The question is, what does a musical add to this intense theatricality by virtue of having a book-and-number alternation?

Maria's final number falters and stops. She sings a few bars of "A Place for Us." Tony tries to join her, then he dies. Stephen Banfield shrewdly notes that the failed number has the effect of song, song recognized in its denial.[2] The orchestra continues beyond the singer, leading to the procession that follows, when the two gangs together carry off Tony's body, Maria following behind, to the music of their earlier dream ballet about getting free of the tenements. The music organizes their grief. Maria has certainly changed. She has been a charming and passionate ingénue through the action, but when Tony dies, she acquires a sudden forcefulness. Her voice hard and flat with rage, she takes up a gun and asks how many gang members she can kill while saving one bullet for herself. Then she takes charge of the gangs instead, having them join hands and carry the body away, in the real final number. "Te adoro, Anton" is her spoken farewell to her lover. She breaks out in tears, but she will never be girlish again. The dramatization is strong and believable. Mordden must have moments like this in mind when he calls the young lovers "real."

Think back to Maria's earlier numbers. Sondheim has accused himself of miswriting her lyric in "I Feel Pretty," giving her rhymes that seem too witty for a Puerto Rican girl relatively new

[2] Banfield, *Sondheim's Broadway Musicals*, p. 290.

to the country. No one else has ever thought this a problem—only Sondheim, who seems worried over the consistency of her character in this song. But characters always go into a different register of expression when they sing. Numbers call for characters to express themselves in new ranges of voice and lyric. None of Sondheim's characters in any of his shows could "really" speak in the brilliant rhymes he gives his singing characters.[3]

Maria's musical high point occurs in the love duet "Tonight," which is *West Side Story*'s version of Shakespeare's balcony scene. "Tonight" seems to be an outpouring of spontaneous passion, the sort of expressive ability we are prepared to believe real young people have at their disposal. They don't, but this is another peak moment in the musical, where Maria passes beyond stage convention to the point of requiring a nontheatrical word, so we call upon "real." Yet the tune she and Tony are singing turns out to be a standard format AABA song, with the same overall structure as thousands of other popular songs. Bernstein and Sondheim have disguised the pop song format with an inventive introduction and with a change of key on each section of the tune. The key changes give the impression of young people being carried away by passion, yet the standard thirty-two-bar structure of repeats and rhymes lies behind the key changes, and the attraction of the song comes from the way the rhymes lace up the repeats of A, bringing the piece to a close on the word with which it began, "tonight," sung seven times in Maria's chorus:

A

Tonight, tonight,
It all began tonight,
I saw you and the world went away.

---

[3] See Sondheim's comments in Guernsey, ed., *Playwrights, Lyricists, Composers on Theatre*, pp. 84–85. At other times Sondheim has belittled the characters in *West Side Story*, saying they were "one-dimensional" and fit only for a "melodrama" (Secrest, *Stephen Sondheim*, p. 117). Yet Sondheim writes the occasional melodrama himself. The characters in *Sweeney Todd* are worth taking seriously, and so are the characters in *West Side Story*. In neither case are they to be taken as "real" without thinking about what the term means in musical drama.

Maria sings that in B-flat, then the music rises to D-flat for the repeat of A.

A

Tonight, tonight,
There's only you tonight,
What you are, what you do, what you say.

At this point the harmony could return to the original key of B-flat or remain in D-flat. But instead, the soaring effect is intensified by a half-step rise in the melody, from F to G-flat, which is sustained by a new key, also G-flat. This is the bridge or B in the AABA format, utterly conventional in structure but leaving the impression of a breakthrough in feeling.

B

Today, all day I had the feeling
A miracle would happen,
I know now I was right.

This is a marvel. At the beginning of B the peak note of the melody occurs with the second syllable of "today," a surge of the singer's voice that seems spontaneous, impassioned, young, and the lyric even supplies a sudden excess of rhyme. "Today" at the start of the bridge picks up "say" from the end of the previous section just as the harmony changes to G-flat. The AABA ordinariness of the song is hidden by this blending, so that the melody seems to be generated from within the singers.[4]

Then the return to A, which is also a return to the original key of B-flat:

A

For here you are,
And what was just a world
   Is a star—
   Tonight.

[4] Knapp, *The American Musical and the Formation of National Identity*, p. 212 and p. 333n24, discusses the flatted sixth in this song as the subjunctive.

This is a conventional ending, with the double rhyme on "star/ are" and "right/tonight" tying the final A together and connecting its conclusion back to the bridge even as it manages to end on the first word of the song, "tonight."

What is real about Tony and Maria in this song is not their identity as young Polish boy and young Puerto Rican girl but their ability to sing this song. They are able to stop talking and do something different, something that requires unusual talent, something that has a different structure of feeling to it, although this structure is the same closed stanzaic format that young love has been sung about thousands of times in popular tunes. They are able to transform the standard, able to make it their own, and this is what young lovers all want to do, in or out of the theatre. Out of the theatre the standard is different, marriage perhaps. Inside the theatre, it will often be an AABA tune.

But at the end of *West Side Story*, all this they have lost. The grief is earth-bound prose, a fragment of song, nothing more. "Te adoro, Anton." It is powerful, for the music that is sung earlier can't be sung now. This is what Banfield means by the denial of song. To enlarge Maria into song at the end would be to highlight her role, concentrating the drama on her performing self. Always this story has balanced the two lovers: Romeo *and* Juliet. The musical changes the ending by keeping Maria alive, but it preserves balance by shifting it to the two gangs, the Jets and the Sharks, as they join into a procession and carry Tony's body away. There is underscoring for the procession. It is "Somewhere," a grim reminder of the fantasy these people have danced about getting free of the tenements. What is real is the combination of elements: the orchestra recalling the fantasy of freedom, the gangs joining into formal procession, Maria forced to become mature, and the musical selves of the young lovers, silenced now. It is real in the sense of being convincing, and it is convincing because so many distinct elements are held in balance together.

LOVERS

Maria is the Puerto Rican girl unlike other Puerto Rican girls, the one who can reach up to that unexpected G-flat at the beginning of the B section of "Tonight." She is nervy and vibrant, qualities that shine in her singing. Tony is the Polish boy who sings with or about Maria. He does little else, but on the "Maria" theme he is terrific. Everything he sings refers to Maria. She is "Something Coming" and "Maria" before she joins him in "Tonight." Actually, she sings the main theme of "Tonight" first, and he proves that he can catch her melody and sing it too. He can repeat the structure and rhyme scheme of her song. That is the kind of young man he is, the kind that can sing with Maria. He is the only one like that. Compare Chino, and the point will be clear. Can you imagine Chino singing a duet with Maria?

We do not think of real people while we watch the performance. We think of performance people, people who can sing and dance, numbers people. Chekhov and Shakespeare characters are performance people too, but the song-and-dance performance is not the same as the Chekhov or Shakespeare performance. If a suspension of disbelief occurs when we watch characters in a Chekhov play, it occurs twice when we watch characters from the book scenes of a musical open themselves into musical performance in the numbers. They are changed by the music. The film director Atom Egoyan in speaking of opera calls this "the transfiguration of real people into a separate reality."[5]

In an early scene of *Guys and Dolls*, the gambler Sky Masterson and the Salvation Army worker Miss Sarah Brown sing a duet in their first encounter. They are bragging to each other about how they will know when the real thing comes along,

---

[5] *Time Out*, 10–17 June 1998, p. 24. Chapin, *Everything Was Possible*, pp. 90–94, discusses the deepening of character that comes from song, using the example of "Losing My Mind" from *Follies*—Sally's song as it turned out, although the disunity of book and number is shown by the song's having been tried for Phyllis too.

neither realizing that it has just come along. They do not know they are falling in love at first sight. In fact, they are sure they are on different wavelengths. Sarah has a diagram in mind for her lover and is looking for the right man to fit it, while Sky is leaving the entire business to love at first sight, what he calls "chemistry." One thing is certain on the surface: these two think they are at odds with each other. That they sing the same tune to the same accompaniment lets us know what is going on beneath the surface. They are already falling for each other. When Sarah hears Sky sing his "chemistry" lyric, she is so obviously drawn to him that Sky puts a move on her—and she hauls off and socks him. So this is a love duet in which the lovers say they haven't fallen in love and which ends with a sock on the jaw. No matter. They are intimate with one another's tune, one another's harmony.

The duet makes it clear that their differences can be adjusted into an ongoing relationship. That could be said of people who fall in love in real life, too, but the musical can condense the relationship into the difference between chromatic and diatonic, which can be perfectly resolved. Sky is the chromatic one. He will show this later, in "My Time of Day." Sarah tends to remain diatonic, even when she gets tipsy and reveals a nice feel for swing in "If I Were a Bell." These differences are musical, and they will come out on the diatonic side (with Sky playing the bass drum in the Salvation Army band), after Sarah has a minor-key fling with Miss Adelaide in "Marry the Man Today." But the early "I'll Know" duet offers a shared diatonic harmony even while the characters think they are at odds with one another.

Why do we take these figures as real? In performing their numbers they impress us not by their reality but by their musical talent. The singers and dancers take these elaborate structures of repetition, the numbers, into their bodies and voices. They are joined by the orchestra. There is a voice of the musical that sings through them, and the drama lifts onto a plane that is different from the plane of a book scene. This plane of the number does not represent real life. The book scenes are already once removed from real life; the numbers are twice removed.

Character in a musical, then, is an effect of song character as well as book character. There are pairs of lovers in most musicals, but their song characters are of different kinds. "All er Nothin'," sung by Will Parker and Ado Annie in *Oklahoma!*, lets us recognize character at the same time as we recognize syncopation, which is one of the ways character comes across in a number. The melody of this tune works by one pattern of repetition while the rhyme scheme works by another. "With me it's all er nuthin'!" depends on an alternation of major and minor thirds that is repeated in the second line ("Is it all er nuthin' with you?"), the fifth line ("No half-and-half romance will do!"), the tenth line ("If you cain't give me all, give me nuthin'"), and the eleventh line ("And nuthin's whut you'll git from me!"). The rhyme scheme connects lines two and five (you/do), lines seven and eight (type/pipe), and lines nine and eleven (be/me), while off-rhymes link lines three and four (between/then) and hint at the "nuthin'" that itself joins lines one and ten. Ado Annie's "Not even sumpin" sets up the exact repetition of lines eleven and thirteen ("nuthin's whut you'll git from me!") with which the song ends. There are other patterns running through this ditty, but the point is that the layers of repetition combine into differing overlaps that syncopate in their interaction.

That broad syncopation has always been true of the American popular song, but the invention of ragtime around the turn of the twentieth century made the device explicit in the syncopated music itself. The result was syncopation that could be danced, and with the beat of ragtime giving rise a generation later to the equally danceable beat of swing, the American popular song became a classic form.

With me it's all er nuthin'!
Is it all er nuthin' with you?
It cain't be "in between"
It cain't be "now and then"
No half-and-half romance will do!
I'm a one-woman man,
Home-lovin' type,

All complete with slippers and pipe.
Take me like I am er leave me be!
If you cain't give me all, give me nuthin'—
And nuthin's whut you'll git from me!
—*Ado Annie:* Not even sumpin?
Nuthin's whut you'll git from me!

This tune trembles with danceability, and it goes without saying that Will and Ado Annie dance it together. What should be added is that two other girls dance into the middle of the song, making up to Will and luring him away from Ado Annie. They are not from the plot. They are song dancers who can enter into the rhythm of this number and bring into view the "wild and free" side of the male, whose "all or nuthin," as Ado Annie is coming to see, is "all fer you and nuthin' fer me." So she does an oriental dance aimed at getting him back. It is true to Annie's batty skills that she should be able to do a comic oriental dance when she is in her number mode. There is no sign of this in the plot. She transforms when she goes into numbers— they all do. And the oriental dance doesn't work—it is a comic failure (which takes talent to perform). "That's Persian!" Will shouts, thinking of the fling Ado has been having with the peddler Ali Hakim in the plot. This kind of cross-referencing between book and number is great fun. There must be two registers for the cross-referencing to occur.

This tune was done "in one" in the original staging—out in front of the traveler curtain, while the set was being changed for the next scene. What happens to the characters of Will Parker and Ado Annie when they perform out front, while the set is being changed? They are separated from the scene of the book, they are downstage close to the audience, they are putting on a number, and they are being enlarged by crossing into song and dance. They project themselves in a second mode of time, even a second mode of space in the "in one" system, and these interruptive modes amplify their roles through patterns of repetition that can hardly arise in book mode. Book mode is for getting on with the story, and it looks like plodding from the vantage point of number mode, which has the lilt of song and dance.

THE CASE OF HENRY HIGGINS

Love duets are worth considering because most musicals have them while most real people don't. Most characters in legitimate drama don't sing duets, either. The love duet is a specialty of musical theatre—full-blown and integrated in opera (again, *Tristan und Isolde* is the culmination) and inserted into nearly every Broadway show. Most lovers in opera and operetta are aware of themselves as lovers and share their melodies and harmonies intentionally and successfully. But a little twist favored by musicals makes true lovers *un*aware they are in love. This is the Sky Masterson/Miss Sarah Brown variety, but Loesser was borrowing an idea from Oscar Hammerstein, who never tired of using it. The classic example is "If I Loved You," from *Carousel*, where hero and heroine fall in love while they sing about the hypothesis of falling in love (the germ of this is in Molnar's *Liliom*, the source play). Hammerstein used the same idea twenty years earlier in the "Make Believe" duet shared between Magnolia and Gaylord in *Show Boat*. It occurs again in "People Will Say We're in Love" in *Oklahoma!*

The need for little twists and variations comes from the danger of blandness that lurks in the love duet. The way Bernstein disguises the AABA form of "Tonight" reminds us that there is something to disguise, a danger of pop tune conventionality strangling what is supposed to be unique passion. Before the advent of the better book, this was not much of a problem, for the affairs were rarely unique or passionate, and the standard-form duet would be an exercise in bright cynicism and dancing. "It's got to be love, it couldn't be tonsillitis," sing the lovers in *On Your Toes*, and since they were Ray Bolger and Doris Carson originally, the sharp lyric sets up some even sharper dancing. They are believable lovers mainly because they can present their mutuality in tap.

The better book brought on a need to disguise the standard-
form love song without giving it up, and the best example of
this revision comes in *My Fair Lady*, where the hero cannot be
imagined singing anything so conventional as a love song, especially not joining a duet. This is not only because the original Higgins, Rex Harrison, could barely sing. The more important reason is that Higgins is devoted to singing by himself.
"Soloist" is a leading note of the Higgins character and one he
must lose before the un-Shavian promise of romance between
Higgins and Eliza can be realized. Let's see how Lerner and
Loewe met this challenge.

No matter how quirky and self-centered Higgins may seem,
his solos are designed for the standard patterns of popular
song. He must assert himself against these patterns throughout
most of the action in order to prove himself singular and original. Then he must change at the last minute and accept these
conventional song patterns in order to prove himself fit for
Eliza. Eliza has no trouble with the standard patterns. She's a
good girl, she is. Her "Wouldn't It Be Loverly" and "I Could
Have Danced All Night" are neatly proportioned AABA songs,
lyrical and conventional, suggesting that she can move musically through either of her environments, poverty on Tottenham Court Road or respectability on Wimpole Street. But
Higgins kicks against the traces until the end, when his performance finally comes to terms with a standard song, and he
turns out to be a good match for Eliza after all.

His first solo number, "Why Can't the English Teach Their
Children How to Speak?" has the standard AABA stanza structure, but as Higgins reaches the final rhyme word of the final
A, which would perfect the form, he pushes it into a new
stanza, one that does not fit any other song (it begins at "Set"):

> One common language I'm afraid we'll never get.
> Oh, why can't the English learn to—
> Set a good example to people whose English
> Is painful to your ears?

The intrusion of new material runs sixteen measures, as though
it might belong to a standard format too, but Higgins brings it

to an end on the spoken "In America they haven't used it for years!" and then starts in again on "Why can't the English teach their children how to speak," as though nothing had happened. We are back to an AABA tune, it seems, but this time Higgins cuts the rhyme pattern apart on the second A section with another spoken line, the one about the French:

> Why can't the English teach their children how to speak?
> Norwegians learn Norwegian; the Greeks are taught their Greek.
> In France every Frenchman knows his language from "A" to "Zed"—
> (*spoken*) The French never care what they do, actually, as along as they pronounce it properly.

His idiosyncratic way with a song bursts out in "I'm an Ordinary Man," which is an elongated verse-chorus song, the verse running to twelve measures and consisting of drastic self-idealizations on Higgins's part (I'm a very gentle man, I'm a quiet loving man, and so on), followed by an AABA chorus that balloons each time into seventy-six measures of misogyny. Higgins finally destroys this chorus by switching on his instruction phonographs of women's voices and making them into a cacophony of female disorder.

Misogyny is what he has to get over, obviously, before he can become fit for a romantic ending, and it is a stroke of sentimental genius on the part of Lerner and Loewe to show this change of character through a song structure that Higgins does not finally want to destroy, although he certainly tries for a while. "I've Grown Accustomed to Her Face" is a gentle, orderly ABAC song. ABAC is another standard format. The B section sets the two A sections apart, letting the repeat occur over a patch of difference, then C appears to break new ground. The sections are even in length, with a coda at the end referring back to A ("accustomed to her face"). Call it ABACA′ with the coda, a trim design. For Henry Higgins to settle for such standardization is a change of character.

He does not settle without a fight. In the midst of the song he erupts into a fantasy about the sufferings Eliza will undergo if she pursues her notion of marrying Freddy Eynsford-Hill. The

eruption that begins "I can see her now" runs to fifty-four measures. Joseph Swain has observed that the melody resembles
Eliza's own fantasy song, "Just You Wait, 'enry 'iggins," hinting
at an underlying similarity between these two,[6] and the fifty-
four measures would be an AABA song in themselves (stretched,
as Higgins is wont to do) were it not for the spoken *Quasi recita-
tivo* he tags on: "Poor Eliza, How simply frightful! How hu-
miliating! How delightful!" Then he talks his way through a
twenty-measure elongated A section of this inner song, reprises
"I'm an ordinary man" (this time it is "I'm a most forgiving
man"), swings into a reactionary reprise of "I shall never take
her back," and comes to what he thinks is a triumphant declara-
tion of the old Higgins, a shouted "Marry Freddy, Ha!!"

At this point the orchestra intrudes to tell him he is wrong.
In a wonderful bit of scoring, "*appassionate e rubato*," the orchestra plays the opening phrase of "I've Grown Accustomed
to Her Face," and the old Higgins gives in to the new. He simply sings the song. ABACA', period. "I've Grown Accustomed
to Her Face." This time Lerner gives him a touching rhyme to
end with:

> I've grown accustomed to the trace
> Of something in the air;
> Accustomed to her face—

and he ends there. Before he could never *end* songs. He had to
run on with them, carrying them into other songs, refusing to
give standard endings to standard formats, but at last he becomes eligible for a singer-character like Eliza by ending the
song simply and unassertively. One may argue about changing
Shaw's plot to a conventional romantic outcome, as Lerner and
Loewe did, but one has to admire the skill with which they
brought this piece of sentiment about.

The heart of the musical is the projection of musical ability,
which takes the performers into the second order of time, lyric

---

[6] *The Broadway Musical: A Critical and Musical Survey*, pp. 195–96. Swain's
entire discussion of "I've Grown Accustomed to Her Face" is outstanding.

time, and lets them extend their characters musically. Those who do not sing and dance are lesser characters. They stand out because they have no music. They are like the psychoanalyst in *Lady in the Dark* or the Narrator in *Into the Woods*, a bit weird for lacking song, a bit off-center. (Sondheim has a good joke with this off-center narrator by having him fed to the Giantess in act 2.) The larger characters are capable of living in two worlds, one belonging to the book, the other belonging to the numbers, and the musical is a complex form of drama because it welcomes the challenge of presenting both of those worlds as though they were real and normal, and as though characters able to switch from the book mode to the number mode were real and normal, too. They aren't, but we are glad to think they are.

THE VOICE OF THE MUSICAL

I mentioned Joseph Swain's point that Higgins sounds like Eliza in his interlude, "I can see her now." How does this happen? The melody switches into the minor mode and remains virtually confined to the first four notes of the scale. This is also true of the first segment of Eliza's "Just You Wait, 'enry 'iggins." Both characters have to get over the anger expressed in these segments, and their angry reactions are musically similar. I would add that the first four notes of Higgins's "I've Grown Accustomed to Her Face" are identical to the first four notes of the bridge (the B section) in Eliza's "I Could Have Danced All Night." A three-note rise covers the first three diatonic tones of the scale, followed by a leap to the fifth tone. These two share a hidden romantic motif as well as a penchant for anger. One way to think about such similarity is to say that lovers have an underlying similarity no matter how different they appear to be on the surface. Another way, which does not eliminate the first way, is to say that the characters are influencing one another through their songs. Higgins is supposed to be creating a new character for Eliza, but this relationship reverses, and by the end, as Higgins sings some of her motifs, she is creating a new character for him.[7]

These are valid points, but they center on dramatic character in the usual sense, and I would look to a third way of understanding the shared motifs. It is not so much that the characters learn from one another's musical motifs as that they sing their way into the "voice of the musical"—a voice that is not exactly their own but in which their voices can join. I am borrowing Carolyn Abbate's phrase "voice of the opera" here, for Abbate catches the key idea that a musical drama is disrupted by moments of vocalese and can thereby attain a kind of narrative voicing, a melodic and harmonic world into which various characters enter at various times, not so much because they are like one another psychologically (although they may be), but because they belong to the same aesthetic design.[8] The similarities of melody and harmony shared among different characters are not psychological or sociological similarities. They are aesthetic similarities.

Take Alfred Doolittle in *My Fair Lady*. His songs have rhythmic similarities to the songs of Higgins and Eliza, as Geoffrey Block has noticed.[9] Doolittle is a problem for the character-

---

[7] See Block, *Enchanted Evenings: The Broadway Musical from* Show Boat *to* Sondheim, pp. 235–40. Swain, *The Broadway Musical*, p. 200, makes a similar point.

[8] See Abbate, *Unsung Voices: Opera and Musical Narrative in the Nineteenth Century*. Abbate is dealing with Edward Cone's sense of voice in *The Composer's Voice*, rejecting the transcendent implication of that meaning in favor of a poststructuralist definition. I am borrowing from her discussions of singing characters in opera, especially in chapters 1 and 3. Her discussion of narrativity in musical sonority itself (chapter 2, especially) results in a single voice that is not Cone's "composer's voice" but does not step entirely free of the transcendental nevertheless. I do not engage the argument at that level, although I do wish to record the penetrating sentences that sum up this position: music has "a terrible force to move us by catching us in played-out time. When music ends, it ends absolutely, in the cessation of passing time and movement, in death" (Abbate, p. 56). In answering to this aesthetic quality, nineteenth-century opera remains distinct from the musical. In Kierkegaard's terms, which I call on in chapter 8, "recollection" is being caught "in played-out time." The musical seeks what Kierkegaard called "repetition" instead.

[9] Block, *Enchanted Evenings*, pp. 238–40.

centered approach because there is no way to think that Eliza and Higgins are "like" him or are "learning" from him. But he belongs to the musical universe of *My Fair Lady* from his first number to his last. How about Freddy Eynesford-Hill? His "On the Street Where You Live" has a close approach to one of the motifs we have been discussing for Eliza and Higgins: three ascending tones, then a leap to a sixth rather than a fifth. Freddy share the motifs of the other characters because he inhabits the same musical universe as the others. Each well-composed musical has a style of its own, a characteristic sound, and there is a drive among the singing characters to join this voice. So when Freddy sings outside the Wimpole Street house, or when Alfred Doolittle and his cronies sing and dance their way through "With a Little Bit of Luck" or "I'm Getting Married in the Morning" in the Tottenham Court Road area, they are performing their way into the voice of the musical too.

Love duets can now be seen as a special version of the voice of the musical. When Sky Masterson and Miss Sarah Brown sing the same melody in "I'll Know," or when Ado Annie and Will Parker sing the same melody in "All er Nuthin'," or when Tony and Maria sing the same melody in "Tonight," we can say that lovers harmonize with each other, sometimes even before they realize it themselves, but they are also voicing something broader that runs through the universe of their musical. A well-composed show has a style of its own, a voice for its own range of character and incident, which works its way into the voices of many characters (especially the lovers), works its way into the orchestration, works its way into the ensembles, the dances.

Sometimes characters will sing the same melody at quite different points although there is no rationalized reason for one to know the other's tune. When Nathan Detroit finally declares himself in song before Miss Adelaide, the melody of his "Sue Me" briefly resembles Sky Masterson's lovely "My Time of Day," which is much more harmonically and poetically complex. The resemblance is in the melody of "When the smell of the rain-washed pavement / Comes up clean and fresh and cold," compared to Nathan's main theme, "Sue me, sue me, shoot bullets through me." Nathan does not literally lift Sky's music—these are vastly different songs. Yet the touch of similarity in their melodies does mean something. One can say that these two gamblers are alike—they sing the same tune for a minute. That would be right as far as it goes, but it does not go far enough. Musicals have broad voices in which various characters share, and this tune shared at different points in the show between Sky and Nathan comes from the voice of *Guys and Dolls*. The orchestra gives Sky a richer and more mysterious harmony under the tune. The richer harmony lies beneath "Comes up clean and fresh and cold" in "My Time of Day," and it is based on a flatted fifth. The flatted fifth is a distinctive harmony for the gamblers and their dolls: Adelaide has it in "Adelaide's Lament," and Nicely-Nicely and Benny have it in the title tune, "Guys and Dolls." The flatted fifth is one way the voice of *Guys and Dolls* is created. *Carousel* uses an augmented triad to the same effect, and *Sweeney Todd* uses the interval of a ninth.[10] Repeated distinctive harmonies are a way to create a musical universe. The melodic bits shared between Sky Masterson and Nathan Detroit, or among Eliza, Freddy, and Henry Higgins, are another way, and this kind of shared motif brings into focus the actual sharing of tunes sung in a duet, like "Marry the Man Today," sung by the heroines in *Guys and Dolls*, or the duets sung by lovers in most musicals. These are all instances of the voice of the musical making itself heard.

The Kurt Weill/Elmer Rice/Langston Hughes *Street Scene* (1947) creates a beautiful moment when the theme of Anna's major aria from act 1 is sung by another character, the young law student named Sam, when he realizes in act 2 that Anna is dead. There is no reason to ask how Sam came to learn Anna's aria. He is not a learner of arias. Music can be heard within a musical or an opera even when there is no book reason for hearing it, and the heard music can be shared. Anna projected this major piece earlier, as what seemed an entirely personal

---

[10] For *Carousel*, see Swain, *The Broadway Musical*, pp. 101–27. Banfield, *Sondheim's Broadway Musicals*, pp. 292–305, gives further examples of repeated motifs in *Sweeney Todd*.

account of lost hopefulness, and now Sam is the one character responsive enough to hear her song after her death and express it in his own voice. That is why it is such a powerful moment— not because one character learns the tune from another, but because these two, so different in situation, the man with a future before him, the woman trapped in a deadly marriage, share the ability to project themselves in this music. Suddenly there is an emotional connection between them, carried across on this melody from the lost woman to the young law student. If the orchestra simply played Anna's theme as underscoring in act 2, no one would be puzzled, for orchestras do this kind of thing all the time: they know the musical environment better than any characters do. It is rare for a character to share in this knowledge. Characters who know everything can be a danger to the musical, as we will see, but characters like Sam, who know something unexpected and can suddenly perform it, are alive to the voice of the musical.

We are talking about a shared musical formality even when characters are expressing their deep musical uniqueness. The characters are voicing themselves, yet they are joined by a formal element that lies beyond them. It exceeds their awareness. Its clearest location is in the orchestra, a point to which we will return, and when the singing and dancing ensembles suddenly perform a number all together on stage, they are capturing the spirit of this musical universe. A wonderful example occurs early in *Show Boat*, when the black chorus and the white chorus (the two ensembles are distinctly identified and usually hold apart) sing the same number, "Cotton Blossom." The white singers, all dressed up and ready to see a show, are singing about the showboat itself, which is called the "Cotton Blossom." The black chorus is singing about the cotton blossom they have to pick in the fields, which is their "heavy burden" when it is packed into the bales the men have been heaving about on the levee. By putting these two choruses together and giving them the same melody, the musical pretends that the racial difference can be overcome in the spirit of exuberant singing, but in fact the lyrics that are sung concern two very different kinds of "cotton blossom," and the kind the white people sing about depends on the work that goes into the kind the black people sing about. But this point of racial difference is occluded by the blending of the shared tune. Hammerstein had strong political ideas, but his politics are often smoothed out by this tendency of the voice of the musical to take ensemble forms, as though everyone shared equally in the same world. The challenge of the post-Hammerstein musical is to sharpen the political realism of the form without losing the consistency of the musical composition.[11]

The convention of the shared tune can be extended to an explicit disagreement between the singers. The duet "A Boy Like That" between Anita and Maria in *West Side Story* works this way. Anita sings an AABA song on the need for Maria to find "one of your own kind" to love, but Maria then turns the B section of that song her own way, "It isn't true, not for me," and invents an obbligato melody—"I belong to him alone"— over Anita's reprise of "A boy like that." The beauty of the duet is that Maria's obbligato becomes the lead melody by the end, with Anita singing it too, in harmony with her. Then the voice of the musical is enlarged to a quintet when Anita, Maria, Tony, and the leaders of the rival gangs sing different lyrics over the "Tonight" harmony. In this case, Anita's lyric, which is about sex, squares with the rival leaders' lyric, which is about violence. Maria and Tony sing the "Tonight" lyric to this harmony too, their passion soaring over the gritty chromatic singing of the others. Love, sex, and violence operate in the same harmonic pattern. It is a startling transformation of leading ideas from *Romeo and Juliet*.[12]

"A WEEKEND IN THE COUNTRY"

The ending of act 1 in *A Little Night Music* (1973) shows the voice of the musical in full form. The succession of events

[11] For the musical's tendency to assimilate otherness to an acceptable standard, see Knapp, *The American Musical*, especially pp. 179–281, and Most, *Making Americans: Jews and the Broadway Musical*.

[12] See Knapp, *The American Musical*, p. 213.

looks like book material. The Egermanns receive an invitation for a weekend in the country. Anne Egermann does not want to accept, because her husband is having an affair with Desiree, who invited them. Her husband does want to accept, for the same reason. Anne visits her friend Charlotte and admits her apprehensions. Charlotte tells Anne to accept the invitation, wear her white dress, demonstrate her youth, and put Desiree to shame. Thus Anne and her husband will accept the invitation.

The plot thickens when Charlotte proceeds to tell *her* husband about the weekend to which the Egermanns have been invited. Her husband is having an affair with Desiree too, and Charlotte hopes his anger over losing out to his rival will cure him of his adulterous urges. On the contrary, his adulterous urges flame up. He announces that they too will attend this weekend, although they have not been invited. There is no stopping him. Charlotte must accompany him on this gate-crashing adventure. The act ends with both couples planning to attend the weekend.

The amazing thing about the first-act ending is that it is done entirely in a number, "A Weekend in the Country." This is a secure example of the integrated musical, one would think, for the plot is being advanced along several lines, yet it is all being done through song and Hal Prince's fluid staging, whereby Anne can visit Charlotte merely by crossing the stage. When she returns to her husband, the two couples can be seen making their plans simultaneously. At the end of the number, which is also the end of act 1, we know these characters are going to converge at the Armfeldt estate in act 2, where discord is inevitable. This is the stuff of a book, but it all happens in a number.

Yet the point of the number is something else. We will later find it possible to replace *integration* with a different word for the musical, *coherence*, which means different elements holding simultaneously together without losing their differences. "A Weekend in the Country" is an example of coherence. Its dramatic quality depends on its means of performance—there is no other way to create its effect of simultaneity. These strands

FIGURE 3. The original cast of *A Little Night Music* singing "A Weekend in the Country." Used by permission of the photographer, Martha Swope.

of plot are all sung to the same tune, a standard AABA structure in fast 6/8, which allows every character to join into the
same music no matter the differences among their motives and
attitudes. In terms of plot, the relationships are reaching an
impasse, but in terms of the number, all four characters are
singing one tune, even rhyming with one another, and we
know that they are going to end harmoniously. That is not to
say they will end as married couples. I left Henrik, Anne's stepson, out of the description a moment ago. He wants to go for
the weekend too, keen on observing these "devil's compan-
ions" as he puts it (Henrik is a Lutheran), but actually keener
to stay close to his stepmother, whom he adores (he is a
Lutheran who would rather be a lover). So three plot strands
are being sung simultaneously, and I have also not mentioned
Petra, the maid, or the five lieder singers—these people join in
too, at the end of the number. There are many reasons for going to this weekend in the country, some are not connected to
the book, contests abound among these characters, and yet
everyone is singing in harmony and rhyme. They will work out
their plot relationships. Anne will run off with Henrik, her
husband will settle in with Desiree, Charlotte will recapture
her husband, Petra will have a romp in the hay with the butler,
and the five lieder singers will go on singing. But the point is
that they have *already* worked out their musical and lyrical relationships by performing this number in which the plot seems
at sixes and sevens. It is not so much that the plot is being advanced. The plot is being transformed into a musical version
which lets eleven characters express their interests simultaneously, as though they all respond to one voice—coherently.[13]

Many issues follow once the musical is understood to have a
voice of its own. There is a drive for ensemble performance in
the musical that sets this form of drama apart from realistic
prose drama and its focus on the psychology of individualism.

[13] This is not the first time such musical simultaneity occurs in the show,
nor is it the last. The waltz of the principal characters before the action begins
and the waltz at the very end are two other occasions. Musical simultaneity has
a long standing in opera, of which the leading example must be the concluding
garden episodes of Mozart's *The Marriage of Figaro*.

Most American literature, and most American drama, is cast
in a realist mode and takes the portrayal of the individual character as the normal intention. That is not true of the musical,
in which the shared formality of song and dance leads to an
awareness of multiple performance as a logical outcome—
duets, quartets, ensemble singing and dancing. Often a number seems to express a character's deep feeling, as though song
and dance can reach into the area of subtext and transform the
private motivations found there into performability. But the
private motivation does not matter so much as the performability. If subtext is to be explored by the realistic actor in the legitimate theatre, it is to be changed into accessible song and
dance formats in the musical. There is no subtext the musical
cannot get to, and once gotten to, the hidden motive will be
obvious to everyone, transformed into a different beat, into a
melody that can be shared, into a lyric others can join. When
others join, the musical is moving into its ensemble tendency.
The sentimentality of the genre is one result of this shared
performability. Rodgers and Hammerstein clarified the ensemble tendency of the musical and they also clarified its sentimentality. They opened a great opportunity for later writers to
play off against the sentimentality. Most successful writers of
musicals after Rodgers and Hammerstein took up this opportunity and turned the musical toward ironic or satiric versions
of the ensemble outcome. I am thinking of Loesser, Kander and
Ebb, Cy Coleman, Sondheim, William Finn, among others—
writers who may use the ensemble outcome too, and do not
turn away from the occasional moment of sentimentality themselves, but who also test these things, challenging the Rodgers
and Hammerstein legacy while using its capital. This double attitude toward the musical's past is one reason why the musical's
future is turning out to be deep and complex.

The chapters that follow unpack these ideas and spread
them out more fully. First, there is the musical's challenge to
the codes of "rugged individualism" to which a great deal of
nonmusical American literature and drama seems to be devoted. The musical's ensemble tendency has ideological implications that we have not yet explored. I then take up several

basic questions as the next steps. What does it mean for individuals in a musical to break into song, and how does this convention differ from songs that are called for by the book? Speaking of ensembles, what gives the orchestra its omniscience from its hidden position in the pit, and how is this quality changed when the orchestra is placed on the stage (as happens, for example, in *Cabaret*)? And if the orchestra is an all-knowing ensemble, what are the special conditions of narration from within the book of the musical? Why, given these conditions of narration in the book, does the musical nearly always take its plot from a preexisting text—a novel, a play, or with increasing frequency in recent years, a film? These are questions worth discussing before we can proceed to the heart of the matter and discuss the final question, what kind of drama is this?

Chapter Four

THE ENSEMBLE EFFECT

Chorus Lines

W E HAVE just seen why singing and dancing choruses have been such a long-standing convention
in musicals. "A Weekend in the Country" is an effective version of what happens at least once in all musicals: the
enlargement of singing and dancing from one or two characters to an ensemble. There is a drive toward ensemble performance in the musical dramatic form, and this drive is the
fullest rendition of what I have been calling the voice of the
musical. In smaller shows, such as William Finn's *Falsettos* trilogy, the ensemble may amount to a quintet or sextet, but the
drive toward an inclusive group performance will still be there.
It is especially strong in the most successful rock musicals,
Hair (1968) and *Rent* (1996).[1]

The ending of *Candide* amounts to a formal dramatization of
this principle. In his disillusionment over the failure of Pangloss's "best of all possible worlds" philosophy, Candide sends
everyone away and prepares to live alone. This would be the
antithesis of a musical's normal ending, but one by one the
characters return to the stage, Pangloss bearing a fish for dinner, the Old Woman twigs for a fire, Maxmillian a broom for
sweeping; the final number, "Make Our Garden Grow," takes
shape as a sextette. Then the entire company enters and the
number becomes a chorus. The muted optimism of the num-

---

[1] The theme of community in both rock musicals receives smart discussion
in Scott Miller, *Rebels with Applause: Broadway's Groundbreaking Musicals*. Two
broad surveys of inclusiveness in the American musical have recently appeared:
Most, *Making Americans: Jews and the Broadway Musical*, and Knapp, *The American Musical and the Formation of National Identity*.

ber softens Voltaire's original "we must cultivate our garden" ending, but it sets forth the penchant for inclusion that the musical format thrives on.

Legitimate drama has its large scenes, too, but the ensemble numbers of a musical do something that does not happen in legitimate drama. The characters express themselves simultaneously. And the build-up of a number to a simultaneous performance is often a dramatic event in itself. Normally, the build-up occurs toward the end of each act of the book, and the act reaches its climax when that ensemble potential is realized. The earlier climaxes were sometimes called *finalettos* and the ending of the entire show the *finale ultimato*. They were important enough to need fancy names.

The ensemble as a dramatic event could have its impact earlier as well, especially in the kind of number that begins as a solo and expands. At an early moment in George and Ira Gershwin's *Lady, Be Good!* (1924), Ukulele Ike comes on carrying his favorite instrument and sings a chorus of "Fascinating Rhythm." Why he is singing this song is a mystery in the plot, but the answer is obvious when it comes to the performance, which has Adele Astaire and her brother Fred join Ukulele Ike on the second chorus, with the orchestra coming in to replace the ukulele as accompaniment. This number exists to spread out to the other performers, from Ukulele Ike through the Astaires to the chorus of singers and dancers who have now been drawn to the stage for the third, fourth, and fifth choruses of the number. By now everybody is singing and dancing "Fascinating Rhythm," which has grown into an ensemble number, the first showstopper of *Lady, Be Good*. I have used the names of the original performers in 1924 to suggest the impact the number originally had (Ukulele Ike was the stage name of Cliff Edwards, who was well known, and the Astaires were just then coming into their own as stars). This number was geared to its original performers rather than to the plot, but the principle operating here is the same as the principle operating at the end of act 1 in *A Little Night Music*: the musical fulfills its intentions in the teamwork of ensemble performance, no matter how many good solos are heard along the way.

The older musicals normally began with a chorus number in order to establish the ensemble convention from the beginning. This was often said to be an excuse to put the chorus girls on display from the start—a likely enough reason, which coexists with the other reason. The other reason is that the older musicals were declaring themselves an ensemble kind of theatre even before the stars of the evening made their appearances. The old story about *The Black Crook* becoming the first American musical when a ballet troupe was merged into a production of a melodrama is a good story from the aesthetic point of view, whatever its historical accuracy. Two ensembles are better than one at the point of origin.[2] But the best way to use the ensemble-basis of the musical is to dramatize its build-up as an event within the show. The drama lies in the build-up itself. The plot has been converted into the advance of the number to more and more singers and dancers. Sometimes the plot of the book is more or less forgotten, replaced by the build-up of the number—this is "Fascinating Rhythm." The more sophisticated version retains the plot of the book and illustrates it through the build-up of the number—this is "A Weekend in the Country." In both cases the number has overtaken the book, turning book time into number time and making the drama occur through the spread of song and dance to the entire company. The choreographer Susan Stroman has commented on the excitement felt when a number builds to the point where it "explodes into unison."[3] The ensemble effect is what she is talking about.

The expansion of a number into a united ensemble is the voice of the musical making itself heard. When Sam reprises

[2] A French ballet company had been booked to perform at the Academy of Music on 14th Street, but the theatre burned down. At the same time in 1866, William Wheatley, manager of Niblo's Garden at Broadway and Prince Street, had a failed melodrama on his hands, *The Black Crook*, by Charles M. Barras. The producer simply combined the two—at dull moments in the plot, the ballet girls would come on and dance in flesh-colored pink tights. The story is told in Flinn, *Musical! A Grand Tour*, pp. 81–89, and Knapp, *The American Musical*, pp. 20–28. A Romberg musical of the early 1950s, *The Girl in Pink Tights*, is about this supposed episode in theatre history.

[3] Quoted in the *New York Times*, 1 March 2002, section E, p. 1.

Anna's aria after her death in *Street Scene*, one could say that Sam is a sensitive character, but that is not the full point. The full point is that the chorus of tenement dwellers sings the context for his sensitivity. They sing "The Woman Who Lived Up There," the choral number that makes room for Sam's sudden reprise of the aria. They do not know who she was, exactly, or how she came to be murdered by her husband, and they do not share Sam's sympathy for her at first, but their chorus sets the harmony for Sam's reprise of the aria. Then they join him, and the aria ends as a chorus. This number reaches its full-throated beauty because they *all* share in Anna's death. Real tenements are not like this. Tenements in legitimate plays are not like this. The tenement in the source play for the musical is not like this. "The crowd surges about uncertainly, not knowing what has happened, and buzzing with questions which nobody can answer" is Elmer Rice's stage direction in his *Street Scene*, the play on which the musical is based, and Sam's role in the play at this point is to sympathize with the daughter of the murdered woman, Rose. He has nothing to say about Anna.[4] It is music that lets him share Anna's aria, music enlarged to choral performance in the background.

A fine opportunity for sentiment lurks in this ensemble tendency of the musical. Or it did lurk there, until Rodgers and Hammerstein drew it out and made it so obvious that a reaction set in. Rodgers and Hammerstein perfected the "Clambake" version of the ensemble number, whereby groups of fellow citizens get together and demonstrate through singing and dancing that a community spirit prevails. I am thinking of

[4] The concluding perception of the play is that one must belong "to oneself" before one can depend on anyone else. This is what Rose tells Sam after the murder of her mother, when she rejects Sam's offer to go away with her. Rice originally wrote it this way: "I don't think people ought to belong to anybody but themselves. I was thinking, that if my mother had really belonged to herself and that if my father had really belonged to himself, it never would have happened. It was only because they were always depending on somebody else, for what they ought to have had inside themselves." That is full-blown American individualism, more congruent with the "legitimate" drama than the musical. The musical retains those lines, incidentally, but counters them with the ensemble effect of "The Woman Who Lived Up There."

"This Was a Real Nice Clambake," sung by the citizens of whatever Maine town one imagines as the setting for *Carousel*, who have just had a picnic on an island across the bay and who are now lolling about in "languorous contentment," singing one of Hammerstein's brilliant essays into pure corniness. "The vittles we et / Were good, you bet! / The company was the same." This could just as well be called the "Hayride" type of number, for it was first written as "This Was a Real Nice Hayride" for *Oklahoma!* and then cut, but hayride or clambake, the ideology is the same. People in their best moments voice the joy and reassurance of community. I want to glance at this ideology in the most famous Rodgers and Hammerstein musicals in a moment, for it is a defining achievement in the genre, but I also want to add that some of the most interesting musicals of the past fifty years have questioned the Clambake version of ensemble, have placed it under ironic examination, turned it inside out, disbelieved it. Rodgers and Hammerstein carried the idea of ensemble to a peak of sentimentality that could hardly be imitated. The 1960s brought new attitudes and new musical styles into play—the 1950s could not be imitated, either. Some good shows of the 1950s did match up to the Rodgers and Hammerstein model, but for the most part the influential musicals of the past fifty years have reversed the code of the sentimental ensemble and questioned its platitudes. They have not given up ensembles, but have used them in new ways.

Rodgers and Hammerstein

Mark Steyn has remarked that Oscar Hammerstein wrote about one subject above all others, community.[5] The close fit between this preoccupation of Hammerstein's and the ensem-

---

[5] In *Broadway Babies, Say Goodnight: Musicals Then and Now*, p. 97, and in his program notes to the Royal National Theatre production of *Oklahoma!*, directed by Trevor Nunn.

ble basis of the musical helps to explain the enormous success of *Oklahoma!*, *Carousel*, *South Pacific*, and *The King and I* in the 1940s and early 1950s. No writer was so constitutionally attuned to this element of the form than Hammerstein, and Rodgers had a wealth of operetta-like romantic melody at his command to give resonance to the community ideology. Rodgers had it both ways. With Hart, his romanticism created a lively tension with the snappy wit of the lyrics. With Hammerstein, the romantic melody was freed from the resistances that gave it bite, and the melodies sang in the same vein as the lyrics.

Rodgers and Hammerstein were writing about community at a time when the United States was emerging from the Depression and the Second World War to become a worldwide military and industrial power. The image of community in the shows has nothing to do with the country's new power, which was founded on an economic system that drives people apart at least as often as it brings people together, but it was not hard for Americans to believe that their cause was founded on the kind of good-heartedness that could be turned to song and dance in the hands of the Broadway masters. So the time was right for Rodgers and Hammerstein, but there is something more. They thought about their conventions. They experimented with them, rather than merely using them for the sake of getting a show on the boards, and their experimental attitude toward the conventions of the musical is what drives the genre ahead after their time.

Not one of the big four Rodgers and Hammerstein shows begins in the conventional way, with a singing and dancing chorus. Their theme of community emerges as part of the drama itself. Musical ensembles take shape as an outgrowth of the book, and that is one reason integration seems to be the hallmark of their style. Open small and let the numbers spread—that is the technique, although *Carousel* finds a way to open large and let the numbers spread anyway.

The first and most famous opening was an opportunity handed to them. Curly's offstage "Oh, What a Beautiful

Morning," even a cappella for a minute, is a classic case of an unusual opening,[6] but the basic idea came from the source play. *Green Grow the Lilacs* begins with Curly singing a cowboy song offstage while Aunt Eller is churning butter in the front room of the farmhouse, then Curly can be seen, still singing, outside the window. At first Rodgers and Hammerstein tried various ways to get the chorus into the opening minutes of the plot. "Strawberry festivals, quilting parties, sewing bees were suggested and rejected," Hugh Fordin reports in his biography of Hammerstein.[7] Finally they kept the opening to Curly's solo, then added the nice touch of having Laurey sing the same tune when she first comes out of the farmhouse. One is not quite sure if she is mocking Curly, or loving him, or just singing.

What they really changed from the source play was the setting of the opening scene. They moved it from inside the farmhouse to the yard in front of the farmhouse, where ensembles could be brought onstage after a time (and where Aunt Eller must now churn her butter, improbably, in the great outdoors). Groups of boys and girls come in as the first scene goes on, offering little outbreaks of support for the soloists and teasing them, three ensemble groups in the first scene alone: the male chorus joins Will Parker for "Everything's Up to Date in Kansas City," the female chorus joins Laurey for "Many a New Day," and the male chorus joins Ali Hakim for "It's a Scandal, It's an Outrage." Indian Territory this may be, but the ensembles make it clear that the white settlers are already in a statehood frame of mind. Riggs's play has a sharper edge about this issue. The pressure for statehood actually impedes the love story in Riggs (Curly has to break out of jail to spend his wedding night with Laurey, and he will go back to jail in the morning). In *Oklahoma!* the expansion of the first scene into ensembles tells everyone that "Oklahoma" is already present in these

---

[6] Mordden, *Rodgers and Hammerstein*, p. 46, names *Peggy-Ann*, *Music in the Air*, *Anything Goes*, *Pal Joey*, and *Lady in the Dark* as earlier shows with intimate openings.

[7] Fordin, *Getting to Know Him: A Biography of Oscar Hammerstein II*, pp. 186–87.

unison-minded singers and dancers, so when in the second act they all come down to the footlights and sing the number "Oklahoma!" itself (I am recalling the downstage move of the original production, which was a defining moment), the show is likely to be stopped because the community philosophy implicit in act 1 is now coming across to the audience as a full-throated ode.[8]

Carousel is the Rodgers and Hammerstein musical that comes closest to declaring for an individualist ethic in the face of the community ideology. Billy Bigelow likes to think that he is cast in the mold of rugged individualism, as though he could hold out against the community tendency of these New Englanders.[9] We know before he does that he has the potential for community himself when he comes upon Julie Jordan in the bench scene and sings the same words and melody, "You're a Queer One, Julie Jordan," which her friend Carrie sang a few minutes before. This is the voice of the musical being heard and Billy shares in it. This is the first book scene. We have already seen the power of ensemble design, for the overture to this show involves most of the company in a pantomime enveloped by the orchestra's splendid "Carousel Waltz," but we

[8] For the development of the song from solo to chorus, see Wilk, *The Story of Oklahoma!*, pp. 200–3. The "forgetting" of the American Indians in this moment of community is discussed by Most, *Making Americans*, pp. 101–18. Knapp, *The American Musical*, p. 124 notes that the nationalistic expropriation of land to form the new state was being celebrated in 1943, "when America had recently entered into a war against an enemy whose behavior was uncannily resonant with the actual history of Oklahoma." Rugg, "What It Used to Be," pp. 46–47, treats such cultural amnesia as a form of "nostalgia," which is especially evident in the showstopper, the number that lets the audience join the performers in a moment of pure presence—as though the narrative could be halted and the musical might never end. In my terms, this would be number time taking over from book time as though the number might not end. There are times when the showstopper response requires a spontaneous encore of the number. Thus the number, built on repetitions in itself, is itself repeated. The spirit of community in the musicals of the Rodgers and Hammerstein era is discussed from a gay male perspective in D. A. Miller, *Place for Us*. For a feminist lesbian response, see Wolf, *A Problem Like Maria*.

[9] Swain, *The Broadway Musical*, pp. 99–127, has a good extended discussion of individualism and community in *Carousel*.

did not know who the characters were in the pantomime. Now we are finding that the sexy barker from the carousel, who wants to be different and his own man, is drawn by some romantic power to voice the same tune that the utterly conventional Carrie sang minutes before. Billy did not hear Carrie's song. He just knows it, and it indicates that he belongs to the community no matter how determined he is to prove himself unique.

Still, he *is* determined. In his would-be individualism, he is the character who deserves a "Soliloquy," and the length of the solo, and its vocal demands, make it seem almost operatic. We have already noted that it is not—that it is really two standard popular song formats joined by several good bridges. Billy has realized that he must prepare himself to be a good father. I have mentioned that Molnar let this all remain unsaid in the corresponding moment of *Liliom*, a tactful and deft decision. Rodgers and Hammerstein are using the musical's conventions to extend and double Billy's role through explicitness, and one has to admire the complexity of the result even as one notes the obviousness of the method. Then Billy goes back to being the Molnar character and bungles the robbery that is intended to enable him to provide for his daughter. Over his body, the play's representative of community values, Cousin Nettie, asks Julie to call to mind the message from "the sampler I gave you." The message is "You'll Never Walk Alone," an overblown ditty straining to become an anthem, perhaps the most pretentious song Rodgers and Hammerstein ever wrote.

Why, then, is this moment heartbreaking? Audiences find the shared lyric—Julie attempts to sing it, cannot, and Nettie takes it over as her solo—profound and moving, and I think they are right. It is because the performance of the shared music has its own weight of meaning. The performance catches the feeling of community fully and gives it substance. Billy has failed to realize what community means. Now he is dead, his wife faces poverty with a baby on the way—and yet the community value provides the strength to survive. Julie cannot sing it yet, but Nettie can, and Nettie has already sung herself into the heart of community in "June is Bustin' Out All Over." The

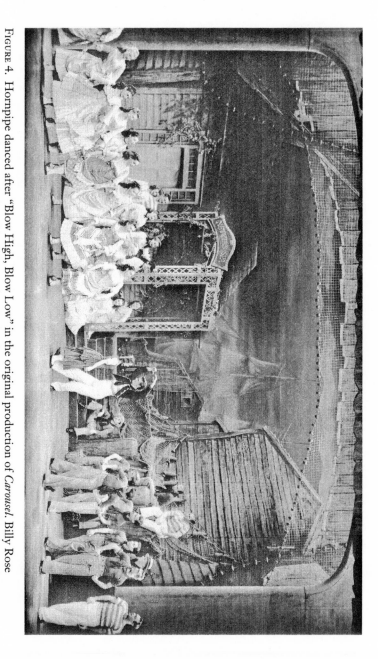

FIGURE 4. Hornpipe danced after "Blow High, Blow Low" in the original production of *Carousel*. Billy Rose Theatre Collection, The New York Public Library for the Performing Arts, Astor, Lenox and Tilden Foundations.

reason the song is so powerful is that its sentimental message coordinates with the means of its performance. Nettie can sing it for Julie and to Julie because Nettie has community in her heart, community and perhaps nothing else. And eventually, at the end of the show, the song will be sung as a chorale, when Louise graduates from high school. For once not the loner in her class, the outcast daughter of the reprobate Billy, Louise joins with the others (and Nettie) in singing this same number. The only person who does not sing is Billy. He is standing by as a ghost, learning the Rodgers and Hammerstein code at last. He has seen himself reflected in his daughter's isolation in the beach ballet, and now he sees her being drawn into the graduation chorale. Something is finally breaking through Billy's simplistic individualism, and it is the spirit of community performance that just about everyone else in this musical has understood all along.

South Pacific opens at a far remove from the ensemble number. First, a children's duet, "*Dites-Moi*"; then, after the principals enter, a solo for Nellie Forbush, "A Cockeyed Optimist"; then twin soliloquies for the would-be lovers, showing that they share a melody even though they think they are ruminating to themselves; then—in what may be the smoothest transition into a romantic solo in all musicals—"Some Enchanted Evening," in which the love-at-first-sight being sung about has already happened and may have happened too late. The entire scene is brilliantly intimate in its introduction of the love story from different perspectives, but it is also setting up the contrast with the male chorus to follow in the next scene, a bunch of Seabees and Marines roaring out "Bloody Mary is the girl I love." The ensemble is held back, in favor of something entirely different in the intimate opening, but then they come on, these horny hell-raisers, and the musical is hitting its stride. Somehow at least one of the characters from the delicate scene will have to work into performance mode with these Seabees, an event that transpires in the "Thanksgiving Follies" of act 2, especially when Nellie joins Luther Billis in "Honey Bun."

By the time of *The King and I*, it was virtually expected that a Rodgers and Hammerstein show would open quietly (after the overture). Anna Leonowens and her young son are on a ship approaching Bangkok, courage is required, and Anna's solution is "I Whistle a Happy Tune," with the boy joining in. There follow two solos for women ("My Lord and Master" for Tuptim, "Hello, Young Lovers" for Anna), before the first ensemble number picks up the theme of Anna's relation to children. This is the pantomime presentation of the royal children to Anna, a long number that demonstrates the bonds that will hold even as the cultural differences between the main characters are being dramatized.

The opening numbers of the major Rodgers and Hammerstein shows consistently break away from the rousing chorus numbers of standard Broadway fare. They are often solos or duets involving children, quiet moments of reflection or joy, but it would be a mistake to overlook the ensemble numbers waiting in the wings. The ensembles will set the solos into a context of group performance, and without that context the musical lacks its basic performance mode, which matches Hammerstein's social philosophy exactly.[10]

SHAW'S *PYGMALION* AND *MY FAIR LADY*

"Legitimate" drama is different from the musical in this regard. Ensemble moments are possible, but they are not necessary. Theatre is such a collaborative form in the first place that there is always a carryover from the teamwork involved in the production to the coordination of large groups in the play, but "straight" plays can nevertheless be based on images of individualism for which the musical has little time. There are one-

---

[10] The leading Rodgers and Hammerstein flop, *Allegro*, does begin with a chorus and is something of a crash course in Hammerstein's concern for ensembles and community. The ultimate in their unorthodox openings was the original version of *Me and Juliet*, which was supposed to begin with no overture, just stagehands coming out to work on the set. They were actors in the play within the play, and the show was actually beginning, but the tryout audiences thought they were real stagehands and paid them no heed. See Secrest, *Somewhere for Us: A Biography of Richard Rodgers*, p. 320.

character plays, but how many one-character musicals? Hamlet is not an ensemble performer. Romeo and Juliet build their characters through one another, but their tragedy is that they cannot survive in a context larger than two. The ending of *West Side Story* refuses Shakespeare's device of having a single authority figure, the Prince, summarize the moral lesson of the play and bring about reconciliation between Montague and Capulet. Instead, *West Side Story* ends with a procession of the two gangs, which repeats the earlier procession from the ballet number "Somewhere." The ensembles participate in this number, with Maria joining the procession and with Tony being carried away, and we are meant to remember the "Somewhere" ballet. Authority is left standing on the stage with nothing to say. The ending is a far cry from Shakespeare, but it is an epitome of musical theatre performance.

This difference between legitimate drama and the musical can be seen clearly by setting Shaw's *Pygmalion* against the musical it gave rise to, *My Fair Lady*, as we did earlier when we noted that the musical supplies the turning-point "Rain in Spain" scene not in the play. The musical also adds two "working-class" numbers in the early scenes. "Wouldn't It Be Loverly" is inserted at end of scene 1, to take the place of Eliza's routine with the taxi in Shaw's play (in the play, she uses some of the money Higgins has flung at her to ride home in a cab; in the musical, the new money gives her thoughts of spending it to live in a comfortable room somewhere). And new scenes are added in a tenement section of Tottenham Court Road, to give Eliza's tipsy father, Alfred P. Doolittle, a chance to sing "With A Little Bit of Luck" (Shaw's play never moves to this setting). Both numbers are meant to provide early solos for major characters, but both also involve ensemble performance. A male quartet behind Eliza helps her act out a fantasy about the "loverly" comfortable life. Doolittle's "Little Bit of Luck" number grows from solo to trio to chorus, an expanding song-and-dance carrying over two scenes. The whole neighborhood swings around to Alfred's view on drink and laziness. Thus poverty is sentimentalized into song-and-dance routines for happy tappers, but both numbers are intended to create a contrast between the ensembles for the poor and the ensembles for the rich, which have also been added to Shaw's play. The Ascot scene and the ballroom scene are large assemblies of snobbery on display. Unlike the tappers and stompers of Tottenham Court Road, the rich dance along the coordinates of stilted elegance (which puts their clothing on display, for the costuming of Cecil Beaton in these two scenes was part of the show's original success).

The happy ending provided in the musical, which brings Higgins and Eliza together for the promise of an ongoing romance, is often thought to be the most significant change from Shaw's plot. We have discussed the achievement of Henry Higgins in learning how to control the format of a popular song, which changes him from the arch-individualist a musical cannot tolerate into a fit mate for Eliza. *My Fair Lady* ends with just the two characters and is unusual in that regard. But it is moving in the right direction. The romantic ending is appropriate as the conclusion to the musical coordinations that have been running throughout.[11] This is how people live in their most desirable moments in the world of Rodgers and Hammerstein, which is also the world of Lerner and Loewe. They live by social relationships that take the form of song and dance.

CHALLENGES TO SUCH PIETY: *CANDIDE* AND *WEST SIDE STORY*

My Fair Lady looks to the past just at a time when a different future for the musical was in the air. The different future was taking shape under Leonard Bernstein and his collaborators, who were turning Voltaire's *Candide* and Shakespeare's *Romeo and Juliet* into musicals in years when theatregoers were waiting all night along 51st Street for a chance to buy standing-room tickets for the next performance of *My Fair Lady*. Historians of the musical theatre must take 1956–1957 as a defining

---

[11] The happy ending was first used in the 1938 film of *Pygmalion*.

point, with the triumph of the older tradition, *My Fair Lady* (opened March 1956), playing at the Mark Hellinger, a few blocks from Bernstein's *Candide* (opened December 1956) at the Martin Beck, and only steps from *West Side Story* (opened September 1957) at the Winter Garden.

The Bernstein shows invert the Rodgers and Hammerstein ensemble ethos. We have glanced at the ending of *Candide*. Now glance at the beginning. *Candide* begins with Pangloss and the chorus singing "The Best of All Possible Worlds," which takes the notions of weddings and festivities celebrated in *Oklahoma!* and *Carousel* and turns them around. Why are there so many divorces in the best of all possible worlds? the bride-to-be wonders on her wedding day. Because then people can try the wonders of marriage over and over again, sings Pangloss. The chorus backs him by repeating his lines. It is Rodgers and Hammerstein being played through a Gilbert and Sullivan routine with the chorus, and perhaps it seems like good-hearted joshing for a moment. But before the scene is over, a new choral number is the occasion for an outburst of war, pillage, and rape, including the rape of the bride-to-be. This is not "June Is Bustin' Out All Over." The next scene gives us the Lisbon earthquake and the Inquisition. Satire had long been a Broadway genre, of course, but this was a monster satire, out to destroy all the romantic notions that had made the Broadway musical a successful commodity, and the notion that community can be forged through song and dance disappeared early.[12]

Candide flopped in 1956, despite decent reviews and immediate recognition for the score. Broadway was not ready for Voltaire. *West Side Story* was a great success in 1957, however, and its ensemble opening, with the violence of gang warfare being danced in a jazz ballet, is one of the defining moments of musical theatre. One reason for its success was that it concentrated its innovations into one basic convention of musicals,

---

[12] Mordden's chapter on *Candide* in *Everything's Coming Up Roses* summarizes the rewrites *Candide* has received and gives solid praise to the original version.

dance, while *Candide* diffused its satire into narrative conventions, which never work well in musicals. Both of these conventions are discussed more fully later. For the moment, recall Agnes de Mille's ballets in the Rodgers and Hammerstein shows. *Oklahoma!* and *Carousel* not only popularized ballet in musicals, they *centralized* ballet for important segments. So did Robbins with the choreography for his earlier collaboration with Bernstein, *On the Town* (which was derived from the ballet *Fancy Free*). De Mille and Robbins were following a path made by Balanchine in the "Slaughter on Tenth Avenue" ballet in *On Your Toes*, by Rodgers and Hart. "Slaughter on Tenth Avenue" is danced at the climax of act 2. "Laurey's Dream" sets up the act 1 curtain. *West Side Story* moves dance to the very opening action and uses it throughout. We have discussed the scene in which Anita is nearly raped by the Jets and retaliates with a decisive lie about the killing of Maria. Powerful episodes involving the warring gangs are danced throughout *West Side Story*, bringing the ensemble tendency of the musical fully into contact with sex and violence.

After *West Side Story* the way was open to many kinds of experiments with the ensemble tendency of the musical. I have argued that Rodgers and Hammerstein changed the history of the genre by basing song-and-dance conventions on more challenging books than had been used before, but they also consolidated the ensemble convention into an ideology of community-mindedness that dramatized the sentimentality of the form. The Bernstein shows of the mid-1950s shattered the community spirit of ensemble, and the "concept" musicals that followed in the 1960s and 1970s found the way open for sharp and lasting experiments with choruses, chorus lines, and company song-and-dance numbers.

CONCEPT SHOWS: *CABARET* AND *COMPANY*

Cabaret (1966) challenges many of the musical's conventions, none more directly than that of ensemble performance. Ensembles in *Cabaret* are for Nazis in the Berlin of the 1930s.

The number that demonstrates this chilling reversal of the Broadway convention is "Tomorrow Belongs to Me," Kander and Ebb's version of a Nazi anthem, first sung by the waiters and the Emcee at the Kit Kat Klub. Its reprise at the end of act 1 is devastating. A good-hearted engagement party for Fräulein Schneider and Herr Schultz is under way. (They are the middle-aged couple who form the secondary love story.) Trouble arises when the one Nazi at the party, Ernst, learns that Herr Schultz is Jewish. Ernst is ready to stalk out when the prostitute Fräulein Kost begins to sing the anthem.

> The sun on the meadow is summery warm,
> The stag in the forest runs free.
> But gather together to greet the storm,
> Tomorrow belongs to me.

"Sing with me!" she calls to Ernst, and after their duet she gives the standard call for singalongs to the other partygoers: "And now—everyone!" Everyone joins in except for the principal characters, the two sets of lovers, Fräulein Schneider and Herr Shultz, Sally Bowles and Cliff. They are left "outside the circle" while the ensemble sings,

> Oh, Fatherland, Fatherland, show us the sign
> Your children have waited to see.
> The morning will come when the world is mine,
> Tomorrow belongs to me.

This is a choral number that excludes the lovers and dramatizes the way ordinary German citizens became swept up in the Nazi ideology. (The concentration on "me" also shows the core of self-isolation beneath the pretense of Nazi socialism.)

This is *Cabaret*'s reflection of the central moment in its source, Christopher Isherwood's long story, "Sally Bowles." To drift with the bohemian, cabaret-oriented life of young people in Berlin in the 1930s is to be complicit with Nazism—that is the realization on which the story turns. The moment of the realization is the funeral of Hermann Müller, the last Social Democrat chancellor before Hitler took power. Sally Bowles and Chris (the narrator, an approximation of Isherwood himself) catch sight of the funeral procession from their window. They don't know who has died. Sally does not care. Chris cares to the point of realizing that they are losing contact with ordinary people everywhere, as they drift into complicity with the rise of the Nazis. "In a few days, I thought, we shall have forfeited all kinship with ninety-nine percent of the population of the world, with the men and women who earn their living, who insure their lives, who are anxious about the future of their children."[13]

Nowhere does the musical use those lines. Instead, it makes "Tomorrow Belongs to Me" into the shared ubiquitous number of the show, the number almost every character seems to know, and lets the number spread into ensemble voicing in the party scene, leaving only the principal characters "outside the circle," unable to speak for anything but a defiant isolation.

The two women of the love-stories voice this isolation most clearly. Here is Fräulein Schneider after she realizes that she cannot run the risk of marrying a Jew:

> All my life I have managed for myself—and it is too old a habit to change. I have battled alone, and I have survived. There was a war—and I survived. There was a revolution—and I survived. There was an Inflation—billions of marks for one loaf of bread—but I survived! And if the Nazis come—I will survive. If the Communists come—I will still be *here*—renting these rooms! For—in the end— what other choice have I? This—is my world!" (pp. 98–99)

Sally Bowles expresses the code of individualism from a young person's perspective, where it seems even more desolate. When she breaks up with Cliff, she says, "I meet someone and I make all sorts of enormous promises. . . . And I suddenly realize I can't keep those promises—not possibly! Because I am still *me!*" (p. 110).

That is how the book makes the point. The numbers make the point more effectively, especially the title song, in which Sally pretends to praise the sociability of cabaret life while she is really focusing on her strange role model, a character unseen

[13] Isherwood, "Sally Bowles," p. 49.

in the musical, a prostitute named Elsie. Elsie gave Sally Bowles this number and then achieved her place in memory when she died and was laid out on her bier, "the happiest corpse I'd ever seen." Both times Sally Bowles sings this climactic number, the chorus of cabaret performers who are with her disappears into darkness, and she is left alone on the stage. Ensembles do not hold together for Sally Bowles. They are for Nazis. In her title number, Sally Bowles ends up singing alone, in memory of a dead prostitute. The reversal this musical gives to the Rodgers and Hammerstein format is rigorous and exact.

Sondheim's *Company* (1970) challenges the ensemble tendency by seeming to be about urban loneliness. Bobby, the hero, does not do ensemble at all well. His friends, who do, are all married. They think Bobby should get married, although the husbands also think he is lucky in his freedom and the wives think he should be attracted to women like themselves. The climactic number, "Being Alive," declares that Bobby is ready to end his isolation through some sort of long-term relationship, but in fact no such relationship develops, and he sings most of "Being Alive" alone. Earlier in the number the married friends do some of the singing, as though this were an ensemble piece in the making, but the song does not take shape until the married friends turn silent and Bobby is free to sing the entire tune through on his own.[14] This is hardly an example of ensemble performance. The orchestration (by Jonathan Tunick) even tucks the "Company" theme into the accompaniment to "Being Alive." This is the ensemble tune with which the musical began. Now there is no ensemble, and their tune has been absorbed into Bobby's solo.

There follows a book scene in which Bobby refuses to appear at his birthday party, and the friends are left with nothing to do. So they leave, and Bobby comes along to blow out his birthday candles by himself. As often happens in a Sondheim

[14] It does not take shape because the B section of the AABA song form does not fully occur until Bobby sings alone. See Banfield, *Sondheim's Broadway Musicals*, pp. 169–72, for a good discussion of the ambiguities and contradictions in "Being Alive."

show, a basic convention of the musical is being turned around. The final episode of *Company* puts the ensemble out of the picture and gives us the individual instead. In the sense that the "company" involved means providing friendship for a lonely bachelor, which is what Bobby's married friends think they are doing, the show is funny and cynical about the relationships. The friends either imagine Bobby becoming one of them through getting married or warn Bobby that he is better off not becoming one of them. In either case the married couples merely refer Bobby to their own situation, and this is not friendship.

But Sondheim shows also have a tendency to solidify the very convention that is being turned inside out. The ensemble has a grip in *Company* (as the name of the show would imply)— not so much in the book or the lyrics, but in the performance of the numbers. That tune to "Company" that Jonathan Tunick worked into the accompaniment to Bobby's solo has a vivid history in this show. It was the number that dramatized the emergence of the six married couples out of the sensational set Boris Aronson designed for the original production. The set was a chrome-and-glass abstraction with different compartments and levels. It separated the members of the company at the beginning, as a metaphor for isolation involved in Manhattan apartment dwelling. But Sondheim timed the opening number to reach a climax just as the singers reached the stage via the elevators that Aronson had built into the set.[15] The blocking brought the singers to where they could become an ensemble at the climax of the number, moving out of the isolation of the set and reaching the stage where a "company" could take shape.

Bobby cannot fit into the ensemble. This is a sign of the limit he would like to overcome. At the opening of act 2, in "Side by Side," he tries to join the series of tap breaks performed by the married couples and finds that he has no partner. He comes up short in the performance sense. That the final number is a solo

[15] Secrest, *Stephen Sondheim*, p. 195.

for Bobby might be taken to mean that the ensemble possibility drains away, but *Company* cannot end with Bobby singing alone. Everyone feels the pressure that calls the ensemble together at the end for a reprise of the opening song. That is how the musical really ends, with ensemble performance, Bobby singing with everyone else. It is a convention, of course, for this reprise sets up the curtain calls (it is Number 22 in the vocal score, entitled "Bows"), but conventions have meanings and reveal the principles at work in the form. Try ending *Company* with Bobby alone, without the company. The audience would feel it had been short-changed, to say nothing of the company.

A CHORUS LINE: THE THING ITSELF

A Chorus Line (1975) tests the convention of ensemble performance in another way, by turning the ensemble itself into the subject of the musical. The book concerns the audition process for more than seventeen young dancers who are trying to make it on Broadway. Only eight are to be selected. The seventeen hopefuls who survive the first cut have to tell stories about themselves in answer to the director Zach's request to learn more about them while they are trying out. Some of these vignettes become musical numbers. Mike remembers watching his sister at ballet lessons and knowing "I Can Do That." Diana tells of her ordeal studying method acting at the High School of the Performing Arts and feeling "Nothing." There are also duet and trio recollections. Three of the girls recall the importance of ballet training in their childhoods and combine into a trio-and-dance, "At the Ballet." Just about everyone joins in the rousing number about adolescence and sex, "Hello Twelve, Hello Thirteen, Hello Love."

These spots of personal recollection can lead to the impression that the show is about individualism in the traditional American grain. For Frank Rich, "*A Chorus Line* stands for the supremacy of the individual, for the right of even the lowliest member of an ensemble to have his own integrity and dreams."[16] It is true that the musical offers temptations toward that interpretation, but the achievement that matters in the show is the achievement of ensemble performances, a point Rich also recognizes when he notes that the stories of these two dozen characters are told "simultaneously." Simultaneity is the real achievement of the musical. Sheila's reverie about childhood ballet lessons may begin as a solo, "At the Ballet," but the number draws others into the reverie and it becomes a trio. "Hello Twelve, Hello Thirteen, Hello Love" begins as Mark's account of reading up on human anatomy when he was prepubescent, but simultaneity develops when all the dancers remember doing this kind of thing. The dancers generate an ensemble number that lasts for about half an hour, giving way here and there for more of Mark's reverie, or for similar individual recollections, or for a solo turn (Diana's "Nothing" is sung within the limits of "Hello Twelve"). The show pauses over individual recollections but then turns the number into ensemble performance, and that is the dynamic that matters.

The temptation to linger over individuals comes to a head in the Zach-Cassie relationship. Director Zach has had an affair with auditioner Cassie years ago, and now he tries to dissuade her from trying out for a chorus line, on grounds that she has "star" quality (which is a problem in a chorus line). No, Cassie insists, she wants to be part of the line. She also wants to restore her love affair with the director, but the line comes first. Is it hard to believe that chorus lines matter more than love affairs? At one point Cassie says she can have both, the line and the director. But we do not see her linking up her romance with Zach at the end. We see the chorus line dancing, with Cassie fitting right in. The ensemble dance is the outcome of the musical, and the drive for simultaneity is perfectly realized.

Fine irony lies in the music they sing and dance, "One," for the number is *about* the individualist, the "one," the star whom they are supposed to be backing up—

[16] Rich, Introduction to Kirkwood et al., *A Chorus Line*, p. xvii.

She walks into a room and you know
She's uncommonly rare, very unique,
Peripatetic, poetic, and chic—

In fact, this sensational "one" never appears. The dancing ensemble rehearses their backup routine to the point where it suddenly clicks into focus as the foreground, all the ones who have told their stories now becoming the many who can do this number in perfect unison. (The ballet film *The Red Shoes*, which the girls of the chorus line remember fondly from their childhoods, should be recalled at this point, for there is a dance without the star dancer at the end of the film too. *The Red Shoes* threads its way through *A Chorus Line* at a number of points.[17]) The climax of the show is actually the curtain call, where all the dancers—the seventeen hopefuls and the dancers who were cut at the very beginning—sing and dance "One" in their brilliant costumes and top hats. Cassie must be one of them, enjoying just what she wanted, belonging to the line, but we cannot see her apart from the others. The shaping of the ensemble is so much the subject of the musical that the curtain call is really the final number and the conclusion of the drama. Where is the book when a number takes over the play?

A Chorus Line is one of the pathbreaking musicals, and we will study it in greater detail in subsequent chapters. For the moment, the point is that *A Chorus Line* does declare for the power of ensemble performance, but it does so by dramatizing a convention of ensemble itself. The expansion of a number into a chorus used to represent some other sort of social cohesion—a Long Island party in the shows of the 1920s and 1930s, Seabees larking about in the South Pacific in Rodgers and Hammerstein—but now nothing else is being represented. This is the convention itself—it is about the chorus line. Such

---

[17] Zach's cruel device of having the losers in the final audition step forward as though they had won also occurs in the film. In an early script, the absence of the star from the performance of "One" was to be indicated by a spotlight moving about the stage in front of the chorus line, but this was abandoned. Information of this sort is abundant in Mandelbaum, A Chorus Line *and the Musicals of Michael Bennett.*

reflexivity does create a kind of integrated musical, but not the kind that is usually meant by that term. This is not the seamless integration of book and number. This is the absorbing of the book into the number, so that the plot is dance and the only time that matters is lyric time. The interplay between Cassie and Zach, along with the autobiographies of the other dancers, are reminders that there is supposed to be a book, but the book never takes shape and the chorus line does. We will see more about this later.

Chapter Five

THE DRAMA OF NUMBERS

The Diegetic Convention

A *Chorus Line*'s way of dramatizing a convention of musical theatre itself leads us to a broader consideration of
"backstage" musicals, which have always been with us
and have rarely been theorized. Backstage musicals are about
putting on musicals, so that the plot is about the means of its
own production. Since the characters are show people whose
job is song and dance, much of the singing and dancing is
called for by the book. *Show Boat* is about entertainers, so they
sing and dance. The Rodgers and Hart *Babes in Arms* is about
kids putting on a show in a barn, and *Pal Joey* is about Chicago
nightclub performers. The improvement in book writing in
the second half of the twentieth century led to inventive variations on this theme. Much of *Cabaret* takes place in a Berlin
nightclub where the heroine, Sally Bowles, is a singer and the
orchestra for the entire show is more or less the nightclub
band, but the cabaret is a metaphor for the rise of Nazism, and
there are strange links between the nightclub and episodes occurring in the city. *Phantom of the Opera* uses an opera-within-
the-musical device—the plot occurs at the Paris Opera where
various operas, including one by the Phantom himself, are being rehearsed or staged. *Follies* takes place at a reunion of former Follies showgirls, who perform some of their old numbers
for one another. There are even ghosts in *Follies*, and they perform, too—they were showgirls once. The backstage musical
has probably taken on more new lives than any other subgenre
of theatre in the last fifty years.

The usual view of this phenomenon is that it is a convenience: it is easier to justify numbers arising out of a book that

is already about the performance of numbers. True, but I think there is more to it than that. Many songs are called for by the book without the need to invoke the backstage convention. When Beadle Brampton sits down at Mrs. Lovett's harmonium to sing his favorite parlor songs in *Sweeney Todd*, or when Frankie writes a song, "It's Got to Be Love," and sings it for her handsome teacher in *On Your Toes*, they bring about the same result—putting a song *into* the book. The hoedown that opens act 2 of *Oklahoma!* is called for by the book. It is a social event for the characters in the book, as is the dance at the gymnasium that is supposed to bring the Jets and the Sharks together in *West Side Story*. I think songs and dances are called for in the books of many shows not because the other convention, that of having characters break into song, is inconvenient to the writers but because the convention of breaking into song is such a mine of dramatic advantages that it becomes worth attention in the book. Books can seem better for recognizing song-and-dance numbers because songs and dances lay claim to the same characters and situation as the book but are in a fair way to improve on the book's version. The book that proceeds as though these song-and-dance interruptions are not going to happen may be a good book, but it is missing an opportunity. Knowing that song-and-dance interruptions are certainly going to happen makes the book smarter about the aesthetic design it belongs to. This is more than a convenience.

The term *diegetic*, borrowed from film criticism, is coming to be used for numbers that are called for by the book. It is meant to cover the backstage musicals plus any other occasions on which characters deliberately perform numbers for other characters. When Beadle Brampton spies the harmonium and sets about singing old ballads, the number is just as diegetic as the show dances that are being rehearsed in *A Chorus Line*. Thus, not all diegetic numbers belong to the backstage convention, but all numbers from the backstage convention are diegetic. What they all have in common is that they are called for as performances in the book. The diegetic number is not a case of someone "bursting into song." Rather, someone has a song to sing, according to the book, and goes ahead and sings it.[1]

The diegetic number would seem to work wonders for the theory of the integrated musical. The number still has its own structure and its own time scheme, but because it is called for in the book, it seems to be integrated into book time. The most famous opening song in a musical, "Oh, What a Beautiful Morning," from *Oklahoma!*, is a diegetic number. It is famous because it begins offstage as an a capella solo, challenging the usual chorus opening of Broadway shows, as we saw in the previous chapter. It is diegetic because Curly is singing it to be heard as a song within the book. Cowboys sing on fine mornings like this, we are to understand. Aunt Eller, churning butter out in the yard on this fine morning, hears the offstage song just as we hear it in the audience. A smile crosses her face. She knows it is Curly, and in a few seconds, there he is, onstage and singing what passes for a cowboy song.[2]

My argument that numbers are set off from the book by virtue of their different order of time needs to take the diegetic

---

[1] *Diegetic* originally meant "narrative" and was opposed to "mimetic" in Plato, a distinction that becomes "somewhat neutralized" in Aristotle (Genette, *Narrative Discourse*, p. 163). See also Puchner, *Stage Fright: Modernism, Anti-Theatricality, and Drama*, pp. 22–28. Film theory has changed the meaning: the diegetic is everything that falls within the frame of the shot. Borrowing from this, recent narrative theory applies the term to the world in which the narrated events occur. The two meanings are distinguished in Prince, *A Dictionary of Narratology*, p. 20. If a scene in an opera calls for an aria to be performed as part of the fiction (as happens in the party scene of *Eugene Onegin*, for example), this can be called a diegetic aria, as opposed to arias that arise apparently spontaneously from impassioned characters. The diegetic convention in musicals is discussed by Banfield, *Sondheim's Broadway Musicals*, pp. 184–87. Abbate, *Unsung Voices: Opera and Musical Narrative in the Nineteenth Century*, p. 5, uses "phenomenal performance" instead of "diegetic." Here is her definition: "a musical or vocal performance that declares itself openly, singing that is heard by its singer, the auditors on stage, and understood as music that they (too) hear by us, the theatre audience."

[2] The flatted seventh that occurs on the first syllable of "morning" in the title phrase marks this as a cowboy song reimagined for the St. James Theatre on 44th Street in New York City. Riggs used the real thing as the opening for *Green Grow the Lilacs*: "Get Along Little Doggies."

convention into account. If numbers are lyrical inserts that bring book time to a pause, what about numbers that are called for in the book? Book time cannot be said to come to a pause. A bit of Aunt Eller's morning is being taken up by Curly's singing. When number time is announced as belonging to book time, how can they differ? This has to be looked into.

"Can't Help Lovin' Dat Man"

Let us examine one of the best diegetic numbers, "Can't Help Lovin' Dat Man," from *Show Boat*. This tune is first sung by Julie, a black woman who is passing for white in order to keep her starring role in the showboat troupe. She sings "Can't Help Lovin' Dat Man" because her friend Magnolia, who has just fallen for a man herself, has heard Julie sing this tune before and thinks it worth hearing again. The black cook Queenie is surprised to hear Julie sing this tune (they are in the kitchen pantry of the showboat) because it is supposed to be known only to black folks. Julie is worried that her secret will now come out. But she acts boldly and sings the song, which Queenie then joins for a chorus herself, along with her husband, Joe, who has come in to hear the familiar tune. Soon a group of blacks are singing it and doing a bit of the shuffle. In a wonderful move, Magnolia gets on her feet and starts to do the shuffle herself. She has been learning it from the black people, and she does it well this time.

This song is carefully joined to the plot, but it still functions as the addition of another order of time, lyric time. It dovetails neatly with the book dialogue calling for it, but it does the job most songs do in musicals, which is to provide moments of lyric elaboration and suspension for song-and-dance performance to become the center of the show. A pause is a pause even when the characters in the book hear it as a pause. Queenie picks up something from the song that will matter when the book resumes, and even mentions her discovery during the song—"ah didn't ever hear anybody but colored folks sing dat song"—but this piece of clever dovetailing is not the main issue.

The main issue is to see and hear this tune to its ending, as it becomes an ensemble performance by the black characters and then a dance that even Magnolia can do. It is a prime example of the ensemble tendency we discussed in the previous chapter—the number spreads to include more and more performers. Magnolia's bit of the shuffle is a sign of her open-mindedness to black culture. It is a sign of her character. But the main delight is to hear Julie's performance of the song through to its conclusion and then to realize that it can be shared and even danced by the black characters who come into the pantry, even by Magnolia. Julie's song has turned into the shuffle and everyone can do it, in the kitchen!

The song has the standard verse-chorus structure, but these units are redistributed. Julie sings some of the chorus first, then after a bit of dialogue in which she realizes that Queenie knows the origin of the tune among black folk she asserts herself, as though to say "I will sing it anyhow, and I will sing it completely," and begins with the verse this time ("Oh, listen sister, I love that mister . . .") This is a nervy moment. The verse takes the form of a twelve-bar blues, the music of black people indeed. When she swings into the chorus, this comes as a repeat because we heard it earlier. The chorus develops as an AABA song. The transition from the blues introduction to the AABA tune is nervy, too. Kern is combining two formats that do not exactly belong together, and he is saying, implicitly, think again, these things do belong together. He especially says this when he inserts a blue note into his AABA chorus at a key moment, under "man" in the repeated phrase, "man of mine." Julie's song, called for in the pantry of the showboat, is Kern's song, too, and as Kern's song it is saying something Julie cannot say as a book character. It is saying that black and white can be brought together in show business, the blues and a Tin Pan Alley song, as long as you accept this tune written by a white Jewish composer, sung by a white woman playing a mulatto (Helen Morgan played Julie originally), and overheard by Aunt Jemima (Tess Gardella, a white woman who blacked up as Aunt Jemima in advertisements, played Queenie). All this happened beyond anyone's particular intention, but it did happen.

THE DRAMA OF NUMBERS   107

And the number that made it happen did intentionally put the blues elements into the pop-song format for Julie to sing. The conditions that developed in the performance of the number were established in the number itself, and when that number expands to include the ensemble, and when the ensemble swings into the shuffle, and when the white ingénue Magnolia proves that she has been learning the shuffle too, the basic conventions of the musical are fully at work. This is complex theatre.[3]

Here is how the chorus to "Can't Help Lovin' Dat Man" works as a melody. The first phrase, "Fish got to swim and birds got to fly," has the same lyric meter as the second, "I got to love one man till I die," and the two phrases span virtually the same intervals. The rhyme "fly" and "die" adds lyrical resemblance to the musical repetition, and these lines belong to a stanza, A, whose format is repeated twice, the second repeat falling after B. The overall structure is AABA, the same as in "Surrey with the Fringe on Top" and "People Will Say We're in Love" from *Oklahoma!*, "Tonight," from *West Side Story*, "Luck Be a Lady," from *Guys and Dolls*, "A Weekend in the Country," from *A Little Night Music*, and thousands of other show tunes and popular songs. The refrain "Can't Help Lovin' Dat Man of Mine" is heard at the end of each A section. By the time Queenie, Joe, and their cohorts finish singing, the refrain has been heard seven times, and it is the concluding phrase of the song, which circles back on itself. It may advance the plot on one important point, but mainly it circles back on itself and gains a lift by doing so.

---

[3] The interracial casting of *Show Boat* was a bold move for the Broadway of 1927. We could add that the song was also meant to be overheard by a Phi Beta Kappa graduate and all-American football star from Rutgers, Paul Robeson, who was making a reputation singing spirituals in New York instead of practicing as an attorney after obtaining his law degree from Columbia University. Robeson undertook a concert tour in Europe in 1927 rather than wait for *Show Boat* to be finished, and Jules Bledsoe, well established as an opera and lieder singer, played the role first. Robeson came to the role in the London production of 1928, then played Joe in the film. See McMillin, "Paul Robeson, Will Vodery's 'Jubilee Singers,' and the Earliest Script of the Kern-Hammerstein *Show Boat*."

By the end everyone onstage is dancing. The shuffle has repetitions of its own, the body in motion with or without the
words. Repetition abounds. The repeated stanzas of the song
contain the repeated rhymes of the lyric and the repeated motifs of harmony and rhythm in the music. This is the musical at
its fullest, and the elation that is felt in the performing group
and in the audience comes from the simultaneous occurrence
of these repetitions within the suspension that is occurring
within book time. This is a number having its effect. "Elation"
is the right word for this effect, for reasons we will come to.

Later in *Show Boat* Magnolia sings "Can't Help Lovin' Dat
Man" for an audition at a Chicago nightclub, and Julie turns
up by sheer coincidence just in time to recognize her friend
from the showboat days. The number is diegetic again. Julie
hears Magnolia's rendition of her song and makes the noble
gesture of giving up her gig.[4] The nightclub manager hears the
song too, and doesn't like it. The onstage accompanist suggests
"ragging" the tune, so Magnolia has to sing an up-tempo
version to land the job. Eventually she goes on to become a
star, and by the final scene, set in 1927 (the year the musical
opened), she is heard singing "Can't Help Lovin' Dat Man"
over the radio, while her father and former husband listen—
diegetic again. Never has so much been done in the interests of
integrating a number with a book in a musical, but the song is
still an insert, a number with time of its own, and utterly detachable. It can go from the Mississippi River in the late 1880s
to a Chicago nightclub in 1904 by virtue of being diegetic
within the book, then it can go to a radio broadcast of 1927
which people on the showboat listen to—and then it can be
broadcast and recorded by Helen Morgan, Ella Fitzgerald,

---

[4] This section of Edna Ferber's *Show Boat*, the novel on which the musical is
based, does not bring Julie into the audition scene, but the novel's audition
does show where Hammerstein took the hint for the diegetic "Can't Help
Lovin' Dat Man." In the novel, Magnolia auditions with spirituals like "All
God's Chillun Got Wings" and "Go Down, Moses," which she learned from
the black people on the kitchen staff of the show boat. Hammerstein took this
idea and carried it back to the kitchen pantry scene by having Julie sing the
black folk's song Kern had written for the occasion.

Barbra Streisand, and a further list of singers, a triumph of detachability within the show and in the song's long aftermath.[5]

Refrain

One reason Ella Fitzgerald could be just as convincing singing "Can't Help Lovin' Dat Man" over the radio as Julie and Magnolia are singing it in *Show Boat* is that all of these singers repeat the same phrase at the end of each A section of music: "can't help lovin' dat man" (the phrase with the blue note). They must really mean it, they sing it so often. Ella does not need a dramatic reason to sing about how she "can't help lovin' dat man." "People will say we're in love," "I could have danced all night," "The guy's only doing it for some gal"—the refrains of popular songs are all around us, and there is no reason for them to be there, no *other* reason. The song gives reason enough. There is something internal to the repetitions in a song that justify the song's projection, regardless of context. What is this?

Words in a song pretend to refer to something outside the song—the dying of a lovely flame, the special face one looks for in a romance, the best meat pies in London—but the repetition of the words several times brings the lyric around to itself as another point of reference. It refers to itself as well as to the other things. "I'm always true to you, darlin', in my fashion, / Yes, I'm always true to you, darlin', in my way." This is heard twelve times when Bianca sings it in *Kiss Me, Kate* (once in French), and for some reason it is a pleasure to hear so often. Its view of love is sassy and cute, but there is another reason for the pleasure. Refrain seeks to become its own signifier through repetition, and this approach to transparency—where the words and tune being heard refer to

[5] See the analyses of this song in Forte, *The American Popular Ballad of the Golden Era, 1924–1950*, pp. 55–59, and Knapp, *The American Musical and the Formation of National Identity*, pp. 191–92.

themselves through repetition—lifts the song to another layer of reference above the normal agony of being "about" love, or "about" the blues. The other layer makes the song about itself.

A good book about Shakespeare, Sigurd Burckhardt's *Shakespearean Meanings*, talks about the "liberation" that music can bring into a verbal text. "As often in Shakespeare, music liberates from the slavery of intention: it suspends, in a momentary harmony, the endless chase of means and meanings." The liberation and suspension Burckhardt has in mind occur most fully in the full-scale repetition of refrain, with its word-for-word, note-for-note semblance of perfection. This effect can be tested by thinking about "Oh, What a Beautiful Morning," where the entire chorus is a refrain. The second time, or the third or fourth, the refrain is heard—

> Oh, what a beautiful mornin',
> Oh, what a beautiful day.
> I got a beautiful feelin'
> Ev'rythin's goin' my way—

it is no longer just the morning that is beautiful. It never was, but on first hearing, we pretended this cowboy is only charged up about the fine weather. That pretense can be abandoned the second or third time he sings the refrain. He is charged up about the repeated lyric and music, which are now on their way to becoming their own signifiers. He is also charged up about his performance of the song. It is beautiful, and he sings this kind of beauty well.

John Hollander points out that in addition to being repeated itself, refrain bears a memory of its own repetition.[6] It is an historian of its occurrences, and if it alludes to words from some other poem or song, it calls that poem or song into play as well. A refrain about "wind and rain" remembers its own repetitions, but it also remembers Feste's song at the end of *Twelfth Night*, which has refrains on "with hey ho, the wind and

---

[6] See Hollander, "Breaking into Song."

the rain," and "the rain it raineth every day."[7] Lyrics to show tunes do not often become so intricate. Hollander would call them the "tra-la-la" variety of refrain, which means that we can stop thinking about meaning for the length of the repeat. I am not so sure. "Always true to you, darlin' in my fashion" is in fact an allusion to a poem by Ernest Dowson, which itself goes back to an ode by Horace.[8] Perhaps this is not a typical example. Cole Porter may have been showing off, although the musical in question, *Kiss Me Kate*, makes substantial allusions to a play by Shakespeare, which itself goes back to other plays. Allusion in popular song formats may be more substantial than "tra-la-la" suggests, but even "tra-la-la" does the basic work of refrain, which is to repeat a line or phrase until it turns into itself. One could say that the line signifies itself, if such a thing were possible, but it does signify itself-in-repetition, which is slightly different. A sign must signify something other than itself to be a sign, but the close call is exciting, and the refrain in poetry or a song is a close call. The repeated line threatens to abandon semiosis by standing for itself, and by actually standing for itself-in-repetition, it gives a lift to the poem. Song and dance thrive on this lift.[9] The reason Ella Fitzgerald does not need a book reason to sing a show tune on a recording is that

[7] Hollander chooses a fine wind-and-rain poem by Trumbull Stickney, "Mnemosyne," and Hardy's "During Wind and Rain." See "Breaking into Song," pp. 79–87.

[8] See Dowson's "Cynara" ("I have been faithful to thee, Cynara, in my fashion"), which refers to Horace, *Odes*, I, 4.

[9] We are touching on a lively debate among music and dance theoreticians at this point, for it is sometimes said that music and dance are altogether free from extrinsic referentiality and are self-contained in the signifier. This formalist position seems impossible to maintain without some yielding on the side of extrinsic referentiality, for the formal elements that might seem to create an intrinsic self-sufficiency are themselves part of extrinsic awareness. The scale in Western music is a condition of experience in the listener, for example. For a full discussion of this issue, see Nattiez, *Music and Discourse: Toward a Semiology of Music*, pp. 118–26, along with the adjustments offered in Rosario Mirigliano, "The sign and music: A reflection on the theoretical bases of musical semiotics," pp. 43–61. Similar conditions of experience allow dance to be understood, too.

good show tunes have their own structures of repetition and refrain, waiting for a good singer to do something with them.

OUT-OF-THE-BLUE NUMBERS

So, diegetic songs have a built-in detachability. The song that is called for in a show has been called for elsewhere and can be called for again. "I thought only black folks knew that song" alludes to the previous history of the song and sets up the possibility that great crowds of white folks are going to be hearing it over the years. But most songs in musicals are not diegetic, not called for. Most songs in musicals seem to be happening for the first time, arising spontaneously from within the characters in the book. We need a phrase to distinguish the diegetic number from the usual kind, where characters burst into song. When Ado Annie sings "I'm Just a Girl Who Cain't Say No" in *Oklahoma!*, she is not said to be singing by the book. She and Laurey have been talking about how to behave with boys, with Laurey trying to teach her friend a bit of restraint. Ado Annie illustrates her approach by breaking into song. The debate comes to a pause and a solo number takes over, uncalled for. This is the standard convention of musical theatre, obvious and commonplace, and therefore requiring attention.

When characters burst into song or dance the number seems to come from out of the blue. That will do for our phrase. Out-of-the-blue numbers are distinct from diegetic numbers because they are not called for as numbers by the book but are forms of spontaneous expression by the characters.

The distinction can be seen in the musical that is practically built on it, *Guys and Dolls*. When the leading ladies are caught up in their work, Miss Adelaide at the nightclub, Miss Sarah Brown at the Salvation Army mission, they sing diegetic songs. When they are caught up in romance, they sing out-of-the-blue songs. Miss Sarah Brown comes into the opening scene singing "Follow the Fold" with the Salvation Army band. This is what Salvation Army bands do—the number is part of the book. Miss Adelaide sings in a nightclub with the Hot Box Girls.

"Take Back Your Mink" and "A Bushel and a Peck" belong to a milieu different from that of "Follow the Fold," but the night-club numbers are like the Salvation Army number in one respect: they are called for by the book and are diegetic. The women who sing them have another mode of song in prospect, the out-of-the-blue mode, and this other mode leads to what is presented as a better life, getting married.

Their love duets are out of the blue. Sky Masterson and Miss Sarah Brown have two out-of-the-blue duets. We have already discussed the first, "I'll Know" (chapter 3), the one they sing before they know they are in love. Later, after they know, they sing "I've Never Been in Love Before," the only love duet sung on the streets of New York at 4 A.M. after a couple has been on a bender in Cuba and the man has proved his worth by not taking advantage of the woman. (While in Cuba, Miss Sarah Brown burst into her tipsy song, "If I Were a Bell," strictly out of the blue, and she and Sky got into a dance brawl with the Cubans that was strictly diegetic.) The duet is introduced by Sky's gorgeous out-of-the-blue interlude, "My Time of Day," an unexpectedly introspective and chromatic meditation that leads into the more conventional "I've Never Been in Love Before." These are both out-of-the-blue numbers.

Miss Adelaide's love duet with Nathan Detroit also comes from out of the blue. This is from an episode we looked at in chapter 2, when Adelaide mistakenly thinks Nathan is lying about going to a prayer meeting. She motors along in her characteristic triplets (Miss Adelaide's "note" as a character is to project her energy and volubility through musical triplets), complaining that she has given the best years of her life to this no-goodnik before her, and the no-goodnik turns the argument into a love duet with his refrain, "So sue me, sue me, shoot bullets through me, I love you." They never do sing the same lyric together in this song, but the comic alternation between their modes shows that they are a match. They are speaking for themselves, bursting into song, showing an extra range of spontaneous expressiveness. Not just love duets but any kind of number can come from out of the blue. When gamblers from across the country gather on Broadway to sing

an anthem in four-part harmony about "The Oldest Established Permanent Floating Crap Game in New York," the number comes from out of the blue. When Adelaide reads from a
medical textbook, footnotes and all, and makes it into a song, it
is out of the blue. But the contrast between Salvation Army
singing and Hot Box singing, which is also the contrast between the leading female characters, is built on diegetic songs.

DIEGETIC SOPHISTICATIONS

Magnolia is introduced into *Show Boat* by means of a diegetic
tune. She is heard practicing the piano offstage, faltering
through a little ditty that sounds like it comes out of an exercise book. Kern's original conception was to transform the
G-major ditty into the final number of the musical, "It's Getting Hotter in the North," which Magnolia's daughter Kim
was to sing at the end of the show. This would have been another diegetic number—Kim is a Broadway star on a visit to
the showboat, and this is the kind of tune she has been singing
on the Great White Way. "It's Getting Hotter" was cut from
the original production and lost from view thereafter, but it
can be heard on John McGlinn's recorded reconstruction of
the original, and the derivation of the jazz tune from the piano
ditty is unmistakable. There are other recollections of the piano ditty (in the convent school scene, for example) and they
usually connect Magnolia to Kim. Ferber had stressed this iden-
tification between mother and daughter, and Kern's various
transformations of the piano ditty form a musical way of creating the same effect.[10]

That is an example of a composer using a convention for a
dramatic point. The diegetic tune shared between mother and
daughter in *Show Boat* dramatizes the relationship between the

[10] The McGlinn recorded reconstruction of *Show Boat* as Kern intended it
is from EMI Records Ltd., 1988. Kreuger, *Show Boat: The Story of a Classic
American Musical*, is a storehouse of information about this musical. Kern's and
Hammerstein's original intentions can be traced through various early drafts
and rehearsal scripts. See McMillin, "Robeson."

women not by means of dialogue in a book scene but by means of shared music in the numbers they perform. This sharing of musical material can happen in out-of-the-blue numbers, but the diegetic convention makes the sharing more pointed. What Kern wanted to do by turning Magnolia's piano ditty into Kim's "It's Getting Hotter in the North" would have been an artful application of the diegetic convention, and sophistication of this kind runs through the history of the musical, increasing as the twentieth century moves along. The convention by which the musicals are performed becomes the thing being dramatized. Rodgers and Hart shows are laced with diegetic innovations of this kind. *On Your Toes* (1936) builds a Russian ballet troupe into the book and makes the plot hinge on whether these classically trained dancers can learn to dance to swing and jazz. Moreover, it works that question into a diegetic number in which American dancers show the Russians how to swing, and the Russians show the Americans what "on your toes" really means. This is the number called "On Your Toes," and it galvanizes the conventions of dance into the turning point of the book. *Pal Joey* (1940) has the nerve to center on second-rate dancing at a seedy Chicago nightclub, thanks to the sophistication of knowing that second-rate dancing can only be made credible by first-rate dancers.

The Rodgers and Hart *Boys from Syracuse* has an inspired moment for a diegetic song built into the plot—a love duet that the heroine sings to her husband's twin brother by mistake. The husband is in the marketplace bragging to the fellows about the wonderful sentiments his wife Adriana expresses to him. To illustrate, he sings the verse and chorus to "The Shortest Day of the Year," based on the conceit that the shortest day may have the longest night, but even that night is the shortest when I am with you. (The verse includes the fine Hart couplet, "I measure time by what we do, / And so my calendar is you.") The husband is singing Adriana's verse within the book, not bursting into song from out of the blue. This is how she sings to him, in their more romantic opportunities. We then discover that at this very moment, Adriana is at home singing this lovely tune to the wrong twin brother, the other

Antipholus, who has come to town unbeknownst to anyone. She thinks it is her husband. Romance is going haywire.

This splendid variation on the lover's duet may sound like the well-known cynicism of Rodgers and Hart musicals, but Shakespeare got there first. In the corresponding scene of *The Comedy of Errors*, the source of the musical, Adriana gives an impassioned speech about marriage, not knowing that she addresses the wrong twin. Husband and wife are "one flesh" she says, thinking she is speaking to her husband. But she isn't. She is speaking to the wrong piece of flesh. She is speaking about "one flesh" to the wrong flesh. Her one-flesh doctrine, which is central to the Christian conception of marriage, comes from St. Paul's letter to the Ephesians in Scripture, and Shakespeare knew exactly what he was doing. He set the play in Ephesus (changing *his* source, Plautus, on this point). Rodgers and Hart redesigned the cynical comedy of the scene into the book-and-number format and highlighted Adriana's plight by having her sing her diegetic tune to the wrong twin.

THE NUMBER TO BE COMPLETED

That songs or dances can be called for within the book raises the possibility that the number being called for is incapable of being completed for some dramatic reason. The drama focuses on the challenge of completing the number, and at that point, the completion of a song or dance may become a turning point of the book, perhaps *the* turning point of the book. This idea goes deep into operatic history, with *Die Meistersinger* being perhaps the best-known example. One of the earliest musicals to use this idea was Victor Herbert's *Naughty Marietta* (1910), in which the heroine has vowed to marry only the man who can complete a melody that came to her once in a dream. This turns out to be "Ah, Sweet Mystery of Life," which fortunately is sung by just the right man at just the right time.

Dance can work the same way. In *On Your Toes* the Russian dancers *do* learn their swing lessons, and the show is able to reach its conclusion when they join the Americans in a jazz ballet, "Slaughter on Tenth Avenue." There is a further diegetic problem that has to be solved before this number can be completed. Gangsters are waiting to shoot the lead dancer when he stops dancing. So he frantically extends his final routine, dancing to gain time until the police arrive and save him from disaster. The plot is daft, but the dancing (originally by Ray Bolger) is sensational.

A better example of the drama of the completed dance is *A Chorus Line*, which we discussed earlier as the epitome of ensemble musicals. *A Chorus Line* builds to a climax about dancing itself, the dancing of the chorus line of the title. (There is also the half-baked plot about the relationship between Cassie and Zach, but the real action is the dance.) But we also see the chorus line rehearsing this climactic number; both the learning process and the result are staged. Why should the rehearsal process be staged? Because the drama resides in the achievement of the dance itself, and an ensemble that does not know the routines is an effective beginning for an action that ends with that ensemble knowing the routines perfectly. Tentatively, awkwardly, the seventeen chorus-line aspirants don their top hats and begin learning the steps for the number called "One." The question is not the dull one of "Will Zach and Cassie get back together?" but the exciting one of "Will this ensemble take shape?" Dancers are missing steps, and Zach is hounding Cassie for being individualistic. The lyric to "One" turns into a cacophony of voices. The first group is counting the beats that dancers must keep in their heads ("five, six, seven, eight") while the second and third groups are repeating the dance steps ("Lift, elbow straight, pose" and "Lift, lift, lift, change") and the fourth sings the lyric: "One moment in her presence and you can forget the rest." None of this can be understood. The dancers are using the words as crutches (as dancers do when they are rehearsing), and the language is a jumble of sound. The hard work involved, the precision required, and the pleasure that can be sensed at the moment everyone perfects the routine simultaneously—these form the climax of the musical. The moment when the imperfections of the rehearsal give way to perfect ensemble dancing is one of the glories of

musical theatre. Everything clicks into focus, the lyric is suddenly clear, the precision moves of the line are perfect. This is
what the show is about.[11]

This achievement is undercut by a last-minute return to
sentimentality, when the chorus line goes into "internal-
thought" mode once more and sings "What I Did for Love" as
an anthem to the theatre. One of the dancers, Paul, has been
injured. His career is probably over. What will you do when
you can't dance any more? asks the tiresome Zach, and the
chorus goes into internal thought mode and sings their hymn
about loving the theatre anyhow. Ken Mandelbaum reports
that the composer, Marvin Hamlisch, demanded a spot for
"What I Did for Love" on grounds that it would become a hit
tune about two lovers who are calling off an affair.[12] The lyrics
are so generalized and trite that they could refer to the ending
of anything lovable. (The song did become a hit outside of the
show, and the film version did turn it into a song about lovers.)
But this last-minute piece of pandering cannot drive away the
real climax, when "One" comes across as a dance number and
the chorus line, which is supposed to support a star, finds itself
in the limelight—it is the star.

Musically, "One" is brilliant as an ensemble dance number.
It is strung out along a series of chromatic harmonies that refuse to deliver a conclusive cadence until the end of the thirty-
two-bar structure of the song. Look for a V–I cadence after the
lead-in and you will see the point at once. There is no B-flat
seventh leading to the tonic E-flat cadence until the chorus is
ending, then one comes along to conclude the climactic three
whole notes—the high pitches of the song, on "she's the one"—
so that the kind of musical closure which normally concludes
each four or eight bar section of a tune is here deferred all the
way to the end. This stringing out of the song's harmony opens
the space in which dance ensembles can do their work, "five,

[11] Unison dancing can be achieved at measure 241 in the vocal score, in
which case Zach interrupts it when he pulls Cassie out of the line at measure
272. Or it can be achieved in the curtain call.
[12] Mandelbaum, A Chorus Line *and the Musicals of Michael Bennett*, p. 185.

six, seven, eight" turning into "one, two, three, four" over a sustaining and open harmonic structure without the pauses by which an individual singer gains a toehold, so to speak, for delivering a star number.

These are all diegetic examples of numbers called for in the book. One of the ways the book can pay attention to the musical time that will bring it to a pause is by calling for a number, finding only part of it, searching for the rest, and making a dramatic moment out of the successful completion. We will see in a later chapter that this search-for-the-completed number can even occur beyond the diegetic convention, in the out-of-the-blue mode (the example will be *Sunday in the Park with George*, where the climactic act 2 duet "Move On" takes song elements from act 1 and combines them into an oversized AABA song). But for the moment, as we are examining the diegetic convention to see how far the book can go toward recognizing the power of the number, the leading example must be *Lady in the Dark* (1941) by Kurt Weill, Ira Gershwin, and Moss Hart.

THE SPECIAL CASE OF LIZA ELLIOTT

The book of *Lady in the Dark* turns on the search for a song the heroine, Liza Elliott, cannot remember. It is buried traumatically in her childhood. She also cannot decide which of her ardent suitors she should accept—Nesbitt, or Randy, or Charley. When Charley is discovered to be the right man, he also knows the childhood song, "My Ship," and sings it with the heroine. They are working together in the offices of the glamour magazine of which Liza is the editor. Liza hums a bit of "My Ship." Charley looks up in surprise and sings a line, himself. "Why—do you know that song?" says Liza in astonishment, and they sing it together. Happily ever after takes shape because two people know the same song. This could only happen in a musical comedy, and that is the point. A book that searches for a Weill/Gershwin song while entertaining us with other Weill/Gershwin songs is better than most plots in the legitimate theatre, which have no Weill/Gershwin songs at all.[13]

How did Liza remember the song in time to sing it with Charlie? Throughout her adult life she has been unable to recover the childhood song, but the breakthrough has occurred in the therapy sessions by which she has been trying to straighten out her psychic life. All the songs in the show, before "My Ship" comes out of repression, relate to her therapy sessions or her mental distress. The lights dim on Liza in her book location, where she is talking to the therapist or undergoing a hallucination. When the lights come up, the stage has revolved or the traveler curtain has parted, revealing the full stage set for the fantasy numbers, which are colorful, splashy musical extravaganzas. Liza herself is the star of these inserts. She is caught up in the anxious jubilation-nightmare of her glamorous life. We cannot see her book-location, so the actress slips away and reappears in the dreams.

The first three sequences represent the dreams themselves. In her real life, Liza is drab in dress and dispassionate in the affair she is conducting with a married man. Her dreams—the Glamour Dream, the Wedding Dream, the Circus Dream— taunt her desires for fashion, ridicule her anxiety over marriage, put her on trial for the indecisive life she is leading (this is the Circus Dream). They maintain a flagrant show-business disregard for the workings of the unconscious, which cannot be said to operate according to the formats of American pop tunes. Liza's "One Life to Live" in the Glamour Dream is a standard verse–chorus combination, with the stanzas of the chorus in the AABA form. Her duet with Randy in the Wedding Dream, "This Is New," has a stanza pattern of ABAC. Yet there is something to this fooling about with the unconscious, for a song—any song, including any pop tune—is prepared to articulate feelings left obscure in social discourse. In the

---

[13] For a full discussion of the show, with an emphasis on the lyrics, see Furia, *Ira Gershwin: The Art of the Lyricist*, pp. 160–75. See also Block, *Enchanted Evenings: The Broadway Musical from* Show Boat *to Sondheim*, pp. 133–58, and Mordden, *Beautiful Mornin'*, pp. 61–69.

FIGURE 5. Gerrude Lawrence in the Wedding Dream from the original production of *Lady in the Dark*. Billy Rose Theatre Collection, The New York Public Library for the Performing Arts, Astor, Lenox and Tilden Foundations.

parlance of modern theatre, there is no subtext that cannot be raided by an AABA tune in a musical, and the dream sequences of *Lady in the Dark* are elaborate testimonies to that potential in song. They are outbreaks of what is normally repressed, and if they also look a lot like Broadway show numbers, the formats may seem inappropriate to the talking cure, but the talking cure may be trying to find the same sources that show numbers can turn into travesty and joy. Liza is certainly a different person in the numbers, but that is the way numbers always work in a musical.

The fourth sequence, where "My Ship" is completed for the first time, is a different matter. This time the flashback scenes do represent what Liza is at that moment recalling for the psychiatrist. As the lights go down on the psychiatrist's office, we see Liza move toward the flashback area, where she is spotlighted as a spectator of her own recollections. The young Liza is played by a child, with the adult Liza explaining the significance of the episodes, as though she were still speaking to the psychiatrist. All of this is happening in book time, which is inventively being given a flashback treatment.

Then the adult Liza herself enters the flashback, which is now about high school. She is playing herself as a teenager. A good-looking boy is making time with her, convincing her that she is not the "ugly duckling" her own parents said she was in an earlier episode, and in the surge of relief at being made to feel desirable for a change, Liza remembers the childhood song "My Ship" and sings it for the boy. The breakthrough in her therapy occurs here. As Liza sings the complete song in the flashback, we know that she is recovering it in the therapy with the psychiatrist. This is a complex moment. The performance of the song is a turning point in two plots at once. This is a diegetic number twice over. The high school boy hears it in the flashback, and so (we imagine) does the psychiatrist in his office. The high school Liza is recovering the song she repressed as a little girl, the adult Liza is recovering the song in her therapy, and this complex psychological moment is accessible and lovely because what is really happening is that Gertrude Lawrence (the original Liza) is singing the Weill/Gershwin tune from beginning to end. We have heard it only in bits before.

"Say, that was lovely," says the high school boy. "I didn't know you could sing, Liza." He then leaves her for a beautiful blonde. Forsaken and ugly once more, Liza "begins to weep uncontrollably." No doubt the song is going into repression once again, in the high school scene. The moment of recovery is also the moment of loss. But in the psychiatrist's office, where the present-day Liza will now be seen (lights down on the flashback area, lights up on the psychiatrist's office, Gertrude Lawrence crossing into position), the song has been recovered once and for all. She has recalled the song by reliving the high school episode where she had recalled it once before, and this time she will keep it—especially when Charlie turns out to know it too, in a few minutes.

So *Lady in the Dark* confines all but one of its numbers to dream sequences that are set off from book time, but it pursues the one number as a mystery to be solved within book time, and it handles the mystery with complex deftness. Why this show is so rarely revived is a persistent question in musical theatre circles, for it has moments of greatness. The answer has to do with that psychiatrist, whose function we will examine later, but for the moment, "My Ship" deserves notice as a number that sets up a drama through its failure to be completed, then resolves the drama in the one way open to numbers, by being performed whole.

WHAT HOLDS BOOK AND NUMBER TOGETHER

The orchestra, of course, knows "My Ship" all along. It plays fragments now and then, as the heroine struggles to remember the song, giving a groundwork of recollection to the proceedings. There is never any real doubt about whether the tune will be recovered, because it has always already been recovered, in the orchestra, which is just waiting for the proper moment to play the whole thing. This is always true when the book turns on the drama of the uncompleted number. The orchestra

knows "Move On" in *Sunday in the Park with George*, as well as
the act 1 songs from which "Move On" is composed. An orchestra knows "Ah, Sweet Mystery of Life" and the "One" music for the chorus line to rehearse by. Does this matter?

The orchestra knows all the songs, not just the mystery song.
And it performs the indispensable function of musical theatre,
accompaniment. The musical is a disunified form, setting out
book time as a medium ready to be interrupted by number time,
and the genre has the spirit of disputing the pieties of high culture, breaking the rules of the mighty and powerful, challenging
the settled beliefs, but it cannot do without its accompaniment. I
believe there is no a cappella musical—it would be a contradic-
tion in terms. (I am willing to be proved wrong, for the musical
likes to deflate solemn pronouncements.)

In other words, the orchestra has a certain kind of power in
musical theatre (a point Wagner made more clearly than anyone), yet the convention by which this power operates usually
passes without comment. It holds the book and the number
next to one another, facilitates the transition from one to the
other. Usually it plays from out of the blue, but on occasion it
can be brought into the book by a special application of the
diegetic convention. The distinction we have been pursuing
about different kinds of numbers applies to the accompaniment
as well. Where the orchestra is positioned is part of the distinction. It usually plays from the pit, an unseen location of power
(Wagner was especially drawn to that feature), but in its tendency to deflate pomposity and render power visible, the musical has lately taken to putting the orchestra on stage, where it
takes on a very different character. What we have observed
about diegetic numbers and out-of-the-blue numbers carries
over to the means of accompaniment, in other words, and the
means of accompaniment raises questions about the difference
between visible and invisible performance in a musical.

I devote the next chapter to the orchestra in order to give
due care to this major convention and to establish a groundwork for the succeeding chapter, on narration. For the orchestra is also a narrative power in musical theatre, yet another kind
of power has come into play recently, the power of stage tech-

nology, creating what I think is a confusion of systems of omniscience. The question of narrative is also related to the musical's penchant for taking up source stories and subjecting them
to the conventions we are talking about. The orchestra leads to
narration, narration leads to stage technology, and both narration and stage technology lead to the sources. We must discuss
these things, slowly and in order.

Chapter Six

THE ORCHESTRA

A Cappella on a Beautiful Morning

AT the beginning of *Oklahoma!*, when Curly comes on
singing a cappella about the beautiful morning and a
smile crosses Aunt Eller's face, something is missing.
We know what it is when Curly gets to "the corn is as high as
an elephant's eye," for the note he sings on "eye" is suddenly
accompanied by a chord from the orchestra. That's what was
missing, the orchestra. Now it is missing no longer, and Curly
is no longer on his own. He has what no cowboy has ever had
on a fine summer morning in Indian Territory, an orchestra to
accompany him.

Who hears the orchestra? Does Curly hear it? The performer playing Curly does, of course, but I am speaking of the
fictional Curly, the character in the book, and that Curly does
not hear the orchestra. If he did, Aunt Eller would hear it too,
and would drive it off the farm for scaring the animals. No one
in the book hears the orchestra in *Oklahoma!*

Only the audience hears it, and the surprising thing to the
audience is that Curly sang a few measures a cappella to start
off. The audience knows that a basic convention of the musical
is slipping into place when the orchestra comes in on "eye." In
the source play, *Green Grow the Lilacs*, cowboys and their wom-
enfolk sing a cappella several times (Lynn Riggs wanted to preserve some real cowboy songs, so his characters sing a lot). In
a musical we expect the orchestra to accompany anyone who
sings. We knew the *Oklahoma!* orchestra was there in the first
place, just waiting to chime in. It has already played some of
the musical numbers as an overture. When the orchestra
comes in on "eye," with its lovely subdominant chord edged

with a seventh (it is one of the notable moments in popular music, and when you listen to it next time, see if you don't find that you have been hearing it all your life, as part of the culture), we are not surprised, for we know that a leading convention of musical drama has asserted itself, after having been silent for the opening bars of the song.

The presence of the orchestra coming in to join Curly beyond Aunt Eller's hearing is pure out-of-the-blue performance. Even when the song is called for by the book and the character is singing by the diegetic convention, the pit orchestra plays from out of the blue, and no one thinks this odd. It seems natural for two dozen musicians to be chiming in when some cowboy is yodeling about a fine morning, and when no one questions such an absurdity, a basic convention of musical theatre must be operating.

The significant point is that no one ever asks about this—it is *obvious*. An orchestra accompanies a song in a musical. It doesn't have to be written into the book. That is nothing but a convention, and no one has to think about it.

So let us think about it. What is the orchestra doing, down in the orchestra pit?

OMNISCIENCE

The orchestra knows everything. It knows when to introduce the numbers, when to bring them to a close, when to keep the beat, when to keep quiet. It knows the difference between book time and number time, and it knows how to set the two apart, or lead from one to the other. One might say the conductor is the one who knows these things, but we may treat him as part of the orchestra, without whom the conductor would look like a fool.

The orchestra is the infallible element of a musical, the agent that always knows what is coming and never misunderstands a character or a turn of the plot. This is the true connection between the Wagnerian aesthetic and the musical—not the unity of all elements, but the omniscience of the orchestra. For

Wagner the orchestra rendered audible the innermost essence concealed behind the visible events on the stage and provided a "musical narrator" in the voice of the composer. The musical will not settle for the layered mystification of such talk, but it does depend on the idea of omniscience in the orchestra, and no one defined that idea more clearly than Wagner.[1]

The overture with which musicals normally begin is no idle affair: it is the orchestra's announcement of its authority. It already can play the tunes that will arise in the plot. (It might even know themes that have been cut, as in the "Misery's Comin' Round" theme in *Show Boat*, which Kern kept in a prominent place in the overture after cutting it from its place in the book.) It puts the tunes in the minds of the audience, too, so that by repetition through the evening a hit song or two will be created, but this is the commercial rendition of an aesthetic fact: numbers are detachable, and can be set into the overture for the orchestra to use in the conventional assertion of its authority and omniscience.

The overture can be a number unto itself rather than a collection of the later tunes. The classic case is the "Carousel Waltz" with which *Carousel* begins. For the first fifty measures this could be taken as the beginning of a conventional overture, but then the curtain rises and the stage is filled with the pantomime we discussed in chapter 4. For nearly ten minutes the orchestra roars on with its gorgeous waltz while the pantomime shows

---

[1] Wagner said that music is the mother of drama, and his term for the orchestra pit was *mystischer Abgrund* (mystic chasm). For further discussion of the importance of the orchestra in the nineteenth century, see Dahlhaus, "What is a musical drama?" "Omniscience" has been tamed in recent literary criticism, and it no longer has the transcendence Wagner looked for. I am grateful to Jonathan Culler for pointing this out in regard to the narrator of nineteenth-century fiction. See J. Hillis Miller, *The Form of Victorian Fiction*, p. 64, and Maxwell, "Dickens's Omniscience." Perhaps "omniscience" should be replaced with "near-omniscience" or "quasi-omniscience" to catch the postmodern feel of things, but I am not going to do this. In rehearsals, the moment when the members of the cast first hear the orchestrations for their numbers is a major experience. For an account of the *sitzprobe* in rehearsing *Follies*, see Chapin, *Everything Was Possible*, p. 137.

a town fair, jugglers, a dancing bear, and especially a carousel, where the local girls flirt with the handsome barker. This is the opening action, the pantomime having been taken from the source play, *Liliom*, but the orchestra's waltz transforms this opening into a grand piece of Broadway assertiveness. Not for a moment does anyone in the theatre think that the music really represents the sound of the carousel, for no carousel organ sounds so magnificent, and everyone knows the convention by which the orchestra plays from beyond the plot, out of the blue. Yet having the orchestra sound a bit like a hurdy-gurdy or a town band (Rodgers insisted on a tuba to keep the beat) is jolly and interesting. In fact the orchestra is playing a full-throated European waltz above the oom-pah-pah beat, reminding us that Molnar's play was European, showing us that transplanting it to America is Broadway self-confidence at a high pitch, and above all impressing us with music that sounds a lot like Budapest or Vienna and a little like a hurdy-gurdy at the same time. The musical is having its way with European culture, and there is no question from this moment on that the theatre world is going to receive the plot of *Liliom* mainly in the form of a Broadway show.[2]

The wordless energy of this pantomime-overture is distributed between the unseen orchestra and the activity on stage. Without any book dialogue, characters are being presented and plot is being advanced. The barker notices one mill-girl in particular, the one who does not sway in motion to his spiel but stands still and gazes at him. The barker places the girl on the carousel and gets his arm around her, to the annoyance of an older woman who seems to be in charge of things. The girl is ecstatic, the older woman furious, the barker nonchalant. We have not yet heard their names. They have said nothing. A plot is underway, and it is happening in this opening number, which does not have a book to interrupt. Integration would be

[2] For a good discussion of the waltz as a main source of the musical material in *Carousel*, see Swain, *The Broadway Musical: A Critical and Musical Survey*, pp. 99–127.

the right name for the achievement, if there were yet a book to be integrated with. I think it significant that a true moment of integration involves the orchestra in the pit accompanying pantomime or dance on the stage, and does not need any words. (*Guys and Dolls* and *West Side Story* also open with dances.) We will return to this point shortly. For the moment, we may note that the other scene for which I suggested integration as the right word, "A Weekend in the Country," from the act 1 ending of *A Little Night Music*, achieved its simultaneous actions, all the characters singing and dancing to the same tune regardless of their disagreements, through the underlying coordination provided by the orchestra. There we were discussing the "voice of the musical," and here we are discussing the orchestra. This is no accident. The orchestra defines the voice of the musical. It is the leading agent by which this voice becomes known. And when an integrated effect is achieved for a moment, the ensemble tendency of the musical is declaring itself on the groundwork of the orchestra. The musical is not a Wagnerian form of musical theatre, but it is an eclectic form, with revue and vaudeville hints still circulating in the most solidly book shows, and there is no reason not to make a slot for Wagner here and there.

UNDERSCORING: *SOUTH PACIFIC* AND *SHOW BOAT*

The unseen, omniscient orchestra knows what is in the minds of the characters even before the characters do. In *South Pacific*, Ensign Nellie Forbush's realization that she loves Emile de Becque after all (despite her racist anxiety over his previous liaison with a Polynesian woman) is first announced by the orchestra. Nellie has come to ask the commanding officer if Emile is indeed the Frenchman who is risking his life to report on Japanese ship movements from a remote island. The orchestra underscores this with the "I'm in love with a wonderful guy" theme, well known from earlier scenes. Captain Brackett unknowingly reflects the theme with his remark that Emile is "a wonderful guy." "Uh-huh," says Nellie, and makes a hasty exit. "Uh-huh" is not the full expression of her realization. The full expression is the orchestra's playing the music that signifies her love, plus the irony of the Captain's casual remark.[3]

The underscoring carries into the next scene, "but now increases in tempo and gaiety" as the nurses cross the stage with their taunting version of "She's in love with a won—" (this is cut short by Nellie's refusal to acknowledge their frivolity). Then Nellie crosses to what is now a moonlit scene on the beach, and the orchestra continues the theme. Hammerstein's stage direction asks for a "symphonic arrangement of that same metrical line, 'I'm in love,' with key changes and heartbreaking persistence in its repetition as Nellie walks on." This time Nellie gets to say something. Her "I know what counts now" soliloquy leads the orchestra to play a reprise of "Some enchanted evening," which Nellie joins on the second line. The underscoring orchestra is in tune with the recognitions and feelings of the characters, and is one step ahead of anything the characters can say.

Underscoring can rearrange the structure of a number and distribute its elements beneath the spoken dialogue. The effect of this melodramatic technique is to maintain a musical continuity during what would otherwise be dialogue scenes. The orchestra's quotations from "I'm in Love with a Wonderful Guy" in the example from *South Pacific* outlined above sustains musical time as the pulse of the scene, replacing what would normally be book time with a sense that a number is on the verge of occurring. This expectation is satisfied when Nellie sings her reprise of "Some Enchanted Evening." She sings only sixteen measures, but the allusion to a complete number heard earlier is distinct. This is melodrama in the true sense

---

[3] Act 2, scene 8. The underscoring, not always specified in published libretti, is spelled out in the earliest New York Public Library script, RM 742, checked against the libretto published in England by Chappell and Williamson Music Ltd., no date. For further discussion of *South Pacific*, see Mordden, *Beautiful Mornin'*, pp. 261–67; Mordden, *Rodgers and Hammerstein*, pp. 107–26; and Most, *Making Americans: Jews and the Broadway Musical*, pp. 153–82.

of the word, a long-standing convention of which composers like Kern, Rodgers, and Sondheim are modern masters.[4]

Underscoring can set dramatic exchanges in motion. One of the finest early examples occurs in the first meeting between Magnolia Hawkes and Gaylord Ravenal in *Show Boat*. Gaylord's lovely piece of self-pity, "Where's the Mate for Me," has been carried by underscoring through to his rendition of "Make Believe," where he is flirting with the good-looking girl he has just met. So far she has sung nothing and is musically known as a child who was heard fumbling with her piano practicing off-stage (the ditty that was supposed to become "It's Getting Hotter in the North" by the end of the show—see chapter 5). After Gaylord's "Make Believe," the dramatic question is how the girl will respond, and Kern's solution is to sustain musical time with an exchange of song segments between the would-be lovers. The orchestra never stops. It keeps the musical mode intact as the segments of song are exchanged. "Your pardon I pray," Gaylord sings, apologizing for the bold flirtation of "Make Believe." His apology runs eight bars and is answered by Magnolia's initial flight of song, one of the great musical entrances for an ingénue, for if she has seemed immature through her off-stage piano exercise before, her burst of song reveals a mature soprano voice that can obviously keep pace with anything this handsome singer of the "Make Believe" solo has to offer. The orchestra's string section gives her an increase of volume, and she answers Gaylord a fifth above his last note: "We only pretend, you do not offend, in playing a lover's part." Her eight bars match his, and she completes the rhyme.

This is musical interaction. It has the length of popular song elements, eight measures answered by eight, but it does not

[4] Melodrama goes back to operatic experiments in the later eighteenth and early nineteenth centuries, when spoken or declaimed dialogue was interspersed with orchestral accompaniment. The Victorian melodrama uses points of musical emphasis as the "melo-" part of what is otherwise "drama," or spoken dialogue. *Sprechstimme* in Schoenberg and Berg and background music in films are two modern versions of "melodramatic" technique. Musical comedy had bits of underscoring from an early date. Kern made a specialty of the technique and brought it to a high point in *Sweet Adeline* (1929).

form a song of its own. It raises the expectation of a song, but it
sustains the drama by underscored segments in the meantime.
Suddenly the orchestra leads Magnolia out of the 3/4 time of
the sixteen-bar exchange into a 2/4 allegretto in a new key:
"The game of just supposing is the sweetest game I know," she
sings, offering a new eight-bar theme that Gaylord then answers in eight-bars too. This is actually the verse to "Make Believe" in the sheet music version, but here it seems another
sixteen-bar continuation of the flirtation, to which the orchestra then gives a further extension into F minor, a *poco animato*
of sixteen bars for Magnolia on the theme of "banishing all regret" through make-believe. Magnolia takes the lead in the allegretto and *poco animato* segments, with the orchestra setting
the pace and the key changes. On her word "regret," which is
what she imagines can be "banished" through make-believe,
the orchestra transforms the expected A-flat chord into a new
key and follows that with a half-diminished chord that shadows
the optimism of the lovers' game with the sorrow that will follow from it. Regret will indeed not be banished, and the young
soprano will be the one to bear its burden. One could learn a
lot from underscoring orchestras if one could stop to think
about what is being implied down there in the pit, but things
hasten on.

The orchestra's darker chords are changing the key for Magnolia's reprise of "Make Believe" in D-flat.[5] We are returning
to a complete song structure now, but the orchestra has modu-
lated up a half-step for Magnolia's version (Gaylord's was in
C), as though a transaction more substantial than Gaylord's
usual offering is now going on. Magnolia's D-flat version is
joined by Gaylord after the first eight measures, making it a
duet. He takes the harmony while she soars to the high note of
the song, the first time we have heard this climax, a high F. She
shines forth, a stunning reversal from the girl of the piano ditty.

[5] I follow the revised keys of the 1946 revival, which are now reflected in
the piano-vocal score. Swain, *The Broadway Musical*, pp. 34–40, thoroughly
discusses the music shared between Magnolia and Ravenal in this scene, using
the keys of the 1927 version. Block, *Enchanted Evenings*, pp. 23–27, summarizes revisions made for the 1946 revival.

The musical exchanges are fundamental to the drama being enacted here. Magnolia is showing that she can play a love match with Gaylord, so one could say the plot and character are being advanced in the interests of integration. One could also say—and this would be the more important point—that Magnolia's willingness to play a love match in eight-bar segments of uncompleted songs sets up the true drama of the scene, which is her voicing of the song itself, the reprise of "Make Believe," her response to the song Gaylord has already sung, which then joins as a duet. The underscoring orchestra sets these exchanges in motion, shifts their keys, gives the unexpected half-diminished chord to "regret." These underscored segments of song lead to the achievement of song itself. The reprise of "Make Believe," with Magnolia voicing the high notes as Gaylord supports her through harmony, is the drama of the scene. Song is not serving the interests of character and plot, song *is* character and plot.

THE BENCH SCENE IN *CAROUSEL*

The classic case is the bench scene in *Carousel*, where underscoring and song segments lead into two major numbers, "When I Marry Mr. Snow" and "If I Loved You." The scene begins with Julie Jordan (the girl on the carousel in the previous scene) talking to her friend Carrie about boys. It ends with Julie talking to Billy Bigelow, the carousel barker, about love.[6] The orchestra underscores both episodes, putting them into musical time and making song the important dramatic consideration. The scene without music—in book time, in other words—can be studied in the source play, Molnar's *Liliom*.[7] It proceeds by the dialectical method of statement and counterstatement, one thing leading to another. The result in the episode between the girls is a redefinition of the "soldier" Julie's

[6] Mordden describes the two-part structure neatly in *Beautiful Mornin'*, p. 88.
[7] I follow the translation by B. F. Glazer in *The Theatre Guild Anthology* (New York: Random House, 1936).

friend has found as a boyfriend (Julie proves he is a common porter). The result in the episode between Julie and Liliom (the barker's name in Molnar) is a series of five pauses when Julie refuses to be shaken by Liliom's attempts to prove himself dangerous. One of the pauses falls on the line "if I loved you, Mr. Liliom," which is where Rodgers and Hammerstein moved in for their love song. Pauses in dialogue are something like numbers in musicals. They suspend the dialectical progress, as though something is being consolidated in the minds of the characters. Subtext is the concept most obvious to actors at such moments in nonmusical plays, and one way musicals move into new dimensions of characterization is by raising subtext to expressiveness through song and dance.

The bench scene is such a hallmark of musical theatre that we should see exactly how it works. The "Mister Snow" episode begins with orchestral underscoring while the spoken dialogue between Julie and Carrie turns to rhyme. The tenth measure sends Carrie into "You're a Queer One, Julie Jordan," a sixteen-measure segment shared between the two women, which leads to the different song material of "When we work at the mill," twenty measures in which Carrie details Julie's daydreaming habits on the job. A return to "You're a Queer One, Julie Jordan" makes this entire musical exchange between Julie and Carrie seem like a lop-sided song in itself, AA'BA, with a long B section formed by "When we work at the mill," but this impression is bound to change later, when the segments are repeated independently by Julie and Billy Bigelow in the latter half of the scene.

The orchestral underscoring continues after Carrie manages to end her "Julie Jordan" segment on a mistake: "Sphink," she attempts, to rhyme with "think." "Sphinx," Julie corrects her, while the orchestra underscores the dialogue with eight measures from "You're a Queer One." I have a feller of my own, says Carrie as the orchestra plays, and Julie asks, what's his name? leading into the next segment, Carrie's "His name is Mister Snow."

This strikes me as the key moment in the scene. "His name is Mister Snow" is an apparent AABA song that refuses that structure halfway through and keeps the expectation alive that the real number is still in the offing. The bench scene is one of the longest in the history of the musical if both the Carrie–Julie and the Billy–Julie episodes are counted, but it is sustained by a musical confidence that keeps Carrie singing eight-measure segments of songs that do not quite take shape, all of them in G major, until she finally comes across with the real song. Here we are still on "His name is Mister Snow," which sounds as if it *might* be the real song as it follows its first eight measure segment with a second eight on "An almost perfect beau." The promise of an AABA structure is continued with a B segment of eight measures on "The fust time he kissed me." By now the lyric is turning into a parody of the love song, for the almost-perfect beau smells of fish. And Carrie can't return to A at the right point anyway, for she has to recount Mr. Snow's marriage proposal verbatim in a new B segment—*two* new B segments, in fact, one running twelve measures to give the proposal verbatim and one running eight measures to record her own reaction. This is characterization through music, exactly what integration should amount to, and it is coming about because Carrie can't control the B section to a standard pop tune structure. On she goes, B segment added to B segment, twenty-eight measures where there are supposed to be eight. Indeed, she never does get back to A. Here is the ending of the extended B section, one of Hammerstein's inspired moments:

Next moment we were promised!
And now my mind's in a maze,
Fer all it ken do is look forward to
That wonderful day of days.

The amazing thing is that this is the lead-in to another song. Carrie's "days" rhymes with "maze" as the end of a verse, but it belongs syntactically to "When I marry Mr. Snow," which is the beginning of the next song, the real song, the one we have been waiting for her to sing. The forty-some measures about "His name is Mr. Snow" have been the verse to a chorus that this loquacious Carrie has been leading up to, Carrie and the orchestra. When it finally arrives, the "Mr. Snow" song has great piquancy. The way is prepared for something solemn and grand, which is how Carrie thinks her marriage will be, and yet the tune itself is slightly beautiful and utterly conventional—what the marriage will actually be, at best. Finally she has the AABA structure under control. The drama is about finding that structure as much as it is about these young people falling in love.

The lead-in music to "If I Loved You" in the second half of the scene (when Billy Bigelow replaces Carrie) is also formed of eight- and sixteen-measure segments, ninety-two bars in all, before Julie is in position to sing the formally structured AABA love song. Again, the drama concerns the achievement of the song. One of Billy's segments is "You're a Queer One, Julie Jordan," Carrie's song from earlier in the scene, which he has not heard. He knows it because he enters into the voice of the musical, which in this case allows a tune to carry across from one character to another. Billy's "You're a Queer One, Julie Jordan" opens the way for Julie to sing another of Carrie's ear- lier themes, eight measures on "When I worked at the mill." But now the orchestra is changing the key. Instead of Carrie's unceasing G major, there are seven key changes in the ninety- two measures of musical segments exchanged between Billy and Julie. The orchestra is deepening the musical texture, but the dramatic issue still concerns song—when will there be one? The eight bars that lead to the establishment of D-flat for the real song—"But somehow I can see, jes exactly how it'd be"—give Julie a power she has been promising, a musical power that the orchestra knows intimately, the power to pass through E-flat as the way to modulate into the serious expres- sion of song, then to an A-flat dominant as an outline of the real key, D-flat, on "exack'ly how I'd be." It is hard to believe there is anyone who attends theatre at all frequently who doesn't know this modulation and where it leads, as Julie and the orchestra reach the beginning of "If I Loved You." It is one of the memorable moments of modern drama.

What is happening in these cases of underscoring is that musical time is being called away from the tight structures of the popular song formats and arranged into a kind of avenue that leads to song or that connects one song to another. The avenues are made of song elements, eight-, twelve-, or sixteen-measure segments that may have been heard earlier (although new material can be introduced in the segments too). That the segments lead to a destination makes them seem progressive; that the destination is a song makes their outcome into lyrical suspensions of progress. They are something like the verse in the verse-chorus combination, only less structured and capable of greater length. Their effect is to sustain the lead-in to formal song, making song into the issue of the drama and rendering the book mute for perhaps five minutes at a time.

As song emerges from these lyrical introductions, one gains the impression that the action could be conducted entirely in music. Yet no one supposes that the musical is striving to become an opera in these long stretches. The segments of the lyrical introductions are cut from the pop song lengths and remain tied to the strophic arrangement of the numbers that they do not quite attain. We have usually heard these segments before, and even when we haven't heard them before, we know the kind of structure they belong to. This cannot happen in the dialogue of the book. These are formal repetitions of music and lyric, and yet one gains the impression that a lot is happening. Billy is finding Julie a deeper person than he is used to in a woman. But he does not say this—he is singing her melody. Their characters are not the same as they were in the book scenes. They have resources we wouldn't have expected in a circus barker and a mill-girl. Julie is discovering expressive power in her music, and Billy is responding to this. They are drawing closer, and the woman is declaring herself the stronger of the pair (as happens in the Gaylord-Magnolia scene in *Show Boat*, too). One could say that characterization and plot are being advanced by the song, as integration theory would have it, but that is not exact enough. The song *is* characterization and plot. The achievement of the song is what *Carousel* has become for the length of this extended number. It is a formal achievement for the woman and the man, who seem to be learning about themselves and one another while what they are really doing is giving voice to the same music the orchestra is leading into, this long series of segments that promises a song and then finally delivers one, the woman the first voice, the man the second. The orchestra builds the length of the episode, using its underscoring ability to link the segments together, changing the key to suggest that something important is approaching, then leading the soprano into the formal structure of "Make Believe" or "If I Loved You" so that she can declare the musical resonance of her character and so that the man can respond with his own musical character in the same song. That is the drama of the moment, the song.

DANCE

The same thing can happen in dance. We have seen that in the previous chapter, in the example of *A Chorus Line* as it builds to a dramatic climax in the formation of the dance line. But the issue is more complicated than that, now that we have the orchestra under consideration. Dance can be fully performed without words, for example, and the immediate connection that results between performer and the orchestra insists on being formally recognized. Wordless performance raises further thoughts about the drama that results from the achievement of song, for songs can exist without words, but they cannot exist in their full intricacy without words. With words, the systems of overlapping repetition that coordinate in a song are fully engaged, especially when the melody has already been danced. That is what happens in *West Side Story*, the show that brought dance to the forefront of the musical and presented us with a demonstration of what can happen with that kind of beginning.

Here is the beginning of *West Side Story*. The orchestra sets out a dangerous 6/8 meter at the curtain (there is no overture), an unbalanced riff coming in on the anacrusis and crossing hard to the downbeat of the next measure, ta-*da*. There are male dancers snapping their fingers in some angry ritual. They punctuate the measures on the second beat, the orchestra on the anacrusis/downbeat, ta-*da*, then the orchestra has an odd motif, a descending A-major triad ending on a D-sharp, that will have consequences in later numbers, but we don't know that yet. Who are these finger-snapping kids? They are dancers and they seem to own the place, but the place they own is off beat in the orchestra, and where is the tune?

Then for sixteen measures a new dancer is taunted to ominous drum-taps and a rising three-note motif (C, F, B), before the first gang leaves and the newcomer is joined by two others, the trio dancing to twenty-seven measures of fuller 6/8 orchestral playing. Putting this into words is nearly impossible. After 133 measures, the meter changes to 2/4, and two gangs of male dancers close in on each other, then veer away, until one boy is caught and something violent is done to him. The two motifs I have mentioned, the descending major triad ending on a tritone and the rising three-note motif, run through the orchestral playing, sometimes taking new permutations. This dancing is electrifying theatre, and when it is interrupted by book dialogue—with the Jets talking to one another in something like the street language of the 1950s and the orchestra silent—one feels the letdown. The dancing is more interesting than the slangy talk. This is the basic principle of the musical asserting itself, the difference between book and number, only the usual order is being reversed. Traditionally the musical moves the other way, from dialogue in the book to the heightened formality of song or dance. Jerome Robbins and Arthur Laurents moved dance up front and made the book follow after.[8]

What they were showing is that words are not basic to musical theatre. They are good to have, words, people talking back and forth, a plot taking shape in book time, but dance creates an immediacy of action that words can impede. I am taking my lead from Jerome Robbins himself, who heard it from Balanchine. Balanchine once told Robbins that the choreographer gets his fingertips into the land where there are no names for anything. He was describing the core of dance, which does not

[8] The Prologue was originally a song for the Jets, with each character associated with a specific musical instrument. Sondheim says it was Arthur Laurents who saw that wordless dance would be the best opening (Secrest, *Stephen Sondheim*, pp. 118–19).

require words, just music and the dancing body. Dance can use words, but it does not have to.[9]

The opening of *West Side Story* is a true example of the integrated musical. The plot gains narrative impetus in the number itself. Yet something else is going on. The theatrical excitement of dance in *West Side Story* lies beyond the integration of the elements. It lies in the immediate connection between the orchestra and the dancers' bodies, in the land where words are not necessary. The bodies of the dancers become immediately musical, as though they were the orchestra. *Orchestra* originally meant "the place for dancing" in the Greek theatre, and that radical combination of ideas has never ceased to matter. The place for dancing is now called the stage, but dancing materializes the orchestra, gives it body and motion in what I will call the space of vulnerability. The omniscient accompaniment to the musical is being translated into visible bodies without having to pass through words or through the strophic structures of song. Words and strophic song can be called upon, but they are not necessary—dance needs no explanations.

This has always been true of dance, but *West Side Story* makes it known and unforgettable: dance is *orchestra* in the full meaning, with dancers' bodies realized in the music—or is it the other way around? Dancers and poets have talked about this before. Donna McKechnie, who originated the role of Cassie in *A Chorus Line*, said, "you can reach a level in dance beyond words, beyond music."[10] I do not think it is beyond music so much as in music, but Donna McKechnie is the dancer, and she should know. The poet is Yeats, in the famous couplet at the conclusion of "Among School Children":

O body swayed to music, O brightening glance,
How can we know the dancer from the dance?

The meaning of dance is the dancer engaged in dance. The dancing body seems inseparable from its own aesthetic form.

[9] For fuller commentary from Balanchine and Robbins, see Cohen, ed., *Dance as a Theatre Art*, pp. 187–92.
[10] Quoted in Steyn, *Broadway Babies, Say Goodnight: Musicals Then and Now*, p. 183.

FIGURE 6. "The Rumble," from the original production of *West Side Story*. Billy Rose Theatre Collection, The New York Public Library for the Performing Arts, Astor, Lenox and Tilden Foundations.

Where is the music? It no longer seems to be accompaniment. It seems to be the dance itself.

This opening dance number has great formal consequence. Musicologists have shown that Bernstein's score is tightly composed. The two motifs I have mentioned from the opening dance are building blocks or cells that give rise to many of the songs heard later in the show. Raymond Knapp compares this compositional technique to precedents set by Wagner or, more pointedly, by Webern.[11] Opera singers have recorded *West Side Story* (under Bernstein's direction). Yet in the theatre the show remains firmly in place as a musical, and the formal reason for this stability of form lies in the book-and-number patterning that continues to be felt even as the classical rigor of Webern or Wagner seems to be the right context for Bernstein's score. The most important compositional maneuver lies in the unfolding of musical cells into the formats of popular songs, and in this regard *West Side Story* is practicing the technique used by the composers and orchestrators of *Show Boat* and *Carousel*. All of these shows make drama out of the achievement of song itself. What in *West Side Story* reminds one of Webern also heads in the direction of Tin Pan Alley, although Bernstein's classical determination never drops away in favor of pop tune simplicity. The motif of the descending major triad dropping to a pause on a tritone that accompanies the Jets' opening dance takes its place later as the B section of the "Jet Song." ("You're never alone, you're never disconnected"), which is an AABA format. Reversed to a rising tritone, it is the cha-cha melody with which the orchestra accompanies the meeting of Maria and Tony, then it bursts out as Tony's "Maria" number, which is AAB-Coda. (I am following Raymond Knapp's musical analysis here.[12]) The other cell from the opening dance orchestration, a rising C-F-B, delineates a minor seventh, which

[11] Knapp, *The American Musical and the Formation of National Identity*, pp. 208–15, which builds on Swain, *The Broadway Musical*, chapter on "Tragedy as Musical," and Block, *Enchanted Evenings*, pp. 245–73.

[12] Knapp also makes the point that "Maria" is an abbreviated song form that leads to the more complete structure of the "Tonight" duet, an "apex of optimism" in its AABA fullness. See *The American Musical*, p. 212.

is the opening of "Somewhere," an AABA song. Such uprisings of song out of musical cells are basic to *West Side Story*, a lesson that Stephen Sondheim (who wrote most of the lyrics) learned well, as we will see. Sondheim, like Bernstein, keeps this show business technique in touch with classical precedents.

Look at the first meeting between Tony and Maria. The scene is the high school gymnasium, where the Jets and the Sharks are being forced into social harmony at a gym dance. Glad-Hand, a clueless social director, has briefly got the boys and girls from the different gangs to dance with each other. This is a diegetic number—the gym dance is called for in the book. The gym dance breaks out into a wild mambo, Jets and Sharks dancing with their own girls and sharpening their rivalry, to the consternation of Glad-Hand. Then Robbins invents a wonderful way for the lovers to meet. Tony and Maria see each other for the first time during the mambo and are drawn into a special lighting for their own dance, a cha-cha to the musical theme that will soon become Tony's love song, "Maria." The orchestra knows that. It is playing a Latin beat for these lovers, and it knows where the tune will lead. There is no way to think of the cha-cha as part of the diegetic number at the gym, for the mambo dancers fade into shadow. There is also no way to think of the cha-cha as part of the book. Tony and Maria have lighting of their own, and the book is tied up with the high school dance, off in the shadows. Tony and Maria dance to music that cannot be heard in the gym dance. They have entered an area of formality that can best be realized by an aesthetic structure. (Shakespeare wrote a sonnet for Romeo and Juliet to share at this point.) The cha-cha is a suspension of the gym dance, a pause that lifts Tony and Maria into a different range of time, a number-within-the-number.

There is dialogue between the two. Where is this dialogue happening? In the book? In the number? The dialogue is both book and number by virtue of being neither exactly. Tony and Maria speak with each other as easily as they dance: "You're not thinking I'm someone else? / I know you are not. / Or that we've met before? / I know we have not. . . . My hands are so cold. / Yours, too. / So warm. / Yours, too. / But of course.

They are the same." Who says this line, who says that matters less than the saying, for dancing has become the relationship of Tony and Maria and the words are a continuation of the *pas de deux*. The orchestral underscoring sustains them, elevating the tritone motif into a Latin beat. Something is taking shape here. Of course, it is the meeting of the lovers. This is the integrated musical, certainly it is. But the quality of the scene depends on what else is taking shape, the motif that is working its way through the orchestra and into dance, the melody that will soon burst out when Tony sings "Maria." This is the voice of the musical being heard through different scenes. The orchestra leads this voice into its variations, guiding it toward its realization in a popular song structure, "Maria," at which point Tony's character deepens into the performance of the song.

THE DIEGETIC ORCHESTRA

The musical is subversive theatre. We have been taking the orchestra seriously, as a Wagnerian component of the musical, but the musical is always ready to deflower such piety. To the extent that the musical's roots are in burlesque shows and vaudeville routines, subversiveness is part of its direct inheritance. The revue tradition was at its best when refusing to take the ideals of American culture at their word. The routines of Weber and Fields, or Walker and Williams, were underclass exercises in puncturing solemnity, and when vaudeville did become pious, as could happen in Harrigan and Hart routines and in the George M. Cohen shows, patriotism and the like were usually advanced through song and dance rather than through preaching. Even the operetta tradition, where impossibly romantic plots were allowed to pass as valid much of the time, made space for comic routines that brought established values down with a crash. I mention this general characteristic of the musical because if it is in the nature of the orchestra to be hidden and omniscient, an unrevealed goddess controlling the performance, then it is in the nature of the musical not only to use this convention most of the time but also to deflate it on special occasions. Let us look at some of these.

Consider what happens when some of the instrumentalists, or even the entire group, are placed onstage. This may happen as a matter of necessity, when musicals are performed in theatres without orchestra pits (as at the Olivier in the Royal National Theatre of Great Britain, where outstanding productions of *Guys and Dolls* and *A Little Night Music* put the orchestras in full view of the audience), but that is the material condition, and we are pursuing the aesthetic effect. To test the aesthetic effect that can come from a material condition, consider an orchestra placed onstage because there is no pit, and consider further that one of the instrumentalists does not realize that he is in a different aesthetic situation now that he can be seen. He takes up a magazine between numbers, as orchestra members often do in the unseen pit. (I saw this happen in one of the onstage orchestras at the Olivier—the culprit was a reed player.) The effect is disturbing onstage—the instrumentalist does not realize he is now a visible part of the show. He does not know the basic condition of being onstage, that one is seen there. "Theatre" is literally a place for seeing and being seen, a twin condition of visibility, and one indication of the omniscience of the pit orchestra is that it remains invisible, where a clarinetist can read a magazine when he isn't playing.

It is also possible for orchestra players to be placed onstage by the diegetic convention. When there is an onstage band, the audience is invited to wonder if these onstage performers are really playing their instruments or are miming to accompaniment from the pit orchestra. The question itself is the significant thing, for the audience is being teased a little over what level of representation is involved. Normally the onstage orchestra consists of actors who are miming, and the diegetic device is a pretense. When onstage musicians really do play their instruments (as happened when the Matty Malneck orchestra appeared onstage in the Kern/Hammerstein *Very Warm for May*, 1939), they are taking an extra risk. They are playing in front of an audience, where a mistake can be seen and heard at its source, and we tacitly give them extra credit for taking this risk (unless they make a mistake). The onstage players are coming out of the omniscience of the pit orchestra, where a mistake is awful but cannot be seen, and entering the area of vulnerability, the stage, where a mistake doubles up on disaster by being visible.

For a diegetic orchestra that really plays, there is nothing finer than the conclusion of Meredith Willson's *The Music Man*, where the youngsters of an Iowa town try to play Mozart's Minuet in G on band instruments, although they have not had the lessons that Harold Hill has promised. They are an awful diegetic band for a minute. Their mistakes are part of the plot, and their parents are thrilled over the inept performance—at last these kids are focused on something worthwhile. Then comes the curtain call, and (as the show is best staged) the entire cast, young and old, come out dressed in band uniforms, playing "Seventy Six Trombones" on their own instruments. They are suddenly good! Only those who can actually do it are playing the horns, of course, but who knows if they all might not be doing it? The diegetic band has now enlarged to the convention of the curtain call, and Harold Hill's ability to build confidence in people has actually worked to the full. These actors can play! No doubt they are being supported by the brass players in the unseen pit band, too, but I confess that I have never thought to look into this, always being absorbed in the curtain call, where the "Seventy Six Trombones" number is refashioning a basic convention of theatre, the curtain call. There almost seem to *be* seventy-six trombones in this curtain call. It is a large cast.

Return now to orchestras onstage for the entire show. The musical that made the onstage orchestra into a telling aesthetic effect was *Cabaret*. The orchestra in *Cabaret* belongs to the Kit Kat Club and thus has a diegetic relation to the club's scenes. But for the scenes in other parts of Berlin, the orchestra belonging to the Kit Kat Club can provide normal accompaniment for the numbers, as though it were omniscient. The players are onstage and are rather seedy, but they have the strange power to accompany scenes elsewhere. Like the Emcee of the cabaret, who also seems to know what is going on elsewhere, the orchestra has an eerie authority that comes from its contradictory standing, as diegetic accompaniment in the Kit Kat Club and as nondiegetic accompaniment for the other scenes. *Cabaret* is a brilliant musical because of its revision of basic conventions. What do they know, this Emcee and this orchestra? The question begins as an aesthetic ambiguity, but it soon becomes political, a question about Berlin and the rise of Nazism. This orchestra is female, another reversal from the norm. They are bored showgirls at the Kit Kat Club, under the thumb of the rouged and over-elegant Emcee. How do these women know what is going on in the rest of Berlin? How might they be involved?[13]

The onstage orchestra in *Cabaret* is now being repeated in other musicals (the Kander and Ebb *Chicago* among them). It is a brilliant stroke because it subverts the omniscience of the pit orchestra yet retains an aura of ambiguity in its ability to know everything anyway. If the true Wagnerianism of the musical lies in the omniscience of the pit orchestra, it is coming in for a bit of the old razzle-dazzle when the entire orchestra takes to the stage.

A further variation has occurred in a recent production of *Sweeney Todd* under the direction of John Doyle at the Watermill Theatre in England, and then on Broadway, where the singer-actors also serve as the orchestra. When they are not involved in their book and number characters, the actors take up their instruments and accompany those who *are* engaged in book and number. They triple their identities, in other words, doubling through the combination of book and number and then gaining a further identity as instrumentalists. This is an extreme variation on the diegetic convention, but it is not a disruption of the convention (as perhaps it would be if Mimi, Rudolfo, and the other bohemians were also the orchestra in *La Bohème*). The musical thrives on such rearrangments of the norms it is based on. Tinges of experiment and parody have marked the genre all along.

[13] *Finian's Rainbow* begins with a sharecropper playing his harmonica on-stage, and some productions enlarge this with several real instrumentalists—a fiddler, a flautist—in the sharecropper group. With the sharecroppers is Susan, who expresses herself only through her dancing, or "feet talk," as the share-croppers put it. Thus Susan brings dance diegetically into the book too, until the end, when she gains speech.

Chapter Seven

NARRATION AND TECHNOLOGY

SYSTEMS OF OMNISCIENCE

The Character Who Knows Everything

IF the onstage orchestra puts the instrumentalists into an
area where they can be seen, think about the real singers
and dancers. They are always in that area. Under normal
circumstances, the orchestra is in the pit but the actors are
always in the area of "being seen," the stage. The presence of
an orchestra that knows everything emphasizes the fallibility
of everyone else, everyone who is a character in the plot or a
dancer or a singer, but it especially emphasizes the fallibility of
dancers and singers in their numbers. The orchestra also supports the singers and dancers, as everyone knows, but in the
space of vulnerability, the stage, they need support, and the orchestra does not. The musical performers skirt danger before
our very eyes. The foot can slip, the voice can crack, the memory can fail. The performers are visible in the success of their
performances, which means that the danger of failure is visible,
too.

All theatre thrives on this danger, but the performers in
a musical must also handle the enlargement of their characters into lyric time. They are actors who must also be singers
or dancers. The omniscient orchestra, asserting its authority
from its unseen place in the pit, is supposed to be perfect (one
reason why a bad moment in the orchestra is so devastating),
and the fallible characters, performing above this groundwork
of omniscience, are thrown into a highlight of possible failure. They do not fail, of course (hardly ever). But they are

vulnerable, and the danger of failure adds to the excitement of their performances.[1]

It can be a costly mistake to disturb this balance by having an *infallible* character on the stage as a second source of omniscience. If there is to be an approach to omniscience, it is to be the orchestra's approach. This is one of the sharpest distinctions between opera and the musical. Through-sung nineteenth-century opera can double the orchestra's role by building omniscient narration into the action, as in *Lohengrin*, where the hero's narration in act 3 is the dramatic climax. The drive toward unification in Wagnerian opera can at the same time be a drive toward omniscience occurring both on the stage and in the orchestra pit. If all is to be one in the theory of the form, omniscience running through the elements of the work is a logical outcome. This is a totalizing drive that the musical resists in its book-and-number format. The musical relies on song-and-dance performances to stop the show, bring the book to pause, and skirt the dangers of fallibility in their disruptive performance.

Thus an omniscient narrator is out of place in a musical, and any other kind of character who "knows everything" is equally inappropriate. The classic case of the all-knowing character troubling a musical is the psychoanalyst in *Lady in the Dark*, who puts Liza Elliott through the talking cure and understands her problem thoroughly—he even cures her. The psychoanalyst is the dead hand at the center of this bold show, because he lacks the fallibility of musical performance. He never sings or dances. Lyric time is beyond him. He cannot be imagined singing or dancing. Because he knows everything, he has no enlargement into song or dance, nothing musical to be fallible about. His only text lies in the book. The riskiness of the number is beyond him, and there is nothing that he cannot reduce to psychoanalytic explanation.

God poses problems for musicals on this score. Fallible gods, like the Greek Olympians Rodgers and Hart wrote about in

---

[1] This quality of live performance is fully described in States, *Great Reckonings in Little Rooms*, and Goldman, *The Actor's Freedom*.

By Jupiter, or Kurt Weill and Ogden Nash in *One Touch of Venus*, can be delightful in song and dance, because they have little claim to omniscience in the first place. The Judeo-Christian God the Father is a different matter. He is not brought into musicals very often, although the impudence of the genre does tempt some people to try. God comes into the second act of the recent *Jerry Springer: The Musical*, for example. His number is called "It's Not Easy Being God," which is questionable on theological grounds. The number tries to deflate omniscience into human ruefulness. Rodgers and Hammerstein flirted with the God problem in the Starkeeper of *Carousel*, a stand-in for the Almighty, but his role is to take Billy Bigelow back to earth where he can hear the music and see the dances of the show's final scenes. So the Starkeeper likes musicals even if he doesn't perform them. Other examples of God in musicals could be mentioned, but the point is that He doesn't fit the form, because He possesses the attribute already possessed by the orchestra, omniscience.[2]

DELIBERATE DOWNGRADING: THE NARRATOR WHO DOES NOT KNOW

On this side of God, however, there are the omniscient narrators who have written the books on which some musicals are based. These narrator-authors do enter into musicals, and something must be done to prevent them from clashing with the true source of omniscience, the orchestra. Cervantes appears briefly at the beginning and end of *Man of La Mancha*, but he is then downgraded to the role of Don Quixote, who is anything but infallible and is certainly capable of song and dance. The original version of *Candide* (1956) places Pangloss in the troubled position of being both narrator and character, a

---

[2] Musical versions of the medieval mystery play sometimes use Christ as the performance version of the Almighty. God sends a part of himself into the world as a man, which is theologically correct, and the man, being something like the rest of us, can do song-and-dance. This happens in the South African *The Mysteries*, which played in London in 2002.

piece of awkwardness not entirely solved in the revised versions of the 1970s and 1980s, which divides the role into Voltaire (narrator) and Pangloss (character).[3]

Into the Woods has an author figure standing to the side of the stage, introducing scenes, making comments, and acting for all the world like one of the Brothers Grimm. Sondheim has a joke up his sleeve, though. The Narrator is a deeply unwanted person in his omniscient complacency, and when in act 2 the Giantess demands a human sacrifice, all the other characters, fallible as musical performers must be, slowly turn and look at Mr. Know-It-All. To the Giantess he is thrown, and the characters are now faced with the need to make their own plot. This is a relief. Narrative infallibility has been removed, and the remaining human characters must sing their way toward an uncertain future. The Narrator is not quite infallible, it should be added. When he does venture a bit of singing at the end of act 1, he gets things wrong by announcing a "happily ever after" conclusion to the plot. The same actor normally doubles as the Mysterious Man, a fallible character who does have a song ("No More"). This is a complex moment. His singing delivers a piece of wisdom to his son, the Baker, who will as a result follow through with his commitments to the remaining human characters—exactly what the Mysterious Man has not done in his time. "Don't run away" is the moral lesson learned by the Baker, and it seems that the Mysterious Man has the moral capacity to teach this point. But then he runs away himself. Perhaps he is touched with omniscience after all, this weird father figure who flits here and there in the woods, but he is a bumbler as well as a sage.[4]

Most narrators in musicals fall well short of omniscience. Tevye often takes a narrative position in *Fiddler on the Roof* (1964), but he never acts as though he knows everything. On the contrary, he gains humor from knowing very little and having to speak to the Lord Himself about important turns in the

---

[3] For a fuller account of the various revisions *Candide* has received, see Mordden, *Everything's Coming Up Roses*, pp. 170–85.

[4] A point I owe to Lindsay Wilczynski.

action. "With Your help, I'm starving to death," Tevye says to
the Lord in scene 2. "You made many, many poor people. I realize, of course, that it's no shame to be poor, but it's no great
honor either."[5] He is the narrator who cannot control his circumstances, and this allows him to sing. The quotation I have
given leads into "If I Were a Rich Man," for example. *Fiddler
on the Roof* actually has a fiddler on the roof, a bit of humor that
pretends to bring one musician to the area of fallibility, the
stage. Tevye's first lines spell out the issue of fallibility: "A fiddler on the roof. Sounds crazy, no? But in our little village of
Anatevka, you might say every one of us is a fiddler on the
roof, trying to scratch out a pleasant, simple tune without breaking his neck. It isn't easy."

Some characters preserve a note of ambiguity between musical projection and all-knowingness. The leading example is
the Master of Ceremonies, the Emcee, in *Cabaret*, who hovers
between being one thing and another in his every appearance
(between male and female, tolerant and anti-Semitic, amus-
ing and cruel). On the narrative question, he seems wise to
everything that happens in the plot involving Cliff and Sally,
Fraulein Schneider and Schultz, but his way of expressing his
knowledge is to summon a performance from the Kit Kat entertainers, himself included, so that the possibility of omniscience is always deflected into the performance of a cabaret
number, and one cannot be sure where anyone stands, certainly not of where the Emcee stands. When Cliff and Sally
find themselves living together and end their scene with an
embrace, the Emcee has two chorus girls ready to perform a
number about three-way sex. When Cliff accepts the assign-
ment of bringing in money for Ernest's Nazi cause, the Emcee
and his girls are ready with their "Sitting Pretty" or "Money"
song. Always the Emcee knows what has just happened in the
love stories and always he has a cabaret number ready that will
give a sardonic turn to the latest events. When Herr Schultz
and Fräulein Schneider are first attacked by the Nazis (a brick

[5] Quoted from the libretto in Richards, *Ten Great Musicals of the American
Theatre*, p. 500.

is hurled through Schultz's window the day after he is recognized as Jewish), the Emcee does a vaudeville turn with a gorilla, concluding with his notoriously ambiguous "if you could see her through my eyes, she wouldn't look Jewish at all."[6]

Hal Prince's staging of *Cabaret* in the original production of 1966 had an area of the stage for what Prince called "Limbo" scenes.[7] The Emcee stood there more often than anyone. The ending of act 1 had him on the spiral staircase in the Limbo area, watching the partygoers at the celebration for Fraulein Schneider and Herr Schultz become caught up in singing the Nazi anthem, "Tomorrow Belongs to Me." The Emcee descended, and crossed the stage, still in the Limbo area, while the figures on stage froze against a black background. The Emcee was looking at them. He knew this would happen. "Then he turns to the audience," reads the stage direction. "He shrugs, he smiles, and exits."[8] He is bearing witness to the rise of Nazism, but this is nothing special to an Emcee in a cabaret, who is also the welcoming figure for the audience in the theatre, us.

Sondheim's *Assassins* has a Balladeer who can attain omniscience from time to time, as when he narrates the assassination of McKinley (scene 8). But Sondheim is experimenting with the narrative problem. Later, when the Balladeer enters into Guiteau's cakewalk up the scaffold steps, playing banjo while the two blend into a duet, "Look on the Bright Side," he gains in effectiveness because he now is joining Guiteau's song. He has abandoned his privileged position of knowing everything and has entered into song and dance, for a change.

---

[6] The ambiguity of the Emcee is to the fore here. Perhaps his line is a satirical hit at the Nazis who think so foolishly, but in calling the gorilla Jewish, the line might speak for anti-Semitism after all. For a fuller discussion of this show, see Mizejewski, *Divine Decadence: Fascism, Female Spectacle, and the Making of* Sally Bowles, and Garebian, *The Making of* Cabaret. Useful briefer discussions are in Scott Miller, *From "Assassins" to "West Side Story,"* chapter 2; Mordden, *Open a New Window: The Broadway Musical in the 1960s,* chapter 9; and Knapp, *The American Musical and the Formation of National Identity,* pp. 239–48.

[7] Hal Prince, *Contradictions,* pp. 130–33.

[8] *Cabaret* libretto, p. 84.

The *Assassins'* narrator is forced out of the action too. In scene 15, as he tries to moralize about America as a country where the mailman can win the lottery and the usherette can become a rock star, the gathered Assassins advance upon him and drive him from the stage. Then they are free to sing "another national anthem" without hindrance, and this modulates into the country-and-western ballad that Lee Harvey Oswald is listening to in the next scene, as he considers suicide in the Texas Book Depository. (In most productions, Oswald is played by the same actor as the Balladeer, further emphasizing the displacement of authority.) In the Oswald scene, omniscience is taken over by Booth and the other assassins, who know Oswald's complete story and can read his mind. They talk him into killing President Kennedy as a way of justifying those assassins who came before and making possible those assassins who will come later. It is one of the most nerve-wracking scenes in modern drama, a moment when the implication that the assassins are heroes worthy of this much attention is fully dramatized, and it comes about after the moralizing Balladeer is driven from the action. The problem of omniscience has been enlarged into a sort of nightmare of misplaced authority among the rest of the cast.[9]

THE SET

The contemporary musical has brought a new form of omniscience into the picture, the omniscience of the set. Stage technology has advanced to the point where the set can move itself into position before the eyes of the audience, as though magic or the almighty were creating the effect for us, and this miracle of backstage inventiveness can overwhelm song-and-dance performance and become the new groundwork or matrix of the musical. Do modern musicals sometimes seem ponderous and

[9] Sondheim's use of the narrator in *Pacific Overtures* is especially deft. He is a reciter (from the Kabuki theatre tradition), knowing more than the other characters but decidedly not knowing everything.

overdone? The reason lies in the doubling up of all-knowing forces—the orchestra in the pit, where omniscience belongs, and the computerized lighting and set design, which covers song-and-dance with another layer of infallibility.

The set looms as the new mother of musical theatre. This is a special feature in shows produced by Cameron Mackintosh, working with such designers as John Napier, Maria Bjornson, and Timothy O'Brien.[10] A theatre chandelier seems to crash onto the stage in *Phantom of the Opera*, and a helicopter takes off in *Miss Saigon*. The crashing chandelier reminds one that the Phantom is a technologist himself, capable in his magic of destroying the stage on which he is represented. When he sends the chandelier crashing to the stage, the event is contained within the fiction that this is the Paris Opera, but later, shooting fireballs out of a skull he has at his disposal, he seems to set the entire stage on fire, and this seems to be the stage of the musical itself. (We will return to *Phantom* for an extended discussion later in this chapter.) These things would be exciting in a theme park, but in the musical they turn the drama into spectacle, gliding the sets into place before our eyes, stunning us with wondrous lighting, and integrating the show into the interplay of special effects. *Sunset Boulevard* had a set for which the theatre had to be redesigned and which eventually cost so much that the Broadway show had to close, for it was losing money even on full houses. (A Harold Rome show from the 1950s, *Wish You Were Here*, had its own usable swimming pool, and huge pool effects had earlier been practiced in shows like *Neptune's Daughter* at the Hippodrome, but these efforts at least made money.)

The set goes with the theory of the integrated musical. No longer is it only the book that is to be integrated with the music or the dance that is to be integrated with the book; now it is the *mise-en-scène* within which everything else is to be integrated. This is one of the outcomes of Wagnerianism in the musical theatre, and the set-driven shows also have a ten-

---

[10] See Goodwin, *British Theatre Design: The Modern Age*, for a solid account of design in musical theatre.

dency to be through-sung. The director Trevor Nunn dates the change from *Evita* in 1978, and credits the government-subsidized companies in England and Europe with giving the designers of musicals budgets large enough to create not just scenery but total environments.[11]

The fluid, gliding set that can materialize before our eyes has removed the need for the in-one system of the older musicals, in which a number was inserted for downstage performers while the new set was being established behind the traveler curtain. No one wants to return to the in-one system, but its aesthetic effect should be remembered, for the new design technology aims for a different effect, which is less germane to the musical. The in-one system separated a moment of performance from the larger *mise-en-scène* and isolated it downstage, giving a spot to a song-and-dance duo or a big solo voice, keeping the musical in touch with its vaudeville roots. When Carol Channing stepped before the curtain to deliver "I'm Just a Little Girl from Little Rock" or "Diamonds Are a Girl's Best Friend," both in-one numbers in *Gentlemen Prefer Blondes*, the audience knew the set was being changed and the book was being disrupted for something else, but the something else was the heart of the matter. Dramatic character was being established apart from the book, in terms of song and performance, the performance was being spotlighted in an area of keen vulnerability downstage, and Carol Channing was stopping the show.

Sometimes the set was not even being changed during the in-one number. Moving to the downstage position in front of the traveler was seen as an advantage in itself. The scene I discussed in chapter 1 from the Gershwins' *Funny Face* is a classic example. As Fred Astaire and the Boys finished their song-and-dance "High Hat" in the huge living room on Jimmy Reeves's estate where act 1 mainly took place, the curtains closed and a traveler was brought across to mark an in-one wall at the nearby house of the famous aviator Peter Thurston. Adele Astaire (called "Frankie," this time) came along to let Peter Thurston fall in love with her, an event marked by their singing "S'Wonderful."

[11] Goodwin, pp. 156–57.

As that number ended, the curtains opened to reveal Fred Astaire and the Boys *still* singing and dancing "High Hat" back in the living room. They were reprising the number, but the pretense was that the two numbers had gone on simultaneously, one performed by Fred Astaire, one performed by Adele Astaire. The book was being stopped twice over. "High Hat" was Fred Astaire's first number ever in top hat and tails. This was a major moment in the musical, the definition of a longlasting character for Astaire to play. "S'Wonderful" was the birth of a standard tune that everyone in the Western world has heard by now. That these numbers were going on simultaneously in act 1 of *Funny Face* gives pleasure in itself, owing to the in-one convention.

The day of the in-one staging is gone from Broadway, although it is still used in high school auditoriums and town halls. Alongside Broadway's blockbuster shows with computerized sets, however, there has developed a tradition of plain staging in which a refusal to use the available technology becomes part of a show's theme. *Rent* is the leading example. It has virtually no set, a bare-bones decision in keeping with the poverty these modern-day bohemians choose to live in. The technology of rock music is called on, but not the technology of the self-generated set change. *A Chorus Line* has no set either, apart from the stage on which the auditions are being held and the mirrors to the rear in which the dancers are sometimes reflected. Cassie's self-absorption in her "Music and the Mirror" number thematizes the reflective device. The Encores series of musicals done in concert versions has spun off several hit revivals on Broadway—*Chicago* and *Wonderful Town*, for example—and these are staged with minimal sets and costumes. Chamber musicals like William Finn's *Falsettoland* trilogy and the Stephen Cole/Matthew Ward *After the Fair* specialize in plain staging.[12]

[12] *After the Fair* is based on Thomas Hardy's story "On the Western Circuit." The libretto has not been published, but there is a 1999 cast recording from the York Theatre production in New York. I call it to attention as an indication that there is a class of small musicals that are relatively inexpensive to stage and worth following as a countertrend to the technologized Broadway shows. *Fermat's Last Tango*, book by Joanne Sydney Lessner, music by Joshua Rosenblum, is another, and there are dozens more.

Nevertheless, the theatre will use its new technology and the set does not have to run away with the show. *South Pacific* was one of the first musicals to abandon the in-one convention in favor of fluid set changes in view of the audience, but Rodgers and Hammerstein were careful to underscore the changes so that orchestration would lead the way from one set to another. Hal Prince and Sondheim emphasize musical performance while the set pieces are gliding about in *A Little Night Music*. There are trees visible throughout the entire show, hinting that behind the urban interiors of act 1 there is a pastoral magic that the weekend in the country will bring about in act 2. In the pastoral scenes of act 2, groves of trees can turn, hiding someone and revealing someone else. It is the obscuring and disclosing of characters that matter in the Sondheim/Prince method, not the mystifying movement of the set pieces themselves. When the trees turn to occlude Henrik and Anne making love and reveal Petra and Frid doing much the same thing (act 2, scene 7), the lovemaking is the important thing—plus the change from book to number, for Petra is not only making love to Frid, she is also singing about making love to many more men, in "The Miller's Son." These ubiquitous trees are like the ubiquitous lieder singers who can peer in on any scene while belonging to none of them. The singers are another Sondheim variation on the issue of the omniscient character, for they seem all-knowing and a bit weird ("Who are these klutzes?" Sondheim's agent Flora Roberts said when she first saw them).[13] But they are not primarily narrative in their presence. They are singers, and their role is to weave their numbers into a perspective of uncanniness for the show. Together with the always-present trees, they create a fluid stage space that in act 2 can be anywhere or everywhere on the Armfeldt estate.[14]

---

[13] Zadan, *Sondheim & Co.*, p. 186.

[14] Prince compared this to a film effect: "The last scene in *Night Music*, which takes place *everywhere* on the estate, appears to be happening only on the lawn. What no one else realizes is that the young wife and her stepson are running along a hall and down an alley and off to the country. Desiree is having her scene with her lover in her bedroom. The countess and Fredrik are having a conversation on the lawn. . . . It's actually a situation that can't be

In *Les Misérables*, to choose a contrasting example, when the tables and chairs from the tavern scene slide together to form the peoples' barricades, there is no point beyond sheer stage technology. If the people really did have such magical power behind them they could not lose. But no one thinks of this possibility. The stage technology is merely showing its omniscience, while the orchestra plays some underscoring from *its* position of omniscience, and the interlocking systems of unseen authority have taken over the drama.[15]

The Source, and the Special Case of *Sunday in the Park with George*

There is a further issue here. Musicals usually have a source they are adapting. The source can be a novel or a short story, a nonmusical play, a film, a group of poems, a painting—but a source of some sort usually lies behind the show. Why? I would not settle for the standard answer, which is that source stories are there for convenience. Having a strong plot to begin with is supposed to make it easier to find slots for numbers, according to the convenience theory. But is it really easy to build numbers into an Edna Ferber novel, or an Ingmar Bergman film, or a book of poems by T. S. Eliot, or a play about Chicago women who kill their lovers and get away with it in court? If we think further about sources, we will also be thinking further about sets and narrators, for it is the resetting

---

done on a stage, but I told Hugh Wheeler not to worry about it, to write it as though it were a movie." Quoted in Zadan, *Sondheim & Co.*, p. 192. But the effect of the combined actions depends on their occurrence in a single space, the stage. Film space is fundamentally different, as the unsuccessful film of *A Little Night Music* shows. See the conclusion of this chapter for a fuller discussion of theatre versus film.

[15] The designer John Napier said of *Les Misérables*: "My starting point was the centre of the play's biggest moment, the barricade. Once that was solved everything else fell into place. The barricade could split, lift, and revolve, and was a mass of *objets trouvés* which the actors picked up from time to time and used." Quoted in Goodwin, *British Theatre Design*, p. 151.

of the source that is involved, along with the reinvention of the
original narrative.

The stage director Nicholas Hytner has said that musical
dramatists use old plots "for the excitement that is to be found
in the acquiescence of a story to the musical form."[16] That
seems exactly right to me. The musical transforms something
that already exists on its own terms into a set of different terms,
the book-and-number combination we have been discussing. It
is not a matter of convenience so much as a matter of formal
desire that the musical be based on something else, something
ripe for dislocation. The numbers reformulate the sources,
taking a settled mode of representation—a Ferber novel, say—
and turning it into a new mode of representation—a stage play
for one thing, and a stage play with numbers for another. A
narrator who knows the source stands in the way of the transformation into song and dance. *He* is part of what must acqui-
esce to the new form, and he must be fed to the Giantess in
some way.

What I have called the area of vulnerability where performance takes place is thus tinged with subversiveness. The
singers and dancers have a touch of transgression about their
performance. They are making time with settled things—
singing and dancing into the book narrative, turning Ferber's
Magnolia into the soprano who must rise to the lyrical heights
of "Make Believe." There are two stages of dislocation here.
Magnolia, who begins as a character in narrative prose in Ferber's novel, is dislocated to the stage when an actress takes on
the role, and this dislocation is doubled when the stage actress
bursts into song. Ferber's narrative has now become unmoored
twice, first by being acted and then by being sung. The musical
thrives on changing its source into something new.

The most sophisticated treatment of a source and its authority figure in a musical is Sondheim's *Sunday in the Park with
George*. The source is the famous *Sunday Afternoon on the Isle of
La Grande Jatte* painting by Georges Seurat, which is created
in tableaux at the end of each act of the musical. So the source

[16] Hytner, "When Your Characters Are Speechless, Let 'Em Sing."

does not lie behind this musical but is actually represented *in* the musical, taking shape as a tableau before our eyes. This might seem to give a special kind of omniscience to the painter, Seurat himself, the leading character of act 1 and the main male singer. How can he sing so much if he is omniscient? Song is for fallible performers. But most of the time Seurat hasn't finished the painting, and the painter who is not finished with a painting knows he is anything but omniscient. While he is sketching his work, Seurat is prone to sing for his characters, give voice to them as he sketches them. Some of these figures are also his actual acquaintances, and they have lives of their own beyond his control.

His mistress especially has a life of her own. She is also the model for the leading female figure in the painting, and she wants more of Seurat's time than an artist absorbed in his work is willing to give. She is an invention of the musical, and her name, Dot, is a joke about Seurat's pointillism. She eventually marries Louis the Baker, another figure shared between the painting and "real" life, and Seurat has to finish the act 1 painting despite the disaster in his personal life when Dot leaves. So Seurat's control over his painting, which is a struggle in the first place, leads to his lack of social and romantic control.

The real omniscience throughout this show is where it belongs, in the orchestra. When Seurat does complete his painting at the end of act 1, he calls for "Order, Design, Tension, Balance, and Harmony," and each aesthetic term is answered by a chord from the orchestra. Seurat is moving figures around, on the verge of finishing, the orchestra is accompanying his every move with chords for Order, Design, Tension, Balance, and Harmony, and suddenly the design is perfected (when Seurat dashes into the painting, snatches the eyeglasses from a young girl, then dashes out again) just as the orchestra announces its final chord. The orchestra retains its position of omniscience while George completes the design, on a perfect chord. Imagine this scene without the orchestra's final chords and the importance of the orchestra will be clear. Seurat could not create this marvelous effect alone—not in a musical. He has to have the chords.

Seurat is long dead at the beginning of act 2. His great-grandson is there instead. The new George cannot get his modernistic light sculpture to work, relates badly to the New York art scene, has been through a divorce, and is uncertain about the direction of his career. Omniscience is hardly the issue. Then he visits the site of his great-grandfather's famous painting, encounters the Ghost of Dot, and together they sing a climactic duet, "Move On."

"Move On" is climactic because it takes elements left hanging from songs in act 1 and composes them into a finished song, an outsized AABA number. It is an example of the drama of the uncompleted song that we discussed in chapter 5, but in this case the number is not diegetic. "Move On" arises from out of the blue, but it recombines segments from earlier out-of-the-blue songs—"Sunday in the Park," "Color and Light," and "We Do Not Belong Together."[17] The book does not concern characters who are trying to remember old tunes or perfect dance routines. The book is about completing artistic designs. Seurat completes his *Grande Jatte* painting at the end of act 1. Sondheim completes the song "Move On" in act 2. What the lyric of "Move On" says is trite: an artist has to move on. The power of the number lies in its completion and in its doubling of the theme of artistic completion.

At the end of act 2, after the duet, George repeats his great-grandfather's words: Order, Design, Tension. . . . On each word the orchestra plays the chord from act 1. It is an uncanny moment. The modern buildings that surround La Grande Jatte lift away, revealing the island rather as it was in act 1. If George had this power to dismiss the buildings, he would be omniscient and no one would pay much heed. With the power coming from the orchestra's chords, one knows that something appropriate is happening. It is actually a scenic effect from *West Side Story* being repeated (the tenements lift away at the beginning of the "Somewhere" dream-ballet). The theatre is quoting its own scenic effects, and as the figures of the Seurat painting return to the stage, standing in different places this time, a sort of visual quotation of the act 1 ending is taking place, and this is also a visual quotation of Sondheim's earlier *West Side Story*.

The orchestra's omniscience is at work, but the quotations come with residues of difference. There is grief and beauty in this ending. Completing a design puts loss into the accomplishment. The figures in the painting stand differently now, and the composition does not exactly take shape. The figures in the painting are singing the gorgeous "Sunday" music with which act 1 concluded—music can be restored, but not the rest. Dot is, after all, dead. The figures in the painting depart. George is left alone with the blank canvas his great-grandfather had at the very beginning of the musical: "White. A blank page or canvas. His favorite. So many possibilities."

These are almost the words his great-grandfather spoke in front of the blank canvas at the beginning. The young George is reading Dot's version of his great-grandfather's words. She wrote them into her lesson book, and she did not get them exactly right. Seurat earlier said, "The challenge: Bring order to the whole." Dot's book reads, "So many possibilities." The first points to the completion of the painting. That is act 1. The second points to the need to step free from that completion, the need to find a valid form of repetition, the musical form. "Move on." That is act 2.[18]

THE PHANTOM AND THE DEMON BARBER: A CONTRAST

The source acquiesces to the book-and-number format of the musical. The book-and-number format puts the performers into an area of fallibility, where their characters take on musical dimensions. They seem like additional selves, these singing and dancing characters, bringing the source to life in lyric ways before going back to the give-and-take dialectic of the book

[18] For additional explanations of what needs to be accomplished in act 2, see Scott Miller, *Deconstructing Harold Hill*, pp. 153–89.

scenes. But they are not omniscient. Omniscience is for the orchestra, unless the orchestra is placed on the stage. These are some of the ideas I have discussed, and I summarize them here because I want to take up two musicals, *Phantom of the Opera* and *Sweeney Todd*, which differ in their treatment of these conventions. In many ways they are similar shows. Both become virtually through-sung in their final scenes, challenging the distinction between book and number that I have been taking as a basic principle of the musical. Both have sources that reach back—one century for *Phantom*, at least two centuries for *Sweeney*—to lurid and melodramatic tales of urban violence in Paris or London. Oddly, both took hold in the minds of their composers during visits to the Theatre Royal at Stratford East in East London, where Sondheim saw Christopher Bond's melodrama *Sweeney Todd* in 1973 and Lloyd Webber saw Ken Hill's melodrama *Phantom of the Opera* in 1984. The musicals that resulted used vast stage sets in their original productions, and both were directed by Hal Prince. Yet the two musicals occupy vastly different worlds, and in addressing the differences between them we will also be addressing a contrast in the ways the basic principles of the musical form are put to use.

Phantom of the Opera works its way into a through-sung series of episodes in its final scenes. Those who love *Phantom*—there are many who do—might say that it fulfills the promise of Rodgers and Hammerstein on the ground that Rodgers and Hammerstein intended to write integrated musicals and did not quite manage. Where Rodgers and Hammerstein fell short, Lloyd Webber carries through. Thinking on the contrary that Rodgers and Hammerstein mastered the principles of difference that formed the earlier musicals, I find that *Phantom* deviates from those principles in ways that make it pretentious and overblown, but I do not have the last word on these things and I can see the logic of claiming that the drive for integration has finally been achieved in Lloyd Webber. Perhaps *Phantom* should be celebrated for being a musical on the verge of becoming an opera.

There is more to be said about this operatic tendency. *Phantom of the Opera* contains a parody of nineteenth-century opera in its comic scenes of rehearsal of the so-called "Hanni-bal" and performance of the so-called "Il Muto." Scornful of what the Paris Opera is doing, the Phantom writes his own opera and insists that his beloved Christine sing the soprano role while he surreptitiously takes over the role of Don Juan. The staging of the new "Don Juan Triumphant" as an opera within the musical is Lloyd Webber's invention, one of the ways his many sources are being subjected to a clever recre-ation in the musical form.[19] At the same time as he is in-venting the opera-within-the-musical form, Lloyd Webber is turning his own musical into quasi-operatic realization by making it virtually through-sung. (Lloyd Webber was thus paralleling the Phantom as composer, and was in fact writing for his wife, Sarah Brightman, who played Christine.) Once the Phantom sings "Point of No Return" with Christine in the "Don Juan" opera, the musical itself becomes a through-sung opera, so that the Phantom's opera opens out into the Lloyd Webber musical and the aesthetic principles of the two are joined.

Modern stage technology comes to the fore in *Phantom*, not just in the crashing chandelier conclusion to act 1 but also in the mysterious lake-and-lair lighting effects of the Phantom's hideout in the fifth basement of the Paris Opera, in the disap-pearing acts the Phantom himself can perform, and in count-less touches of self-generated set changes and alterations. The modern stage effects could all have been managed in the late nineteenth-century theatres, certainly at the Paris Opera, but more arrestingly at Her Majesty's Theatre in the Haymarket, where *Phantom* opened in 1986 and is probably still running (the Phantom never finally leaves his theatres). The fabulous staging could not have been managed so well in the old the-atres, but it could have been managed, and the program for *Phantom* even includes some illustrations of the wooden ma-chinery at Her Majesty's, showing how it *would* have been man-aged. So the staging comes from nineteenth-century melodrama

---

[19] The sources are discussed in Perry, *The Complete Phantom*, which also gives the Lloyd Webber libretto and many illustrations.

but is being turned into twentieth-century computerized technology, and this is smart thinking about the craft of theatre.

With mysterious staging effects constantly in view, and with a large orchestra in the pit exercising its total knowledge of the show and driving toward the through-sung final scenes, *Phantom of the Opera* is loaded with systems of omniscience. There is no escape from these intertwined systems of authority, the set and the orchestra. The Phantom himself, with his ability over the apparatus of the Paris Opera, his ability to appear and disappear at will, and his dreadful fireballs, sometimes stands in the position of omniscience within the plot. Yet he sings a lot (he does not dance). This show does not care about this excess of authority, and of course the Phantom does not have the power he desires, the power of being loved, because his face is disfigured. Perhaps this is why many theatregoers sympathize with him.[20]

Otherwise, the plot lies beyond the control of the characters. The heroic decisions of Christine, first to unmask the Phantom (act 1) and then to unmask him again and go on to kiss him full on the lips (act 2) are meant to be turning-point moments of decisiveness, but these gestures fade into insignificance as soon as they are made. They are outclassed by the technological power of the Phantom and the staging. That is finally the problem with the integrated musical. It is attained at the cost of human agency. The quasi-Wagnerian synthesis of music, staging, and plot in a genre which counts on disjunctions between the elements is attained by dismissing the doubleness of time and character by which human agency is represented.

Look at these moments of Christine's assertiveness. When she removes the Phantom's mask and sees his disfigured face for the first time, in act 1, a theme that runs through *Phantom* is reaching a crisis point. Masks of various kinds are worn by normal people in *Phantom of the Opera*, an idea given elaborate demonstration in the "Masquerade" that begins act 2. Is the

---

[20] Behind the role is an adolescent male fantasy about being unlovable, as Jerrold Hogle argues in *The Undergrounds of* The Phantom of the Opera.

Phantom in this regard like other people? Is he different? What lies behind his mask, and how can Christine and the audience respond? These are valid questions, and the play has not skirted them until now. When Christine tears away the mask, only she can see the face—the Phantom stands in profile and in shadow. But what does Christine see? How does she respond? The heroism of the gesture is hers, but she is given nothing to say or sing. The Phantom sings instead, damning her first, then swinging around to the hope that she can love him anyhow. Can she? Should she? We do not know, because Christine has no response. She merely gives back the mask, and the Phantom sings that it is time to be getting back to the opera rehearsal (they are in the fifth basement). Off they go, and the issue of the reality behind the mask is not taken up.

Perhaps the second time Christine removes the mask is meant to be more significant. This occurs in the opera within the musical, when the Phantom has taken over the role of Don Juan (having murdered the tenor backstage). This could be the turning point of the action, because the Phantom's disfigured face is revealed to the audience for the first time, and he and Christine are singing about being "past the point of no return." But the scene dissolves into technology. The tenor's corpse is being discovered. Everyone is catching on—the Phantom is playing Don Juan himself! So the Phantom sweeps his cloak around Christine and they disappear. There is nothing but seamless unity in the composition at this point where the performers of the number disappear into technology before their song is over. The orchestra continues playing "All I Ask of You," which is what the duet has become, the chorus is bursting on to the scene to no purpose, the magic of stage technology is producing a disappearing act, and there are no characters.

Later, in the Phantom's lair again, Christine makes her courageous decision to kiss her abductor in order to save her true lover, who stands off to the side with a magical rope around his neck. The kiss comes after she sings:

God give me courage
to show you

you are not
alone . . .

Whereupon "she kisses him long and full on the lips" while
the orchestra plays gorgeously in approval. But once again the
turning point is addressed through technology. The Phantom
takes a lighted candle and burns through the magically suspended rope coiled around the true lover's neck. The lover is
saved! And before Christine or the lover has time to sing anything in response to this astonishing turn of events, the mob
breaks in again, singing their pursuit song ("Track down this
murderer—he must be found!"), and the Phantom has to find a
new way to disappear. Christine does not sing anything in response to the Phantom's decision to release her. The depth of
the decline from Wagner is visible here, in the inability of
the modern through-sung musical to address its main issues
through music and the need to resort to the wonders of stage
technology instead. I believe it will be found that the through-
sung musical typically resorts to stage technology at these
challenging moments instead of seeking a lyrical and musical
climax in the singing of the principals. Operatic composers
can trust their singers and their orchestras (and themselves)
to dramatize their climactic scenes musically, although operas
do sometimes resort to technology. The through-sung musical
characteristically turns to technology. Let the orchestra play
rhapsodically while the staging takes over the plot (by making
the Phantom disappear, for example) and the seamless whole
will have been achieved before our very eyes, in a truly unified
effect between the orchestra and the stagehands.

There is one earlier moment when a recognition or turning
point is voiced in song. After Christine and her abductor reach
the lair, Christine sings:

This haunted face
holds no horror
for me now . . .
It's in your soul
that the true
distortion lies . . .

This seems promising, as though it might be a recognition scene for the Phantom too. But he has no response. Instead, there being a lake within the lair, with the true lover swimming across it at this very moment, the Phantom is allowed to be distracted from what Christine has sung. His lyric veers off to the oddity of a hero who is climbing out of the water dripping wet:

> Wait! I think, my dear,
> we have a guest!

Then the magical rope descends to coil around the hero's neck, there is some singing back and forth about Christine's need to save her lover by leaving with the Phantom, she kisses the Phantom, the business of burning through the magical rope is performed, Christine and her lover sail away in a boat, and the Phantom pulls off one more disappearing trick.

This kind of musical dodges the challenges and opportunities offered by the genre. Contemporary shows written in the through-sung mode (such as *Les Misérables*, *Miss Saigon*, *The Lion King*) resort to the wonders of stage technology in order to preserve the illusion of a seamless whole. (Sometimes the technology is not computerized and can be wonderful, as in the opening procession of *The Lion King*.) I wish to set *Sweeney Todd* in contrast to the *Phantom* type of show because it is Sondheim's closest approach to the quasi-operatic mode and yet it shows how the principles of the musical can be used to create a different dramatic quality.

For example, *Sweeney Todd* does face up to its recognition scene. In fact, it is two recognitions occurring simultaneously, Sweeney's that he has murdered his own wife, Mrs. Lovett's that the damper has been put on her own hopes of marrying Sweeney. The solution to the problem of how to express two recognitions simultaneously is entirely musical. Sweeney reprises the "Lucy lies in ashes" segment from his earlier "Epiphany," Mrs. Lovett reprises her earlier "Poor Thing" (with new lyrics, which try to justify her having misled Sweeney about his wife), and Sondheim wedges the two into simultaneity by varying the meter of "Poor Thing" from 6/8 to 5/8 in order to get a fit. The orchestra is a partner here too. It is playing

Lucy's earlier "Alms" motif. This is a deliberate "clash" (Sond-heim's word for it) among reprised segments of earlier songs, and the purpose of the clash is to accomplish exactly what *Phantom of the Opera* avoids, a dramatization of the major recognition on the part of two characters at once.[21]

That is the recognition scene, avoided in *Phantom* and dramatized through music in *Sweeney*. Now look at the turning point of the plot, which occurs at the end of act 1. Sweeney's opportunity for taking revenge against Judge Turpin has slipped by, in the "Pretty Women" sequence we examined in chapter 1. The turning point occurs as his revenge motive loses its focus and becomes a desire for indiscriminate murder-ousness against all men, as retaliation against the oppressive structure of industrialized London. Mrs. Lovett has no room for revenge in her heart, but she is a practical woman with a meat pie business to run. Business is not good, the price of meat being what it is, so Sweeney's murderous intention against the human race becomes in her eyes a way of lowering the costs of production. This double reversal is dramatized through an alternation between book and number character-istic of the musical genre at its best. I refer to the two final numbers of act 1, Sweeney's terrific assertion of madness in "Epiphany" followed by his comic duet with Mrs. Lovett, "A Little Priest."

Sweeney's "Epiphany" is a furious number, with no trace of humor. The height of savagery is an unrhymed threat on the men in the audience:

Who, sir? You, sir!
No one's in the chair—
Come on, come on,
Sweeney's waiting!
I want you bleeders!
You, sir—anybody!
Gentlemen, now don't be shy!
Not one man, no,

[21] For Sondheim's comment on the music of this episode, see Horowitz, *Sondheim on Music*, pp. 146–47.

Nor ten men,
Nor a hundred
Can assuage me—
I will have you!

The final line—"And I'm full of joy!"—is the musical climax of
the role, standing out in harrowing detachment from the rest
of the song and demanding the kind of voice that allows opera
singers to play this part gladly.

What tells everyone this is a musical and not an opera, however, is the aftermath of the song. We are into a book scene
now, where Mrs. Lovett is not all that impressed with Sweeney's
rage. "That's all very well," she says, but there is the problem
of corpses. Sweeney's first victim, the rival barber Pirelli, already lies slaughtered in the barbershop. "All that matters is
him," says Mrs. Lovett. What should be done with the corpse?
Sweeney has conventional ideas about burying it, but Mrs.
Lovett is thinking more imaginatively, and within two minutes
she has swung into *her* number, the real climax of act 1:

Seems an awful waste . . .
Such a nice plump frame
Wot's his name
Has . . .
Had . . .
Has . . .

Sweeney's aria has given way to something entirely different, a
music-hall waltz tune on the taste treats that will follow from
the barber's wide-ranging revenge if only the corpses are used
profitably, as the filler for meat pies. This may be the height of
incongruity in dramatic literature—comic cannibalism in 3/4
taking over from Sweeney's passion for revenge. It is certainly
the epitome of the musical, for the sense of parody and incongruity that runs through the history of the genre has never
been used to such disconcerting perfection before. "It's fop,"
Mrs. Lovett sings as she thinks of new flavors,

Finest in the shop
Or we have some shepherd's pie peppered

With actual shepherd
On top.

Sondheim's superb sense of rhyme makes it certain that the versifying of Ira Gershwin, E. Y. Harburg, and Cole Porter is alive and capable of being challenged. This combination of *two* climactic numbers, the comic one overtaking the serious one, shows the musical's finest quality, the quality of pursuing the implications of its own book with the verbal and musical glee that numbers can attain. *Phantom of the Opera* loses track of its turning point episodes in its penchant for technology, but here the turning point is being dramatized through conventions basic to the musical form. The incongruity between these numbers is drastic and delightful. "Turning the coin from melodrama to farce" is Stephen Banfield's way of describing the combination, just a few sentences before he comments on the "operatic" nature of the refrain in "A Little Priest," which is a music-hall tune.[22] None of these terms is wrong. Melodrama and farce, music hall and opera—the genres of musical theatre are all operating in the same world, yet the world seems coherent and exciting because of the incongruities of its design.

THE FILM MUSICAL: TWO CHICAGOS

I dwell on the Lloyd-Webber and Sondheim shows in order to illustrate the principles of the musical in one negative and one positive example, but there is a further issue in that the negative example is a major phenomenon in the modern musical and cannot be dismissed simply on grounds that it is overtechnologized. The technological musical plays a large role in modern culture, and in saying that it fails to accord with the aesthetic principles that make the stage musical important, I also wish to suggest that it falls into agreement with the aesthetic principles of a different form of musical drama, the film musical.

[22] Banfield, *Sondheim's Broadway Musicals*, p. 307. Foster Hirsch spots the music-hall tune, in *Harold Prince and the American Musical Theatre*, p. 127.

The film musical is now gaining a valid aesthetic form of its own. Through most of its history it has served a long apprenticeship as second way of re-presenting successful stage musicals, as when the Rodgers and Hammerstein musicals were turned into film versions. But the film musical is now finding its unique aesthetic basis, and although the topic lies beyond the scope of this book, we are in position to relate musical drama to the central difference between theatre and film. The difference between theatre and film is that theatre occurs in a series of events in a single space, the stage, where the vulnerability of the performers is visible, and film occurs as a series of events photographed and screened, where the vulnerability of the performers is rendered irrelevant. A film is a system of technological omniscience in the first place, and questions of human agency cluster around the director and the film crew, those who manage the system of technology.

The stage itself, basic to theatre and irrelevant to film, is a key element in the distinction at hand. This can be seen immediately in musicals which exist in both theatre and film versions. The theatre version of *Phantom of the Opera* uses the physical stage sensationally, turning the same space into the Paris Opera or the lake-and-lair hideaway that the Phantom occupies five levels *beneath* the Paris Opera, and at times that space is identified with the stage of the theatre in which we are watching all this showmanship, the one in which the Phantom prowls about behind us or above us. Now that *Phantom* has become a film musical (I am not speaking of the old *Phantom* films that were sources for the theatre version but of the 2004 film that was made of the musical), we can see that as the stage ceases to be relevant, the space of performance becomes a limitless series of photographed locations, now a dressing room of the opera house, now the basement lair of the Phantom, and so on, each capable of close-ups, reverse shots, and unexpected angles. Gone is the concentration of all locations onto one stage. This is a difference, not a loss. The result is that *anywhere* can be projected by the film and the audience will be there to receive it, for the audience assumes it is anywhere, too. In the theatre, the audience is *somewhere*, often somewhere a bit uncomfortable, looking at a stage, which is sometimes said to be "all the world," but there it is anyhow, a stage. Everything happens on it. The stage version of *My Fair Lady* places the Alfred Doolittle numbers like "I'm Getting Married in the Morning" on the same stage as the Henry Higgins numbers like "The Rain in Spain," creating a repetition of space (the set changes, of course) that underlies differences of class (in this case) and that corresponds to what we have called the "voice of the musical." The film of *My Fair Lady* sets up different locations for these numbers.

Musical films passed through a long period of trying to capture its own version of the theatre's fixed space. Shooting a film on location was the simplistic approach. If the plot is set in New York City, shooting it on location in New York City might seem a clever move. The opening of the film *West Side Story* shows how disheartening this can be. There are some brilliant shots of Jets doing jazz ballet turns in streets where nothing else is happening. The street becomes a space to be filled by the energy of something dangerous, this male dancing. (The parking garage for "Cool" works this way too, later.) The street functions as a stage in this regard. But then the Jets come upon a basketball court, where kids are playing. The space to be filled with dancing suddenly becomes a space for dribbling a basketball, and the awkwardness of putting these dancers into the space of these kids intensifies when one of the Jets demands the ball be passed to him! The Jets are ludicrously out of place snapping their fingers on a playground while ordinary kids shoot hoops. (And the kids are better basketball players.) This combination cannot be imagined in a theatre performance of *West Side Story*. No basketballs there, just dancing and a space to dance in, one defined by a high wall perhaps.

The Fred Astaire and Ginger Rodgers film musicals found their own way of defining a single space for the length of the dance. Astaire left the camera in one spot for most of his dances and even did entire numbers in one shot, as though a theatre dance was merely being filmed. No one ever thought these were theatre dances, though. They succeed as film dances because they define a dance space to be transgressed and come as close as possible to transgressing it without losing a step. The band pavilion for "Isn't It a Lovely Day" in *Top Hat* and the railed dance floor for "Pick Yourself Up" in *Swing Time* are such spaces, and "Pick Yourself Up" even does transgress the space when Fred and Ginger leap the rails, go beyond the limit, then dance back into the space. Even when they dance in a nightclub, as in "Cheek to Cheek" in *Top Hat*, they fill the entire dance area with their movement and grace, hinting that they have mastered this space and are on the verge of dancing beyond it. Fred's gimmick dances, such as the wall and ceiling dances in *Royal Wedding*, show the same tendency to let the dancing master the space by which it is confined. But the confining space has to be there, and when a film merely roams about in its "on location" freedom, dancing can seem groundless and uninteresting.

The film musical had to find its own spatiality. So long as it depended on the Astaire-Rogers use of dance floors or the on-location way of filming "real" spaces, it was trying to imitate the stage musical instead of finding conventions within the medium itself. Advances have now occurred. The space of the musical film has come to be interiorized, as though the eye or the dream or the hallucination were the location of the musical element. The film of *Chicago* is a case in point, for it transfers its musical numbers into Roxie's fantasy life and rejects the use of the stage space in the theatre version. The theatre version makes the stage into a nightclub, with show business serving as a metaphor for the system of justice in Chicago. Velma and most of the other imprisoned women are aware that they are in show business, with the lawyer Billy Flynn as their stage manager and leading performer. One woman never understands the metaphor—Hunyak, the Hungarian, who believes in truth instead of show business and is hanged. Roxie Hart does not grasp the show business metaphor at first, but she catches on once Billy Flynn works her over (the precise moment of her new understanding is "We Both Reached for the Gun," in which Billy turns her into a dummy and they put on what is actually an old vaudeville routine). So the stage on which the musical *Chicago* occurs, while it may from time to time seem to be Roxie's apartment or a law court, is really the stage of a nightclub, the space of the metaphor.

The film cannot use this idea. The film space is fluid and under the control of the camera, which opens new areas of spatial and narrative conventions but renders the theatre convention of a metaphorical stage space irrelevant. So the film of *Chicago* opens in a "real" nightclub, not a metaphorical one. Velma is performing in this nightclub at the beginning (just after she has murdered her sister and her boyfriend), and Roxie is on hand as a spectator. Then Roxie and her escort Fred leave the "real" nightclub and go to her "real" apartment, where before long Roxie kills Fred. Then the film moves to the "real" prison, where Roxie's vivid imagination lets her imagine various characters performing *as though* they were in a nightclub. The nightclub now becomes a product of Roxie's imagination. This makes for brilliant film-making, but it is a far cry from the metaphorical use of the stage in the musical as a space that stands for the places of the Chicago justice system. Now it is Roxie's mind that creates this connection, and she becomes the controlling point of view for the musical numbers, as though she and the camera can be one.

Films like *Moulin Rouge*, *Hedwig and the Angry Inch*, and *Dancer in the Dark* all participate in this discovery that musicals can create effects true to their own medium by violating the on-location effect and creating spaces of surrealism or hallucination for numbers to occur in. That is what happens when Roxie's imagination visualizes the nightclub numbers while she is in prison—the "location" becomes a fantasy. The space of the number is brought into congruence with the film medium, which is no longer serving as a nifty way of presenting the stage version.

The stage is for the vulnerability of performance, and it is only by degeneration from its own aesthetic principles that it becomes subject to the omniscience of the set design or the omniscience of the narrator. The *Chicago* dances in the film are so closely edited that Renée Zellweger (Roxie) seems to be a skilled dancer (she isn't). Lip-synching has long been used to make movie performers appear to be singing (they aren't). There is nothing odd about this in a film. On a stage, however, lip-synching is a scandal when it is used (this has happened), and dancers cannot be edited. The reason is that film musicals operate on an aesthetic system different from that of the stage, a system that thrives on the omniscience of the camera and brings all other elements of the performance under its control. It is an integrated form, unlike the stage musical, and it is one of the true inheritors of the Wagnerian aesthetic.

Chapter Eight

WHAT KIND OF DRAMA IS THIS?

STAGE musicals depend on such incongruities as Mrs. Lovett singing about cannibalism after Sweeney Todd has reached a peak of operatic fury in his "Epiphany." Why should incongruity be desirable, even a delight? The simpler pleasure would seem to be unity, a seamless interweaving of book and music, the Phantom disappearing to heart-rending orchestral accompaniment. The answer is that simpler pleasures are not what one goes to the theatre for in the first place. One goes looking for something other than totalizing systems of omniscience, something related to the strange business of watching people pretend to be other people and engage in made-up stories for hours at a time. That odd desire lies behind all theatre, the desire to see actors take on new characters, and it multiplies in the musical theatre, when the new characters break out in song and dance, adding musical selves to their book selves. They become doubly other, more than one person certainly, even more than two.

What kind of drama is this? It is popular and illegitimate, originating in vaudeville and revue as well as in operetta, and retaining links to the tradition of low culture despite its high prices. When *Oklahoma!* arrived in New York in 1943, one would have added that most musicals are comedies that end in marriage between hero and heroine, but the possibility that the genre was becoming a form of romantic comedy was brought to an end by Rodgers and Hammerstein themselves in *Carousel* (the marriage occurs early and the husband is killed) and *The King and I* (the attraction between Anna and the King of Siam cannot develop into romance), and by Elmer Rice, Kurt Weill, and Langston Hughes in *Street Scene* (the young lovers break apart at the end, after the girl's mother is murdered by her husband). Since then, and certainly since *West Side Story* in 1957, the most influential musicals have not had the love-and-marriage outcome of romantic comedy, and the question of what kind of drama this is demands a broad and inclusive answer.

In a central episode of Søren Kierkegaard's *Repetition*, the hero goes to the theatre in an effort to repeat a memorable experience. The hero in search of repetition is named Constantin Constantius. Kierkegaard is playing some jokes with us. This is the comic half of a book that (as with all of Kierkegaard's jokes) is meant to be utterly serious. Constantin Constantius seeks to repeat a memorable experience by going back to Berlin, taking the rooms he stayed in before, going to the same theatre he went to before—not the higher theatre of comedy or tragedy but farce theatre, the mixed-level musical theatre of the *posse*, at the Königstädter. This is a German version of the theatre we are examining—an illegitimate, popular musical theatre. The low-level musical theatre is where one can be "carried away," as Kierkegaard puts it, turned into new variations of oneself by music, dance, and comic routines that depend on the very thing, repetition, that the hero is trying unsuccessfully to create in his journey to Berlin.

Many people have been carried away by low-level theatre, especially when they are young. Kierkegaard says it is where one can hope to be "swept along into that artificial actuality in order like a double to see and hear himself and to split himself up into every possible variation of himself, and nevertheless in such a way that every variation is still himself."[1] Young people who might never read a word of Kierkegaard know this experience of being carried away by the illegitimate theatre. Their experience of growing up is intertwined with seeing their first musical in the theatre, with singing along with cast recordings, with slipping into Broadway houses at intermission to take a standing-room place for free, all in order to catch the excitement

---

[1] Kierkegaard, *Fear and Trembling/Repetition*, p. 154.

of the illegitimate theatre, the Broadway posse. Teenagers in America testify to this experience, as can be seen in recent retrospective books by John Clum, D. A. Miller, and Stacy Wolf. All three books are also about growing up gay—the appeal of double-coding in the subversive format of musicals is a powerful draw. Everyone who is drawn to the musical should listen to these books, for they are urgent accounts that can tell anyone what lies at the heart of the illegitimate theatre itself: it is not the gayness, or not only the gayness; it is the double-coding and the subversion and the repetition. The philosopher, the gays, the teenagers testify that low-class theatre will have its way with us, and readers who are old, straight, and nonphilosophical will have their own versions of being carried away. Kierkegaard knew that these experiences come about through repetition, which is what gives the musical its lift, its deepening, its ability to enter the second order of time, which I have called lyric time.

Constantin Constantius especially wants to see the popular comics Beckmann and Grobecker again and again. The comic Beckmann draws attention because of his pantomime ability and his unrestrained dancing. He has the ability to conjure up an entire environment by his way of walking: "with his little bundle on his back, his walking-stick in his hand, carefree and indefatigable, he is capable of coming on the stage with the street-urchins following him—which one does not see" (pp. 163–64). He is like Chaplin for later writers, a story in himself, thanks to his walk and his props. He is supposed to be playing an apprentice on the road, but really he is an "incognito in which dwells the mad demon of laughter." The demon is released when he dances. "He is now beside himself. The madness of laughter within him can no longer be contained." Bergmann releasing the demon inside him into the form of comic dance—this has happened before, again and again, and it leaves no room for settled thought about the morrow, or what one is going to do after the theatre, or how one's year is going. This is a travesty of ordered and settled life. It has happened before, but when it happens now it is bringing its pastness into fresh awareness of a present that needs no future. It is repetition.

The release of the demon in the time of dance catches one's eye. (The "musical comedy" episode of the television series *Buffy the Vampire Slayer* also has the demons being released through song and dance.) The plot is not being advanced when a number takes over the show; it is being suspended while repetition in song and dance releases its demons. Constantin Constantius does not talk about plots at the Königstädter. The farce is Nestroy's *Talisman*, but that is all he says about the story. The story suspended for the number is the important thing, the drama of release into multiplicity, where Beckmann is beside himself. The onlooker senses "every possible variation of himself," as does the performer, yet "in such a way that every variation is still himself."[2] This is a mirroring effect. The repetitive time of song and dance lets characters and audiences see themselves in a new way. Marriage was that new way when all musicals seemed to be romantic comedies ending in the embrace of heroes and heroines, but marriage is only one kind of new way, and it is the mirroring effect that runs throughout the genre.

MIRRORS: *A CHORUS LINE*, *PHANTOM OF THE OPERA*, *GYPSY*

That is to say, if principles of difference and incongruity are the basis of the form, a mirroring effect will necessarily be prominent. Elements different from one another will merely be incoherent unless they reflect one another in ways that can be grasped. "A Little Priest" in *Sweeney Todd* reflects on Sweeney's "Epiphany" by bringing manly revenge into the broader perspective of Mrs. Lovett's meat pie business. The spirit of travesty takes hold in the reflection—either element could be horrible by itself, but not in reflection on the other, not when the reflection is made through the rhyming contest that occurs in

[2] The non-Hegelian theatricality of Kierkegaardian repetition is a theme of Deleuze, *Difference and Repetition* and is further elaborated in Foucault's review of Deleuze, "Theatrum Philosophicum." See also Kawin, *Telling It Again and Again*, pp. 165–85. Abbate's definition of narrative in operatic music takes repetition seriously. See *Unsung Voices*, chapter 2.

FIGURE 7. Donna McKechnie in "The Music and the Mirror," from the original production of *A Chorus Line*. Used by permission of the photographer, Martha Swope.

the lyric of "A Little Priest." I am using mirroring as a metaphor here, but the metaphor has examples of real mirrors in musicals behind it. Mirror scenes happen often enough in musicals to make me think we can learn something from them.

For real mirrors in musicals, look at *A Chorus Line*. Dancers use mirrors for rehearsing, and *A Chorus Line* borrows this fact of the dancer's life in its solidly diegetic plot, which concerns the audition and rehearsals that lie behind a musical. The story of Cassie and Zach we have looked at before, and have noted that dancing itself is more of a dramatic event than anything that happens between them. Cassie has a big solo number late in the show, "The Music and the Mirror." The number alternates with moments of book dialogue. In the book, Cassie is talking with Zach about their previous relationship, but she is thinking of herself as a dancer too, and the number breaks in upon the book scene with changes of lighting and a shift of attention to the dancer's mirror. She can see herself dance in the mirror, the projection of herself which the number is drawing forth. This matters more to her than her old affair with Zach. Each time the lighting returns to book mode, Zach has a flat line which shows that he does not understand Cassie's intensity, or is backing away from it ("So you're going through a slow period, it happens to everyone"). The business about their old affair is boring, but Cassie's passion for dancing has tremendous power. She sees herself, as we do, reflected in the mirrors at the back of the stage, and her involvement in the mirror image of her dance leaves Zach trailing in the heterosexual dust. (She is saying that dance should have been the basis of her relationship with Zach, as if they could have had both, but he doesn't get it. His recuperation will come soon, in his sympathy for the injured dancer Paul.)

I have said in earlier chapters that the move into a number enlarges the book characters into new versions of themselves, song-and-dance versions. Cassie's mirror increases that effect and makes it visible. She sees herself as we see her, a dancer now and no longer only the woman who used to sleep with Zach, and she is drawn to her multiplied image in the same way we are, as though the multiplied image gives us something beyond our ordinary Zach-bound selves.

This effect of mirrors is called on in the final number of the show, the ensemble performance of "One" that we examined in chapter 5. How many dancers perform this final number? One would think it should be the winners of the audition, eight in number, Cassie included. But because this is also the curtain call for *A Chorus Line* itself, the eight losers also come out, and so does a seventeenth dancer, Paul, who was injured in the auditions. They are all wearing gold costumes. Zach should be there too, shouldn't he? and the dance captain? Some productions (but not the original Broadway staging) bring out the extra dancers from the opening number, who were cut early in

the show and spent the rest of the evening backstage.[3] The
point is that the people on stage in the final number are un-
countable, for the convention of the curtain call has merged
with this number ironically called "One," and with two things
going on at once there is no reason to be counting. The mirrors at the rear of the stage double all this.[4]

When mirrors are working well in a musical, in other words,
there is a surplus of identity in the doubling between book and
number scenes. What I mean by *surplus* might best be understood by looking at a mirror scene where there is no surplus or
doubling but only the use of a mirror by one character to control another. There is a mirror in Christine's dressing-room
in *Phantom of the Opera*, but it is not there for her to see her
reflection. The Phantom makes his spooky appearances in the
mirror, beckoning Christine to follow through the looking
glass, into passageways in the Paris Opera which reach to his
lair in the fifth basement. Christine lets herself be taken into
the mirror and finds herself subjected to high-tech power.
That is the literalization of what happens to Christine more
broadly in the action, where her courageous acts in contact
with the Phantom are shunted off into demonstrations of his
magic. This should be a drama of recognition on her part, but
instead it is a demonstration of Phantom power even up to the
point where the Phantom makes himself disappear for the last
time. We have discussed this effect at some length in chapter 7,
but we are being specific about mirrors in musicals now, and

[3] They have been singing from the wings, adding vocal power at climactic
moments. Giving them costumes for the final curtain call seems only fair and
in keeping with the spirit of the show, but it does add to the expenses.

[4] In one eventful Broadway performance on September 29, 1983, all previous performers of roles in what was just then becoming the longest running
musical in Broadway history were invited back to play their roles, and there
were over three hundred costumed dancers doing "One" at the end. See
Mandelbaum, A Chorus Line *and the Musicals of Michael Bennett*, pp. 227–33.
Nowhere is the drive for ensemble in the musical more fully realized than in
the final number of *A Chorus Line*, where all the dancers, winners and losers
alike, hold forth on the stage as if the jobs were theirs, and where it once happened that the previous dancers were there too, hundreds of them, without
changing the basic point of the show.

the one in this musical is a faux mirror, really a portal into the Phantom's magic, which is appropriate to a musical that increasingly becomes a through-sung opera but is not the kind that turns up in the book-and-number shows we are trying to define.

The mirroring that takes place in the book-and-number musical preserves the distance of reflection, the space over which incongruous images can be seen to cohere. When Boy Louise in *Gypsy* looks into *her* dressing-room mirror and sees a new version of herself reflected there—

> the only light on the stage is the glow of the mirror bulbs; the only figure is Louise. She looks at herself, goes close to the mirror to check her makeup, then suddenly stops. She touches her body lightly, moves back, straightens up, and stares at her reflection—

she has to have distance from her image. She is seeing herself as a girl—"Momma . . . I'm pretty . . . I'm a pretty girl, Momma"—and according to D. A. Miller's account of this moment, gay males in the audience are caught up in a crisis of observation, for they have been seeing Boy Louise in a mirror too, over another distance, and now she is about to become "Gypsy," knowing herself as a woman in numbers that require not dressing up but stripping down. Miller calls this mirror scene "perhaps the most moving but surely the most invidious moment in *Gypsy*."[5] The important word here is "invidious," because the recognition at hand is imbued with trouble—different trouble for different spectators. The point is not that the mirrored moments are pleasant but that they are penetrating, difficult, and brought about over a distance of observation. You must keep some distance between yourself and the mirror—Christine misses that point when she follows the Phantom. Distance is real and necessary to any recognition of the self that is open to change and not caught up in narcissism. The best reason why musicals alternate between book and number is that space is thereby preserved between the modes, a gap of difference that

---

[5] D. A. Miller, *Place for Us*, p. 88, from which I borrow the *Gypsy* quotations.

lets mirroring happen. But the recognition that can result from mirroring can be complex and disturbing.[6]

FOLLIES: WHO'S THAT WOMAN? THAT WOMEN IS ME.

Follies has a mirror scene, and ghostly surpluses to go with it. A reunion of former Follies performers is being held in the very theatre where the shows used to be held. The theatre is being torn down, but the producer of the old shows, Weissman by name (Ziegfeld by lineage), has invited his troupers from the old days for one last fling. The diegetic convention is at work, and many of the numbers consist of Follies veterans performing for one another and for the other partygoers at the Weissman reunion. The show revisits the old revue tradition, slotting in numbers simply because this is what old show people do when they have a party. The accompaniment for these numbers begins with the four-piece stage band Weissman has hired for the occasion, then the pit orchestra joins into the accompaniment, as though there is an ideal Follies performance built into this party, ready to well up in out-of-the-blue accompaniment. Also inherent in the party are ghostly versions of Follies girls, the younger selves of the partygoers, who sometimes mirror the dance steps of the partygoers and add a powerful resonance to the diegetic convention.

There is also a book, which focuses on two of the old-time showgirls, Phyllis and Sally, who have brought their husbands to the party. The husbands, Ben and Buddy, were stage-door Johnnies in the old days, when they were in law school. That is how they met Phyllis and Sally. The book centers on the unhappy marriages that have resulted. So *Follies* is both a revue

---

[6] For the mirror effect in literature, see Dallenback, *The Mirror in the Text*. Abbate neatly brings reflexivity to bear on opera in *Unsung Voices: Opera and Musical Narrative in the Nineteenth Century*. Postmarxist theory has made the mirror and theatricality into a special topos. For a summary, see Fuchs, *The Death of Character: Perspectives on Theater after Modernism*, pp. 150–51.

and a book show, a sort of experiment in the possibility of combining the two formats.

The four main characters spend much of their time feeling sorry for themselves in the book scenes, and one of the enduring puzzles of *Follies* is why it can be fascinating despite this concentration on self-pity. Ben and Phyllis, Buddy and Sally— the book scenes involving these four in their present-day unhappiness are static and humorless. The four become interesting because of the numbers they sing and because of their past, which is represented by the ghostly figures of their younger selves. The numbers add a layer of lyric time to the book, and the book adds its own extra layer of time in the younger selves. The younger selves have numbers too. The time of the present-day book can yield to a flashback book scene, which itself can yield to a number-within-the-flashback, so the discrepancies of time are manifold. It is even possible for the present-day characters to watch their younger selves performing a number, although this happens rarely. When it does happen, Ben, Phyllis, Sally, and Buddy are seeing themselves across two shifts of time at once, a chronological shift into the past and a lyrical shift into music. The younger selves in the number are vulnerable, just as all performers of numbers in musicals are vulnerable, but especially because they are being seen by the selves they will become. Not that they pay it much heed. Young people do not often notice the gaze of their own later selves. But we notice, and the later selves notice.

One of the best numbers in *Follies* is "Who's That Woman," known among the Follies girls who used to perform it as the Mirror Scene, because the performers admit that in singing about "the saddest gal in town" they are singing about themselves. In most productions they look into hand mirrors. At the Weissman party, they decide to do the number one last time. An old trouper named Stella takes the lead as she did in her Follies days, but she insists on being backed by the other Weissman veterans who are on hand—six of them, including Phyllis and Sally of the main plot. Their dancing is mirrored by their younger selves, real chorus girls playing ghosts, identical to one another in their tap costumes. The younger selves dance behind the veterans at the party, then move into line with them so that the two groups can dance together. At the end, the veterans are in the same positions where they began, but now each is paired with her own younger self.[7]

Since the actual performers of the veteran roles are themselves veterans of show business (Mary McCarty was Stella in the original production, with Dorothy Collins, Alexis Smith, Ethel Barrymore Colt, Yvonne DeCarlo, Helon Blount, and Sheila Smith as Stella's backup chorus line), there is a nostalgic realism to having the real old-girl troupers bring off the number while they are pretending to be old-girl troupers bringing off the number. A layer of extra attention is called for by the casting—Mary McCarty really can do this song and dance, which is supposed to be Stella's doing, and the same can be said for Dorothy Collins, Alexis Smith, and the others. Call this the foreground layer—the casting of Mary McCarty and company fronts the diegetic performance Stella and company give at the Weissman party.

The ghosts of Stella and the other veterans now can be seen as the background layer, and the result is a number enveloped by two layers of performance. The ghostly younger selves of the chorus girls in the background are present not because they are at the Weissman party but because they are summoned from some Follies of memory by the performance of this number. They are a function of the performance. They are from out of the blue. But they are imitating the Weissman girls at the party, dancing their every step behind them, so they belong to a diegetic moment.

Now look at the foreground layer—Mary McCarty, Alexis Smith, Dorothy Collins, the actresses who are playing Stella and the other Weissman girls. These celebrity actresses add a patina of their presence to the roles they play. "That's Dorothy Collins!" one is always thinking. "That's Yvonne DeCarlo? I thought she was dead" (which is virtually a line Yvonne DeCarlo

---

[7] Sondheim originally meant to have five veterans and six younger selves, to indicate that one of the veterans had died, but the numbers were evened in rehearsals. See Chapin, *Everything Was Possible*, pp. 39–40.

sang in one of her numbers, "I'm Still Here"). There is a shadow of difference between the celebrated actress and her role. There is also a difference between the ghostly chorus girls in the background and Stella and the other Weissman girls at the party. These identities are supposed to be unified. Stella and her ghostly younger self in the background are supposed to be one person, but the ghost is a young woman wearing a costume from the Follies of 1941, while Stella is getting old and is in party clothes of 1997. What about Mary McCarty, playing Stella? She is supposed to be the same as Stella too, but we are aware that she is really Mary McCarty. Stella and other veterans at the Weissman party are reflections of their own past selves, the ghostly background insists. Stella and the other Weissman girls are also reflections of their present-day Mary McCarty/Alexis Smith selves, the celebrity casting insists. These Weissman girls are double reflections of other selves, the background ghosts and the foreground celebrity performers, which means that the ghosts and the celebrity performers have something in common.[8]

The reason *Follies* is so moving, despite the inadequacies of the book involving the four main characters, lies here, in the reflection between Dorothy Collins and the ghostly Young Sally, or Alexis Smith and the ghostly Young Phyllis, or Ethel Barrymore Colt and the ghostly Christine who dances behind her in the mirror number. The list could go on—ghosts abound. One cannot shy away from the nostalgia of seeing these old-timers do their numbers as though they were young, or the ironic humor that attends the presence of actually young chorus girls mirroring their moves in the background. I am no longer talking about Phyllis and Sally, the book characters. I am talking about their reflections, the foreground and the background performers, for that is the heart of *Follies*. The genius of the show is that it complicates the book characters by layering them with dimensions of performance that can be seen at once, as the number is performed. One dimension is

---

[8] For the "ghost" effect, see Carlson, "Ghosts and *Follies*." My thanks to Tom Herson for information about Ethel Barrymore Colt.

the past selves of Stella and the Weissman girls, dancing a re-flection of their every step. Another dimension is middle-aged actresses like Dorothy Collins and Alexis Smith dancing those steps too, having the nerve to put themselves into the area of vulnerability, the stage, bringing off a song-and-dance number when they could be home with the grandchildren. The result is that the numbers performed by the ghosts and the actual per-formers criss-cross the book characters, the Weissman girls, with dimensions of flashback time and lyric time that encircle the ordinariness of middle age with music.

Why is this called "The Mirror Number"? The lyric is about Stella and the other Follies dancers "seeing themselves" in their account of a sophisticated lady who is really the "sad-dest gal in town." But we are seeing another version of "them-selves" in the mirroring of the ghostly tap dancers performing behind, and in the performances of the real veterans playing the roles. The "mirror" of the lyric is complicated by the "mir-rors" of the ghostly dancers and the celebrity performers. The question of "who's that woman" admits of no single answer, but the dancing is filled with elation. The question of identity is raised throughout the show for the leading male characters too, Ben and Buddy, who are also ghosted by their younger selves and played by celebrities. "Who am I?" is the persistent question of this musical.

Numbers as Resistance to Such Talk

Such a heartfelt, earnest question—the sort musicals refuse to answer. The resistance that occurs between book and number wants to rule out simple answers to questions of identity. Musi-cals have been written on the premise that "I am what I am," but this is a reduction of the form itself, which is capable of rec-ognizing that "I am what I am and then some" through the double order of time. When Stella sings "Who's that woman, that woman is me," her younger self is dancing too, not to men-tion Mary McCarty, and there are the other old-girl/younger self combinations in the number too. "Who are we?" gets closer to the ensemble quality of the musical than "who am I?" but the answer is not going to come in the form of psychological explanation. Hidden depths of character are out of keeping in the musical. The numbers are invasions of interiority, subtext disguised as song and dance—"travesty" is the precise name for this—and "who are we?" receives its answer primarily as a travesty performance of the interior recognition, "that woman is me," in what I have been calling the space of vulnerability.

Hidden depths of character, by contrast, *are* important to the theatre of realism. The wellspring of character is subtextual, lying beneath the spoken text as the source of motivation. Realistic actors are invited to analyze this source in order to gain a deep sense of their roles. The musical evacuates this hidden area through its numbers, which leave no impression of the unspoken behind the performance—what matters is being redressed and opened to view. It is not the only form of theatre to practice this invasion, but it is the one that practices it cheerfully. Greek drama, which also invades hidden motives, tends toward the solemn or frantic in bringing the hidden to the surface, but the musical is always prepared for the gleeful. The women in *Follies* seem cheerful and energetic in performing the discovery—we are all the saddest woman in town. Numbers do not represent the subtextual so much as they pick it up, turn it into forms of entertainment, open it to view as a performance, a travesty.

There are, of course, songs of misery in musicals. The great torch song tradition in American popular music has produced some first-rate show tunes of the "Why Was I Born" variety (Kern and Hammerstein, *Sweet Adeline*), but even in songs with a pathetic or tragic edge, the directness of the lyric and the standardization of the musical structure simplify the ongoing trauma and make it performable. Serious matter is no doubt being trivialized in the process. A forgettable number settles for the trivialization. A memorable torch song pursues the trivial into such overlaps of repetition—what I have called syncopations of repetition, the body and voice of the performers picking up the differences among the meter of the verse, the beat of the rhythm, the pace of the stanzas—that this travesty of the private self touches us and makes us want to join it. The torch song like "The Man I Love" that gets out of its show and becomes a standard makes people hum along, or dance—hum the misery, dance the anguish. Some may think *travesty* misses the tone of such performed anguish. I do not think so. A travesty is a disguising of something more serious than itself, but in articulating the trauma and making it performable, the travesty torch song can be moving and unsettling. It is the disguising of anguish into an accomplished performance that matters most in the torch song. Of course the woman is unhappy. But look at the disguise she is bringing off—it turns anguish into song, a travesty of trauma, a performance deserving applause.

The torch song in *Follies* occurs in the concluding series of numbers, "Loveland," where each of the four main characters suddenly has a Follies routine to perform. There is no book reason for the performance of these numbers. The reunion of former Weissman girls gives way to an eruption of parody Follies called "Loveland," and this ends with each of the four leading characters coming on for a vaudeville routine that dashes the last element of romantic illusion from their lives. Their underlying anxieties turn into show business. Buddy, now a clown in baggy pants with a wooden car around his waist, sings "The God-Why-Don't-You-Love-Me Blues," a clownish routine that demolishes the notion that the girlfriend waiting for him in Dallas, Margie, understands and appreciates him for what he is. The torch song follows. It is Sally's "Losing My Mind," in which the title phrase shakes her with the possibility that this is true. The woman may be going mad in her loneliness. It was originally written for Phyllis, but then was shifted to Sally when it was found to be better suited to Dorothy Collins's style. The unique psyche is not to the point here. The song does not "represent" the subtext of character. Instead it tampers with subtext by turning it into rhyme and the thirty-two-measure AABA structure used for countless torch songs before. This time the torch singer really is going crazy, perhaps, and she is Sally because Dorothy Collins could handle the song better than Alexis Smith could.[9] Alexis Smith was then to do a mock striptease, "Ah, But Underneath," in which Phyllis was to admit there is nothing beneath her surface appearance, but Sondheim then came up with a different solo, a vamp number in which Phyllis is both "Lucy and Jessie"—that is, a split personality. "Ben's Folly," a suave, top-hat-and-tails piece in the manner of Fred Astaire called "Live, Laugh, Love," amounts to a performance breakdown over the discovery that he is worthless, a "nothing."

I have called the stage an area of vulnerability for singers and dancers. Vulnerability is the keynote for all four of these characters in the book of *Follies*, and now, transported to a Follies within the *Follies*, they become song-and-dance figures beyond the range of the book, threatened with the vulnerability of performance itself. Three of them will make it through. They will finish their numbers and be so good at performance that their musical selves will outdistance their self-pitying book selves. Buddy in his clown's routine, mastering the tongue-twisting lyric and making a fool of himself, too, rises above anything else we have seen him do. Sally's "Losing My Mind" is her finest number. Elegant, perfectly dressed and made up, going crazy—she is startling, unexpected, hardly the earnest "little Sally" we have seen before. Phyllis has mastered the vamp routines so that she can swing between "Jessie" and "Lucy" without missing a beat. But disaster is always waiting to happen in the area of vulnerability, and in Ben's number the disaster breaks open. He loses track of his lyric, he asks the conductor—the actual conductor in the pit—for his words, he trips, he collapses, while the chorus line cuties behind him keep on singing and dancing as though he were not even there.

Then, with Ben collapsed and calling for help, the Follies apparatus disappears and we are back into the book, which is all that the main characters have left. Performance is now beyond them. Their subtexts have been played out, and they have no performance versions of themselves left. They cannot be imagined singing and dancing again, and book time may have

[9] See Chapin, *Everything Was Possible*, p. 94.

also reached the end. Buddy makes a remark about what will happen "tomorrow," and Sally, seeing the morning light in the window, says "Oh, my God, it *is* tomorrow." Book time has no future apart from the desolation they feel now.

Ben cries out for help from Phyllis. She and the other two get him back on his feet, and the four leave the theatre, go out into the street. They are being watched by their younger selves, standing to the side of the stage. Do the younger selves see what their lives will become? That question is never answered. It is enlarged instead, not answered but brought across to the audience, for we see the young watching their older selves fade into disrepair and misery, but then the young start into a reprise of the show's opening number. "Hey, up there," the young Buddy and Ben are calling to their chorus-girl sweethearts. They are starting over! *They* have numbers left to perform, the same numbers we have seen. Repetition for the young, into the street for the old.

Think of the audience at this point. The back wall of the Weissman theatre has disappeared, according to the stage directions. We are now seeing the back wall of the theatre in which we sit, the Winter Garden Theatre in 1971, let us say. In the original production, part of the street outside the Winter Garden was supposed to be visible through a window.[10] Ben and the others have gone out there. We will be going out there in a minute. The space of vulnerability includes the older selves, the younger selves, and ourselves. This is mirroring without an actual mirror. We are being brought around to ourselves and our own theatre, not yet rubble, not yet haunted with ghosts, although these things will come in time. Yet the reprise is taking place. This is desolate and beautiful, the ending of *Follies*. The reprise asserts itself as though the show could not help going on, but for the people going out into the morning light, the show is over.

---

[10] Again, I follow the original production of 1971. The 2001 edition, reflecting the London revision, omitted the directions specifying the removal of the rear wall of the Weisman theatre and calling for a street view out the window. The Broadway revival of 2001, directed by Matthew Warchus, was staged in the decaying Belasco Theatre, where rubble was left lying about.

DISCOMFORT

The composer and lyricist Michael Friedman, writing in the *London Review of Books*, has recently asked why the musical makes intellectuals uncomfortable.[11] The expected answer might be that intellectuals tend to dislike popular entertainment, but the answer Friedman gives is better. It's the music that causes trouble. The songs seem designed to make audiences feel good, Friedman says, but they have an unsettling effect anyway, because they resist the book. They stand apart from the book, even from the book with which they might seem to be integrated, declaring that something else is going on here, something that the book cannot observe, something that might be under the surface. We are adding that the numbers do not leave the secret under the surface. They dally with the secret and rearrange it into song and dance, often with a glee that can be disturbing.

In chapter 1 I noted Rousseau's dislike of the mixture of speech and song in opera. Rousseau was presenting himself as an uncomfortable intellectual, and while opera advanced in the next century to create a through-composed solution to the problem, the musical arose in the century after that to repackage the discomfort in its book-and-number formats. The number resists the book even when it closely dovetails with the book, and if Friedman is right to say that it is the musical side of the disjunction that makes us uncomfortable, we are adding that this lyric dedication to tapping into the wellsprings of our behavior, this travesty of our private anxieties and desires, ought to be disturbing at the same time it is being pleasurable. The songs and dances are not very disturbing, and the pleasure can be fine—but even then, we know the disturbance as a silhouette of the pleasure.

Here is one of the finest London drama critics, Harold Hobson, showing his discomfort over a Sondheim musical. Review-

---

[11] Friedman, review of Knapp, *The American Musical and the Formation of National Identity*.

ing the first London production of *Company* in 1972, Hobson wrote: "It is extraordinary that a musical, the most trivial of theatrical forms, should be able to plunge as *Company* does with perfect congruity into the profound depths of human perplexity and misery."[12] The remark about "the most trivial of theatrical forms" sounds like the New Critics of the 1940s and 1950s, but the Hobson of the 1970s is caught off guard by triviality that plunges into the depths of human distress. "Congruity" is the word by which he retains his balance, but the more one thinks about *Company*, with its revue format on the theme of "should Bobby get married?" and its deftness at setting matrimonial anxiety into show tunes, the more the right word would have to be *incongruity*. How can the most trivial of theatrical forms plunge so deep as to throw a good critic off balance? One wonders if a good musical penetrates human perplexity and misery because what seems to be triviality becomes a complex opening of private matters into the gaiety of the numbers.

In Sondheim's *Assassins*, there is a vaudeville soft-shoe number at the beginning and end of the show, "Everybody's Got the Right to Be Happy." That it builds to an ensemble number sung by those who have killed or have tried to kill American presidents is part of its iconoclastic brilliance. The other part is that the tune turns out to be a standard format, the AABA format, the most common in American popular song, the one we have followed in earlier chapters. One doesn't know it will turn out to be AABA until the end of the song. At the beginning the A and B sections are kept apart, interspersed with other elements.[13] At the end, the structure is finally intact, AABA, with the entire company singing. Part of the drama is the achieving of the AABA format.

[12] Quoted in Secrest, *Stephen Sondheim*, p. 195.

[13] To be exact, B is sung when John Wilkes Booth has a solo turn with the number, and it centers an ABA pattern. But the complete AABA structure is for the entire group of assassins, at the end of the show. Swagne, *How Sondheim Found His Sound*, pp. 47–124, shows the extent to which Sondheim extends or revises standard song formats. My point is that one also recognizes the formats that are being extended or revised.

AABA is a trivial form—commonplace, found everywhere, the sort of thing Hobson would have been ready to write off when a musical surprised him with its depth. Some AABA songs do run deep in our culture and become instantly recognizable wherever you are. When Adele Astaire fell in love with her cross-Atlantic aviator in *Funny Face*, it was an AABA format that they sang together ("S'Wonderful"). When Joe and the black male chorus carried *Show Boat* beyond its love-at-first-sight routine to voice the despair and endurance of men trapped in labor, it was an AABA format they sang together ("Ol' Man River"). The balcony scene for Tony and Maria was AABA ("Tonight"). Anyone can make a list of AABA songs that express American values of widely different kinds, but Sondheim works this structure out as a kind of ensemble triumph for John Wilkes Booth, Lee Harvey Oswald, Leon Czolgosz, John Hinckley, Charles Guiteau, Giuseppe Zangara, Samuel Byck, Squeaky Fromme, and Sara Jane Moore, their one common element being the intention to assassinate an American president, and in doing so he is throwing wealth and power off balance.

Cassie seeing herself in the mirror in *A Chorus Line* is seeing herself as dancer dancing. This is the point of resistance that throws power off balance. Zach doesn't get it about Cassie. She puts him off balance. When Louise sees herself in the mirror in *Gypsy*, Mama Rose is put off balance. In the illegitimate theatre Kierkegaard finds variations of oneself when one is still oneself, and this is actually staged in the mirror number of *Follies*, when the veteran showgirls dance in ensemble with their younger selves. The discovery that the saddest woman in town is myself, or that I am beautiful and a woman despite Mama's way of defining me, or that I am a dancer before I am Zach's woman—these look like psychological moments, but they ring truest in their challenge to wealth and power, and that is the challenge of having a surplus of identity which wealth and power cannot fix in place. This is a political challenge.

Kierkegaard was not thinking politically when he sent Constantine Constantius in search of repetition, nor are the mirror scenes I have mentioned political in design, but these instances of multiplied self that put power off balance bear on Brecht's theory of estrangement in the Epic Theatre, where the actor seeks to become a reporter of his character's actions even as he plays the character. Brecht sought political explicitness in the estrangement effect and Kierkegaard did not. Brecht would have objected to the rhetoric of being carried away. But the demon is released in both Brecht and Kierkegaard, in outbreaks of doubleness valued for their resistance to linear plots, and the resistance subverts established norms in ways true to the low and illegitimate theatre.

What kind of theatre is this? Its invasions of subtext turn hidden motives into song and dance, but the demon released in the performance of a number resists definition. Readers of Kierkegaard would say it is non-Hegelian. Readers of Brecht would say it is non-Aristotelian. There would be heated arguments, but they are saying what this theatre is not, and the exchange of negativity would imply that the musical is doubly theatrical, ready to travesty any attempt to think of it as one thing. The numbers counter the book by bringing its agents into a second order of time. Characters expand into song and dance, resisting expectations that action is progressive, substituting repetition instead, and making intellectuals uncomfortable. It is not closet drama at all. It brings what is closeted to the stage in the spirit of performance—one reason why gay spectators are among its ardent followers. But everyone has a closet. This theatre is prepared to open the door and be gleeful with what it finds there. It is not that the contents of repression are represented. It is that they are reformulated into what may look like the triviality of song and dance, catching power off guard, and insisting in its ensemble tendency that this invasion of our privacy is not so much psychological as it is political. Or at least it yearns to be political. Most musicals, including most good musicals, are not overtly political. But they belong to a theatre aesthetic that looks toward the political, not with the direct glare of Brecht and not with the sidelong glance of Kierkegaard, but with full regard for the principles of difference that we have been finding at the heart of the genre.

POLITICAL DRAMA: *CABARET* AND *PACIFIC OVERTURES*

Let us be specific. Here are two examples of musicals that open the political implications of the musical to view. They are not from the 1930s, when in fact there were a number of explicitly political musicals (*The Cradle Will Rock*, *Pins and Needles*), but from a later time, when the political determination of the 1930s might be supposed to have drained away from Broadway. They are *Cabaret* (1966) and *Pacific Overtures* (1976), both chosen because they have proved to be revivable shows and because they mark out the political turn that can be given to the conventions we have found to be basic to the musical.

Cabaret is one of the explicitly Brechtian musicals. It looks back to the Brecht/Weill *Three Penny Opera* and it is a version of Christopher Isherwood's account of the rise of Nazism in *Berlin Stories*. The conclusion of the musical is what interests me here, for it uses the convention of reprising an earlier number to bring about a strange duet between two characters who never interact earlier in the plot. Then, after a reprise of another song, a large mirror swings into position so that the audience may gaze upon itself. (The mirror was part of Hal Prince's staging of the original production, but it is used often in other stagings.) The reprises and the mirror combine to give the musical an explicitly political conclusion.

The final scene shows Cliff on a train, leaving Berlin. Knowing that Sally Bowles has decided to stay and that this episode in his life is over, he begins to write his "Berlin Stories." They will be rather like the source upon which the musical we have just seen is based, Isherwood's *Berlin Stories*. "There was a cabaret and there was a master of ceremonies and there was a city called Berlin in a country called Germany—and it was the end of the world and I was dancing with Sally Bowles—and we were both fast asleep."[14] That is what Cliff is writing on the train. Christopher Isherwood wrote better prose than this, but the idea is that Cliff is becoming the author of the story we have just seen, a narrator after the fact. The pretended source is beginning to appear as a result of the musical.

Then Cliff begins to sing "Willkommen." This is odd, for he is reprising the Welcoming Song that the Emcee sang at the Kit Kat Klub near the beginning of the show. Cliff is leaving, and by now we know that the Kit Kat Klub is a place for Nazis. This is what he wants to leave behind. Perhaps he is just being sardonic with his "Willkommen." Or perhaps we are being welcomed to the pretended "Berlin Stories" that Cliff is beginning to write. But what happens next is even stranger. The Emcee from the Kit Kat Klub enters, comes downstage, and joins Cliff in the song. What are these two doing, singing the same song?

The answer lies in the real source. Isherwood's *Berlin Stories* insists that a neutral observer in Berlin cannot stay free from complicity with Nazism. "I am a camera," Isherwood writes near the beginning, as though he could be pure and objective. In moments of political crisis, however, there is no purity. In the "Sally Bowles" story that is the main source for *Cabaret*, he recognizes the danger of being a mere observer of Nazism in its rise. We glanced at this passage earlier: "In a few days, I thought, we shall have forfeited all kinship with ninety-nine percent of the population of the world."[15] He may be telling a story critical of Nazism, but in belonging to the story himself, he has been complicit with the thing he is criticizing. That has been Cliff's realization toward the end of *Cabaret*. It is why he is leaving, perhaps why he is writing. And in the ambiguity of his position, he is like the ambiguous Emcee, who always seems to know what is going on inside and outside the cabaret even as he seems to remain detached from it.

That is why they belong together for "Willkommen" at the end. The drama makes it clear that one cannot enter into the

[14] *Cabaret* libretto, pp. 112–13.
[15] Isherwood, "Goodbye to Berlin," p. 49 in *The Berlin Stories*.

cabaret, a metaphor for Nazism on the rise, and then leave it behind as though one were free of the experience. We have been in the cabaret too, watching a show. There is ambiguity for us too. Remember the mirror. Cliff fades into a blackout, leaving us face to face with the Emcee, a reminder that we have been assuming, as Cliff did, that watching a cabaret is diverting and nonpolitical. The cabaret reappears, there is a last rendition of the "Cabaret" number by Sally Bowles, we are back in the setting of the show, and suddenly there is nothing but the mirror, which swings into position so that we can see ourselves looking at the cabaret set. There is nothing to look at except a neon sign saying "Cabaret" and the mirror—and the reflection of ourselves, looking. Sally Bowles is gone. Cliff is gone. So is the ambiguous Emcee. But we are still at the cabaret. It is an unpleasant ending, for we are meant to recognize that our own attendance at the cabaret has the same political implications Cliff discovered, and we had thought it was just show business.[16]

My other example is from the ending of act 1 in *Pacific Overtures*, where the disjunction between book and number is carried to such a lovely point that no one can say what is happening in the book. The number is "Someone in a Tree," which Sondheim says he is proudest to have written of all his songs,[17] and it comes at a crucial turn in the book, or what would be a crucial turn if we could see the scene. But we cannot see it. We hear the performance of the song instead, and the song is about the inability of anyone to say what is happening in the plot. The number also divides a character into a younger and an older self, demonstrating the double order of time that numbers always bring into this kind of drama.

The book scene is taking place in the Treaty Hut that the Japanese have built for the first visit of Admiral Perry and his cohorts, who have insisted on landing and forging a trade agreement with Japan. Intent on keeping foreign feet from touching

---

[16] Again, I am following the original staging of 1966, which was Hal Prince's work. In Sam Mendes's long-running production of the 1990s, the audience was left face-to-face with a representation of a Nazi gas chamber.

[17] Quoted in Secrest, *Sondheim*, p. 281.

their soil, the Japanese have rigged a gangway of straw mats leading into the Treaty House. The mats and the floorboards are to keep the soil untouched by foreign feet. There is also a Samurai hidden under the floorboards to cut the Americans down should they draw their guns.

The scene remains outside the hut in which the expected book action is supposed to be occurring. Everyone is out of sight except the Reciter—a narrative figure from the Kabuki tradition, which is basic to the staging of the entire show. The Reciter is far from omniscient as a narrator. He announces that no one really knows what transpired during the meeting with the Americans. A key scene in the plot is about to remain obscure when an aged figure appears to the sound of orchestral music, says "Pardon me" to the Reciter, and announces that he knows what happened in the Treaty House. As a young boy he had been looking on from a nearby tree. The number that is now beginning will supply the information that is obscured by the hut. The number develops into a trio when the old man's younger self, the Boy, climbs the tree to gain the best vantage point, and the Samurai warrior is revealed beneath the Treaty House—he heard everything, he says. But we never do find out what happened in that hut. The book scene remains hidden, and "Someone in a Tree" fails to say what happened inside the hut. The three reporters cannot get beyond the groaning of the occasional floorboard and the sight of some gold on the uniforms. The singers are quite certain they have settled the matter, however—"if it happened, I was there" is the mark of their confidence—and they depart with no advance at all having been made toward revealing the episode inside the hut.

The beauty of the song is that it frustrates our desire for narrative completeness and substitutes the satisfaction of another desire, a desire for lyric and musical completeness, the time of the number. Nothing happens in the book. "It's the fragment, not the day" that matters in this number, "the pebble, not the stream." The Zen-oriented implication is that accounting for bits of things is more important than the Western-oriented drive for narrative closure. Yet the singing of the number does reach its own form of closure, through the kinds of repetition that lyric is capable of, and when the three singers join in their final chorus, lyric time has replaced book time in carrying through to an ending. The singers disappear, the narrator is left with no knowledge of what has transpired, and the displacement of the book by the number has reached a triumphant demonstration. Or is it a triumphant failure? The singers do not deliver on their promise of a narrative, but they do deliver the other order of time, the song. I suspect one reason Sondheim loves this number above his others is that it solves a kind of puzzle: Can a number actually focus on a book scene that remains unknown in the show? It can, and it does.[18]

There is nothing overtly political about that number. It lines up with the aesthetic questions we have been discussing. Yet it also aims for political implications. Keep an eye on what happens next. The Americans troop out of the hut, the narrator pretends to get things wrong by announcing that these invaders are departing never to return, and there appears alone on the stage the one American who has not left, the frightful-looking, lion-maned Admiral Perry himself, who ends act 1 with a ferocious combination of Kabuki dancing and American cakewalk. That no foreign foot has touched Japanese soil is now disproved, and the proof is in this wordless dance. Perry's feet dance over the entire stage, the space that has been Japan so far. The dance is grotesque and unsettling. The Japanese and American elements are jumbled together in sheer assertiveness, and there is no progression toward an outcome beyond this sensationally danced confusion of cultures. The political implication is there, but it is carried by the styles of performance. That traditional Japanese culture has been dislodged goes without saying. That traditional Japanese culture leaves distinct elements behind to be Americanized also

---

[18] Sondheim's own account of how the puzzle works out is strictly musical. "It's sixty bars of one chord. But the rhythm keeps changing, and the texture keeps changing, and *where* the chord keeps getting placed just changes a little bit at a time—maybe every four bars, or every eight bars. . . . It's minimalist music. Nothing's going on, but everything's going on." Quoted in Horowitz, *Sondheim on Music: Minor Details and Major Decisions*, p. 158.

FIGURE 8. Admiral Perry sets foot on Japanese soil. Haruki Fujimoto in the "Lion Dance," from the original production of *Pacific Overtures*. Used by permission of the photographer, Martha Swope.

goes without saying—for that is the show we are seeing at this moment, an American show that pretends to be created from a Japanese perspective, with a Japanese dancer who can turn his body into Kabuki and cakewalking shapes in the same instant.

These numbers stop the show. "Someone in a Tree" stops it because it surrounds a book scene that is not there, a turning point that lies beyond narration. A spot of absence in the plot is being sung about as though it were a presence, and the fullness of the music resonates not against character or action or any other part of the book but against a vacancy. When the book does resume, it leaves behind a demon, the bizarre figure of the Kabuki Admiral Perry, whose Lion Dance reflects the conflict of the entire musical. It is a moment of sheer performance in which one reads the Japanese/American situation through wordless dance.

Why it should be the cakewalk that is imposed on the traditional Japanese dance? The cakewalk was invented by slaves in America, black people who were mocking the fancy ways of white society while keeping in touch with the syncopation of remembered African song and dance. The real Admiral Perry would have done the cakewalk no more often than he did a Kabuki Lion Dance. Assigning it incongruously to this frightful Admiral Perry is a reminder that the United States has engaged other races and other cultures before the Japanese. The cakewalk routine puts Admiral Perry's power into touch with the slavery on which it is founded. Nowhere else in *Pacific Overtures* is this connection made. It is made here without words, strictly in a number that keeps its distance from the book and is capable of adding its wordless meaning by remaining apart.

The difference between lyric time and progressive time is to the point here, and one can dwell on the idea that Japanese culture, capable of the grace and restraint of the haiku, holds more firmly to lyric time than does American culture, with its drive toward narrative progress. The numbers have been largely Japanese in orientation in act 1. A particularly lovely song has been an exchange of haiku verses between two of the leading Japanese characters. It is called "Your Turn," because it turns from one man to the other and back again, a back and forth of haikus that refuses narrative time in favor of repetitive time, although the men are on a journey that will have a disastrous outcome.

The other side of "Your Turn" is "Next," the Westernized rock-and-roll extravaganza with which the show ends.[19] The entire company is now dressed modern and dancing a furious account of the Americanization of Japan over a period of 130 years after Perry's first visit. The jumble of cultures is charged with the energy of the choreography and the orchestration. The drive toward new things is taking over from the lyricism of traditional Japanese culture: so much for "Your Turn." The Japanese air attack on Pearl Harbor was represented in the original production, and still is. For some reason, the ultimate American response at Hiroshima and Nagasaki was not alluded to in the original, but it is now, in the major revivals. An explosion blasts the dancers off their feet, and they must rebuild the dance out of ruin. The four numbers we have been discussing—"Your Turn," "Someone in a Tree," "Lion Dance," and "Next"—mirror and supplement the book of the show even as they interrupt or displace it. They turn the political issues of Japanese/American relationships into harsh pulsations of song and dance. This show is fierce in its politics.

COHERENCE AND INTEGRATION

All the shows we have discussed in this chapter are radical—not in their politics but in their aesthetics, their penchant for getting to the roots of the musical and dramatizing the conventions of the form. *A Chorus Line* ends with a curtain call that is also the culmination of the book, and brings countless singers and dancers to the stage. *Cabaret* ends with a hero beginning to write the book on which it could be based, and then introduces an empty stage where the audience sees itself in the place of Nazi spectators. *Follies* is about showgirls engaged in putting on numbers in a theatre. *Pacific Overtures* removes a

[19] "Next" can also be seen as the counterpart to the opening song, "The Advantages of Floating in the Middle of the Sea." See Knapp, *The American Musical and the Formation of National Identity*, pp. 277–78. Banfield, *Sondheim's Broadway Musicals*, pp. 249–280, and Horowitz, *Sondheim on Music*, pp. 155–64, provide thorough musical analyses.

crucial book scene from our view and supplies a boy singing in a tree about the scene he cannot see either, for the benefit of himself as an old man who cannot remember it. Had anyone described these scenes for Jerome Kern and asked him to write the show they come from, he would have declined. They go too far for Kern. Yet the scenes involve the same conventions Kern helped to establish. They make the genre aware of itself, forming an attitude of aesthetic radicalism that refuses to be controlled by the established conventions even when the established conventions are the source of inspiration.

The mirroring that runs through these examples suggests that the main issue is not how elements of the musical are forged into a unity but how the elements remain distinct enough to reflect each other, as though difference could be the groundwork for coherence. *Coherence* is the word I am after. I have been using the term mirrors because musicals use them too, but when difference is working well in a book-and-number format, coherence is the result—different things holding together by adherence to common principles, when they could very well be flying apart. In calling the stage an area of vulnerability, I mean there is a danger of things flying apart. In referring to the voice of the musical, I mean there is a musical formality that holds them together, songs and dances working by design, singers and dancers recognizing the same beat and going on with it. In saying there are multiple selves projected by the singers and dancers, so that their characters are more than single personages, I mean that these people have the power to exceed their ordinary selves and cannot be pinned down. The deeper feelings are coming to the surface, and gaiety is at work in the upsurge. Actors take on otherness by acting in the first place, then they multiply the otherness by singing and dancing too, and their singing and dancing can be matched by others who share the voice of the musical. They are giving Kierkegaard's demon an outing, and they are only trying to put a number across.

I take "coherence" to be a political word as well as an aesthetic word. I set it forth as a better word for the aesthetics of the musical than "integration," the word that usually attends the form. Integration is a political word too, and it means something different from coherence. Integration means the blending of difference into similarity, as though things are being melted in a pot. It would produce a unified whole, both in its political idealism and in its aesthetic meaning. When I suggested that writers coming after Rodgers and Hammerstein used their accomplishments to turn the convention of ensemble performance in very different directions, harsher directions, directions that reject the "June Is Bustin' Out All Over" kind of celebration, I had in mind writers who have revised the sentimentality of the Rodgers and Hammerstein ethos without abandoning the artistic principles of the form which Rodgers and Hammerstein popularized and broadened. The later musicals we have been discussing show that aesthetic integration was never the real issue in this artistic form. The real issue was always coherence, which could be masked into integration for a time but which would eventually reassert itself.

Coherence means things stick together, different things, without losing their difference. That is literally what the word means. Different elements managing to stick together without losing their individual identities is coherence in a musical no less obviously than in a city or a state. I do not mean that the best musicals are political in themselves. Most musicals are not political, but all musicals depend on conventions that translate into political terms. The political implication comes from the conventions of the musical itself, which establish a groundwork of doubled time and character, source stories reformulated into the routines of the show business, raids on private motives most of us keep to ourselves in normal life, a delight in throwing authority off balance, and a desire to maintain song-and-dance formats that go back to Harlem and the Lower East Side. It is an illegitimate drama that disturbs the managers of our affairs the more it remains true to its roots in popular entertainment. Its aesthetic is radical, and that means its political potential is always there, as a matter of the form.

The future of the musical has two broad paths before it. One is the way of high-tech integration, which I have suggested degenerates from the conventions of song-and-dance performance. These shows push in the direction of aesthetic integration, and their political implications are imbued with conservatism and profitability. The other way opens out from Sondheim and the other writers who use the song-and-dance conventions and reflect upon them. I think writers following the Sondheim way will become increasingly political as the genre matures, because the elation that comes from the best shows, their numbers and books interrupting each other to the point of reflecting the interests of both, resembles the political energy that comes from people with differences coordinating into a productive relationship. Rodgers and Hammerstein expanded the sentimentality inherent in that view, and the writers who followed their lead turned the ensemble tendency of the genre into irony or anger. They did not eliminate sentiment. They have proved that when sentiment is recognized in a structure of coherence, it is one of the elements that stick together. It joins with other interests, such as the aesthetic interest in finishing designs that runs through *Sunday in the Park with George*, or the search for an end to trauma that runs through *Lady in the Dark*, or the determination to reinvent famous plays that runs through *My Fair Lady* and *West Side Story*, and a complex form of drama is created, a drama of difference, a drama of the multiple.

I believe that is the direction in which Sondheim has taken the musical, along with Kander and Ebb, Michael Bennett, Bob Fosse, William Finn, Jeanine Tesori, Lynn Ahrens and Stephen Flaherty—but I have no business making a list. Everyone can add names for themselves. When the lists include the names of African-American and Latino-American composers, writers, and performers, the musical will have overcome its major political limitation. Minorities thrive in the aesthetics of the musical, but the genre has fallen short of reaching people of color. What was learned from Harlem in the earlier years of the twentieth century was essential to the development of the song-and-dance aesthetic the musical puts to use, but the musical has not connected with the African-American theatre, at least not consistently. I single out the African-American theatre because its history is substantial and it has now attained the momentum of greatness in the plays of August Wilson. Many of the conventions we have been discussing for the musical are at work in Wilson's plays too, and if the American theatre can respond to the completion of Wilson's cycle of plays, or to the tragedy of his death, by bringing African-American drama into the visibility it deserves—the long tradition of African-American drama, I mean, which reaches back to the Harlem Renaissance and beyond—the musical may finally learn to include the minorities it has largely done without.

Then the genre will lay claim to the political seriousness inherent in its aesthetics. The power of the genre is largely the power of minorities in the first place, but we are looking ahead to a musical theatre where one does not have to notice who is missing. This will be the theatre of book-and-number aesthetics we have been describing, but it will open the way to thinking about politics and theatre together more fully and more exactly than we can now. I think the new shows will have what we have been talking about: a power of reflection running between the different modes of book and number, a sense of the irreverence of the genre, and a feeling for the anger and beauty of radical multiplicity. The image created by this kind of drama is of people who can create a coherent world accessible to anyone who can catch the beat and who refuse to accommodate themselves to the powerful and their technological tricks. I am not really talking about musicals in that sentence, which I have tried to phrase so as to include other qualities of life and art, but musicals are an image of what I am talking about, a social life worth aiming for.

BIBLIOGRAPHY

Abbate, Carolyn. *Unsung Voices: Opera and Musical Narrative in the Nineteenth Century*. Princeton, N.J.: Princeton University Press, 1991.

Adorno, Theodor W. *Beethoven: The Philosophy of Music*. Edited by Rolf Tiedemann. Translated by Edmond Jephcott. Stanford, Calif.: Stanford University Press, 1998.

Aristotle. *Poetics*. Translated by S. H. Butcher. New York: Hill and Wang, 1991.

Auden, W. H. *"The Dyer's Hand" and Other Essays*. New York: Viking, 1968.

Banfield, Stephen. *Sondheim's Broadway Musicals*. Ann Arbor: University of Michigan Press, 1993.

Barthes, Roland. *Image, Music, Text*. Translated by Stephen Heath. New York: Hill and Wang, 1977.

Bentley, Eric. *The Playwright as Thinker*. New York: Reynal and Hitchcock, n.d.

Block, Geoffrey. *Enchanted Evenings: The Broadway Musical from* Show Boat *to* Sondheim. Oxford: Oxford University Press, 1997.

Bordman, Gerald. *The American Musical Theatre*, 3rd ed. New York: Oxford University Press, 2001.

Bordman, Gerald. *American Operetta, from* H.M.S. Pinafore *to* Sweeney Todd. New York: Oxford University Press, 1981.

Bordman, Gerald. *Jerome Kern: His Life and Music*. New York: Oxford University Press, 1980.

Brecht, Bertolt. *Brecht on Theatre*, edited by John Willett. New York: Hill and Wang, 1964.

Burckhardt, Sigurd. *Shakespearean Meanings*. Princeton, N.J.: Princeton University Press, 1968.

Carlson, Marvin. "Ghosts and *Follies*." *Journal of American Theatre and Drama*, 16 (2004): 36–49.

Carlson, Marvin. *The Haunted Stage: The Theatre as Memory Machine*. Ann Arbor: University of Michigan Press, 2001.

Chapin, Ted. *Everything Was Possible: The Birth of the Musical* Follies. New York: Knopf, 2003.

Clark, Barrett, and William H. Davenport. *Nine Modern American Plays*. New York: Appleton-Century-Crofts, 1951.

Clum, John. *Something for the Boys: Musical Theater and Gay Culture*. New York: St. Martin's Press, 1999.

Cohen, Selma Jeanne, ed. *Dance as a Theatre Art*, 2nd ed. Princeton, N.J.: Princeton Book Co., 1992.

Crittenden, Camille. *Johann Strauss and Vienna: Operetta and the Politics of Popular Culture*. Cambridge: Cambridge University Press, 2000.

Dahlhaus, Carl. "What is a musical drama?" *Cambridge Opera Journal* 1 (1989): 95–111.

Dallenback, Lucien. *The Mirror in the Text*. Translated by Jeremy Whiteley and Emma Hughes. Chicago: University of Chicago Press, 1989.

Davis, Lee. *Bolton and Wodehouse and Kern: The Men Who Made Musical Comedy*. New York: James Heineman, 1993.

Deleuze, Giles. *Difference and Repetition*. Translated by Paul Patton. London: Athlone Press, 1994.

Duberman, Martin. *Paul Robeson*. New York, 1988.

Eliot, T. S. *Selected Essays: New Edition*. New York: Harcourt, Brace, 1950.

Engel, Lehman. *The American Musical Theatre: A Consideration*. New York: CBS Records, 1967.

Fergusson, Francis. *The Idea of a Theater*. Princeton, N.J.: Princeton University Press, 1949.

Flinn, Denny. *Musical! A Grand Tour*. New York: Schirmer, 1997.

Fordin, Hugh. *Getting to Know Him: A Biography of Oscar Hammerstein II*. New York: Da Capo, 1995.

Forte, Alan. *The American Popular Ballad of the Golden Era, 1924–1950*. Princeton, N.J.: Princeton University Press, 1995.

Foucault, Michel. "Theatricum Philosophicum." In *Language, Counter-Memory, Practice*, edited by Donald F. Bouchard, 165–96. Ithaca, N.Y.: Cornell University Press, 1977.

Freedland, Michael. *Jerome Kern*. New York: Stein and Day, 1978.

Friedman, Michael. Review of *The American Musical and The Formation of National Identity*, by Raymond Knapp. *London Review of Books*, 31 March 2005, 25–26.

Frye, Northrop. *Anatomy of Criticism: Four Essays*. Princeton, N.J.: Princeton University Press, 1957.

Frye, Northrop. "Approaching the Lyric." In *Lyric Poetry: Beyond New Criticism*, edited by Chaviva Hosek and Patricia Parker. Ithaca, N.Y.: Cornell University Press, 1985.

Fuchs, Eleanor. *The Death of Character: Perspectives on Theater after Modernism.* Bloomington: Indiana University Press, 1996.

Furia, Philip. *Ira Gershwin: The Art of the Lyricist.* Oxford, 1996.

Furia, Philip. *Poets of Tin-Pan Alley: A History of America's Great Lyricists.* New York: Oxford University Press, 1990.

Garebian, Keith. *The Making of Cabaret.* Oakville. Ont.: Mosaic Press, 1999.

Genette, Gerard. *Narrative Discourse.* Translated by Jane E. Lewin. Ithaca, N.Y.: Cornell University Press, 1980.

Goldman, Michael. *The Actor's Freedom.* New York: Viking, 1975.

Goodhart, Sandor, ed. *Reading Stephen Sondheim.* New York: Garland, 2000.

Goodwin, John, ed. *British Theatre Design: The Modern Age.* New York: St. Martin's Press, 1989.

Gottfried, Martin. *All His Jazz: The Life and Death of Bob Fosse.* New York: Da Capo, 1998.

Graham, Martha. "A Modern Dancer's Primer for Action," in *Dance: A Basic Educational Technique,* edited by Frederick R. Rogers. New York: Macmillan, 1941

Guernsey, Otis L., Jr., ed. *Playwrights, Lyricists, Composers on Theater.* New York: Dodd, Mead, 1964.

Hamm, Charles. *Yesterdays: Popular Song in America.* New York: Norton, 1979.

Hammerstein II, Oscar. *Lyrics.* New York: Simon and Schuster, 1949.

Herrington, John. *Poetry in Drama: Early Drama and the Greek Poetic Tradition.* Berkeley: University of California Press, 1985.

Higham, Charles. *Ziegfeld.* London, 1973.

Hirsch, Foster. *Harold Prince and the American Musical Theatre.* Cambridge: Cambridge University Press, 1989.

Hodgins, Paul. *Relationships Between Score and Choreography in Twentieth Century Dance.* Lewiston, N.Y.: Mellen, 1992.

Hogle, Jerrold E. *The Undergrounds of* The Phantom of the Opera. New York: Palgrave, 2002.

Hollander, John. "Breaking into Song." In *Lyric Poetry: Beyond New Criticism,* edited by Chaviva Hosek and Patricia Parker, 73–89. Ithaca, N.Y.: Cornell University Press, 1985.

Horowitz, Mark Eden. *Sondheim on Music: Minor Details and Major Decisions.* Lanham, Md.: Scarecrow Press, 2003.

Hoyt, Edwin P. *Paul Robeson: The American Othello.* Cleveland, 1967.

Hytner, Nicholas. "When Your Characters Are Speechless, Let 'Em Sing." *New York Times*, 10 March 2002, "Arts and Leisure" section, 7.

Isherwood, Christopher. "Goodbye to Berlin." In *The Berlin Stories*, 1–207. New York: New Directions, 1954.

Isherwood, Christopher. "Sally Bowles." In *The Berlin Stories*, 21–76. New York: New Directions, 1954.

Jarvis, Simon. *Adorno: A Critical Introduction*. New York: Routledge, 1998.

Kawin, Bruce. *Telling It Again and Again: Repetition in Literature and Film*. Ithaca, N.Y.: Cornell University Press, 1972.

Kerman, Joseph. *Opera as Drama*. Rev. ed. London: Faber, 1989.

Kierkegaard, Søren. *Fear and Trembling/Repetition*. Edited and translated by Howard V. Hong and Edna H. Hong. Princeton, N.J.: Princeton Univ. Press, 1983.

Knapp, Raymond. *The American Musical and the Formation of National Identity*. Princeton, N.J.: Princeton University Press, 2004.

Koestenbaum, Wayne. *The Queen's Throat: Opera, Homosexuality, and the Mystery of Desire*. New York: Poseidon, 1993.

Kowalke, Kim H. "Brecht and music: Theory and practice." In *The Cambridge Companion to Brecht*, edited by Peter Thomson and Glendyr Sacks. Cambridge: Cambridge University Press, 1994.

Kreuger, Miles. Show Boat: *The Story of a Classic American Musical*. New York, 1977.

Kristeva, Julia. *Revolution in Poetic Language*. New York: Columbia University Press, 1984.

Kruger, Loren. *The National Style*. Chicago: University of Chicago Press, 1992.

Lahr, John. "O.K. Chorale: An English Take on Rodgers and Hammerstein" (review of *Oklahoma!*). *The New Yorker*, 1 April 2002, 84–85.

Lamb, Andrew. *150 Years of Popular Musical Theatre*. New Haven: Yale University Press, 2000.

Lamb, Andrew. *Jerome Kern in Edwardian London*. Privately printed, 1981.

Langer, Susanne K. *Feeling and Form*. London: Routledge and Kegan Paul, 1953.

Langer, Susanne. *Problems of Art*. New York: Scribner's, 1957.

Lawrence, Greg. *Dance with Demons: The Life of Jerome Robbins*. New York: Putnam, 2001.

Levinson, Andre. "The Spirit of the Classic Dance." In *Theatre Arts Anthology*, edited by Rosamund Gilder. New York: Theatre Arts, 1925.

Lindenberger, Herbert. *Opera in History: From Monteverdi to Cage.* Stanford, Calif.: Stanford University Press, 1998.

Loesser, Susan. *A Most Remarkable Fella.* New York: Donald Fine, 1993.

Lyon, James K. *Bertolt Brecht in America.* Princeton, N.J.: Princeton University Press, 1980.

Mandelbaum, Ken. A Chorus Line *and the Musicals of Michael Bennett.* New York: St. Martin's Press, 1989.

Mander, Raymond, and Joe Mitchenson. *Revue: A Story in Pictures.* London: Peter Davies, 1971.

Mast, Gerald. *Can't Help Singin': The American Musical on Stage and Screen.* Woodstock, N.Y.: Overlook Press, 1987.

Maxwell, Richard. "Dickens's Omniscience." *English Literary History* 46 (1979): 290–313.

McMillin, Scott. "Brecht and Sondheim: An Unholy Alliance." Forthcoming in *Brecht International Yearbook*.

McMillin, Scott. "Paul Robeson, Will Vodery's 'Jubilee Singers,' and the Earliest Script of the Kern-Hammerstein *Show Boat*." *Theatre Survey* 41 (2000): 51–70.

Miller, D. A. *Place for Us (Essay on the Broadway Musical).* Cambridge, Mass.: Harvard University Press, 1998.

Miller, J. Hillis. *The Form of Victorian Fiction.* Notre Dame, Ind.: University of Notre Dame Press, 1968.

Miller, Scott. *Deconstructing Harold Hill.* Portsmouth, N.H.: Heinemann, 2000.

Miller, Scott. *From "Assassins" to "West Side Story": A Director's Guide to Musical Theatre.* Portsmouth, N.H.: Heinemann, 1996.

Miller, Scott. *Rebels with Applause: Broadway's Groundbreaking Musicals.* Portsmouth, N.H.: Heinemann, 2001.

Mirigliano, Rosario. "The sign and music: A reflection on the theoretical bases of musical semiotics." In *Musical Signification: Essays in the Semiotic Theory and Analysis of Music*, edited by Eero Tarasti. New York: Mouton, 1996, 43–62.

Mizejewski, Linda. *Divine Decadence: Fascism, Female Spectacle, and the Making of* Sally Bowles. Princeton, N.J.: Princeton University Press, 1992.

Mordden, Ethan. *Beautiful Mornin': The Broadway Musical in the 1940s.* New York: Oxford University Press, 1999.

Mordden, Ethan. *Everything's Coming Up Roses*. New York: Oxford University Press, 1998.

Mordden, Ethan. *Make Believe: The Broadway Musical in the 1920s*. New York: Oxford University Press, 1997.

Mordden, Ethan. *Open a New Window: The Broadway Musical in the 1960s*. New York: Oxford University Press, 2001.

Mordden, Ethan. *Rodgers and Hammerstein*. New York: Abrams, 1992.

Most, Andrea. " 'We Know We Belong to the Land': The Theatricality of Assimilation in Rodgers and Hammerstein's *Oklahoma!*" *PMLA* 113 (1998): 77–89.

Most, Andrea. *Making Americans: Jews and the Broadway Musical*. Cambridge, Mass.: Harvard University Press, 2004.

Nattiez, Jean-Jacques. *Music and Discourse: Toward a Semiology of Music*. Translated by Carolyn Abbate. Princeton, N.J.: Princeton University Press, 1990.

Norton, Richard C. *A Chronology of American Musical Theater*. 3 vols. Oxford: Oxford University Press, 2002.

Perry, George. *The Complete* Phantom of the Opera. New York: Holt, 1988.

Philip, M. Nourbese. *Showing Grit: Show Boating North of the 44th Parallel*. Toronto, ON, 1993.

Poizat, Michel. *The Angel's Cry*. Trans. Arthur Denner. Ithaca, N.Y.: Cornell University Press, 1992.

Prince, Gerald. *A Dictionary of Narratology*. Lincoln: University of Nebraska Press, 1987.

Prince, Hal. *Contradictions*. New York: Dodd, Mead, 1974.

Puchner, Martin. *Stage Fright: Modernism, Anti-Theatricality, and Drama*. Baltimore: Johns Hopkins University Press, 2002.

Richards, Stanley, ed. *Ten Great Musicals of the American Theatre*. Radnor, Penn.: Chilton Book Co., 1973.

Riggs, Lynn. *Green Grow the Lilacs*. In *Nine Modern American Plays*, edited by Barrett H. Clark.

Rodgers, Richard. *Musical Stages: An Autobiography*. New York: Random House, 1975.

Roost, Alisa. "Before *Oklahoma!* A Reappraisal of Musical Theatre During the 1930s." *Journal of American Drama and Theatre*, 16 (2004): 1–35.

Rose, Jacqueline. *Sexuality and the Field of Vision*. London: Verso, 1986.

Rosenberg, Deena. *Fascinating Rhythm: The Collaboration of George and Ira Gershwin*. New York, 1991.

Rugg, Rebecca. "What It Used to Be: Nostalgia and the State of the Broadway Musical." *Theater*, 32 (2002): 45–55.

Savran, David. *A Queer Sort of Materialism: Recontextualizing American Theater*. Ann Arbor: University of Michigan Press, 2003.

Schoenberg, Arnold. *Fundamentals of Musical Composition*. Edited by Gerald Strang and Leonard Stein. London: Faber and Faber, 1967.

Secrest, Meryle. *Somewhere for Us: A Biography of Richard Rodgers*. New York: Knopf, 2001.

Secrest, Meryle. *Stephen Sondheim*. New York: Knopf, 1998.

Smith, Matthew. *From Bayreuth to Cyberspace: Technology, Commerce, and the Gesamtkunstwerk*. Forthcoming.

Southern, Eileen. *Biographical Dictionary of African-American and African Musicians*. Westport, Conn.: Greenwood, 1981.

States, Bert. *Great Reckonings in Little Rooms*. Berkeley: University of California Press, 1985.

Stempel, Larry. "*Street Scene* and the Enigma of Broadway Opera." In *A New Orpheus: Essays on Kurt Weill*, edited by Kim H. Kowalke, 321–41. New Haven, 1986.

Steyn, Mark. *Broadway Babies, Say Goodnight: Musicals Then and Now*. London: Faber and Faber, 1997.

Suisman, Charlie. "Cue the Pop Ballad, Warn the Critics." *New York Times*, 15 August 2004, Arts and Leisure section, p. 4.

Suskin, Steven. *Opening Night on Broadway: A Critical Quotebook of the Golden Era of the Musical Theatre*. New York: Schirmer, 1990.

Swain, Joesph P. *The Broadway Musical: A Critical and Musical Survey*. Oxford: Oxford University Press, 1990. 2nd ed., Lanham, Md.: Scarecrow Press, 2002.

Swayne, Steve. *How Sondheim Found His Sound*. Ann Arbor: University of Michigan Press, 2005.

Traubner, Richard. *Operetta: A Theatrical History*. London: Gollancz, 1984.

Weill, Kurt. "*Street Scene* Becomes a 'Dramatic Musical.'" *New York Times*, 5 January 1947.

Wilk, Max. *The Story of Oklahoma!* New York: Grove, 1993.

Wolf, Stacy. *A Problem Like Maria: Gender and Sexuality in the American Musical*. Ann Arbor: University of Michigan Press, 2002.

Woolcott, Alexander. *While Rome Burns*. New York, 1934.

Zadan, Craig. *Sondheim & Co.*, 2nd ed. New York: Harper & Row, 1986.

INDEX

Abbate, Carolyn, 68
"Adelaide's Lament," 70
Adorno, Theodor, 31n
"Advantages of Floating in the Middle of the Sea, The," 207n
After the Fair, 158
"Ah, But Underneath," 194
"Ah, Sweet Mystery of Life," 116, 124
Ahrens, Lynn, 210
"All er Nothin'," 61–62, 69; performances in front of stage between scene changes, 62–63
"All I Ask of You," 168
Allegro, 23, 89
American Musical, The (Knapp), 85n8
"Among School Children," 141
Aristotle, 6, 6n12; on the components of tragedy, 7
Assassins, 154, 197; Lee Harvey Oswald character in, 155
Astaire, Adele, 15, 21, 79, 157–58, 198
Astaire, Fred, 15, 21, 79, 157–58; film musicals of with Ginger Rodgers, 175–76
Auden, W. H., 31, 31n

Babes in Arms, 102
Balanchine, George, 51, 93; on dance, 140–41
ballet, 80, 80n2
Banfield, Stephen, 55, 58, 163n
Barras, Charles M., 80n2
Behrman, S. N., 22
"Being Alive," 96, 96n
Bennett, Michael, 24, 210
"Ben's Folly," 194
Bentley, Eric, 4; criticism of musicals, 14

Berlin, Irving, 27
Berlin Stories (Isherwood), 200
Bernstein, Leonard, 20, 22, 56, 93, 143
"Best of All Possible Worlds, The," 92
Bjornson, Maria, 156
Black Crook, The, 80, 80n2
Blake, Eubie, 27
Bledsoe, Jules, 107n
Blount, Helon, 189
Bolger, Ray, 63, 117
Bolton, Guy, 17–18
"Boy Like That, A" 72
Boys from Syracuse, 115
Brecht, Bertoldt, 25–30; on the capitalist economic system, 26–27; opinion of *Oklahoma!*, 26
Broadway Musical, The: A Critical and Musical Survey (Swain), 20n, 85n9, 133
Burckhardt, Sigurd, 110
"Bushel and a Peck, A," 113
By Jupiter, 151

Cabaret (1966), 14, 22–23, 24, 77, 102, 207; challenging of musical conventions in, 93–96; character of Cliff in, 201–2; and the code of individualism in Sally Bowles, 95; Master of Ceremonies character in, 153–54, 154n6; and Nazi ideology, 94; orchestra of, 147–48; political nature of, 200–202; staging of, 154, 200, 202n16. *See also specifically listed individual songs from*
Candide (1956), 78, 92n, 151–52; failure of, 92; opening scene of, 92

musicals (*continued*)
  sophistication, 114–16; and dramatic and recognitions, 41–43, 47, 52; as farces, 17–18; forerunners of, 10; future of, 209–11; incongruity in, 179, 197; intellectuals' discomfort with, 196–97; and the love duet, 63, 69, 115–16; "mirroring" in, 182–87, 198–99, 208; and the omniscience of the set in, 155–60; and opera, 5, 21–22, 22n; and "out of the blue" numbers, 112–14; and performance, 52; and the projection of musical ability, 66–67; as a quasi-operatic form, 21–22; realism and character depth in, 192; and reversal, 43–46, 47–49; and romantic comedy, 179–80; solos in, 52; sources of, 160–64; technological, 173; topicality of, 18; and the two orders of time (book time and lyric time), 6–10, 31–33, 31n, 42, 52–53, 66–67, 119, 191, 199; and the use of mirrors in, 182–87, 187n; and the "voice of the musical," 67–72, 75–76. *See also* characters in musicals, and reality; drama; drama, political; ensemble numbers; film musicals; musicals, books of; musicals, and integration; popular (pop) songs
musicals, books of, 15, 17–22, 41–42; coherence of the book and musical numbers, 123–25; differences between the book and musical numbers, 2–3, 49–50; and integration, 129–30; tensions between the book and musical numbers, 6, 13, 191–95, 196
musicals, and integration, 141, 165, 209; and the book of the musical, 129–30; doubt concerning, 2–3, 3n4; high-tech integration, 209–10; integration theory of, 1–6,

13, 73; and plot advancement, 7–8; and sets, 156–57. *See also Oklahoma!*, integrated song from
My Fair Lady (1956), 7, 47–49, 91–92, 210; Arthur Doolittle character in, 68–69; film version of, 175; Henry Higgins character in, 7, 64–67; and "legitimate" drama, 89–91; relationship of Higgins and Eliza in, 67–68; romantic ending of, 91, 91n
"My Ship," 119–20, 123; as a diegetic number, 122–23
"My Time of Day," 60, 69, 70, 113
Mysteries, The (2002), 151n
mystery plays, musical versions of, 151n

Napier, John, 156, 160n15
narration/narrators: the narrator who knows nothing, 151–55; the omniscient narrator, 149–51; and the role of God as in musicals, 150–51, 151n
Nash, Ogden, 151
Naughty Marietta (1910), 116
Neptune's Daughter, 156
new criticism, 3–4
"Next," 207, 207n
"Nothing," 99

O'Brien, Timothy, 156
Of Thee I Sing, 8
Offenbach, Jacques, 13
"Officer Krupke," 49
"Oh, What a Beautiful Morning," 83–84; as a diegetic number, 104–5, 104n2; refrain of, 110
"Oklahoma!" 85, 85n8
Oklahoma! (1943), 5–6, 14, 15, 20n, 83, 103, 179; and the aesthetics of form, 29–30; ballet in, 93; book of, 19–21; dis-integrated song from, 40–41; dream-ballet scene from, 51–52; and the expansion of